Internal Labor Markets in Japan

Japanese labor market practices have attracted considerable attention in the West, for two reasons. First, innovative human resource management (HRM) is responsible for the development of competitive industrial sectors. Secondly, inner flexibility of the labor market has produced low unemployment and wage flexibility. This study provides a thorough investigation of the distinctive features of Japanese internal labor markets (ILM) and occupational labor markets (OLM), closely analyzes important changes in ILM, and considers future developments. It combines a mixture of descriptive and theoretical/econometric work and builds on the authors' well known previous research in this area. The volume also contains a detailed case study and the econometric analysis of the HRM-policies used by a large Japanese firm. Although the focus is on Japanese ILM, international comparisons are made throughout, mainly with reference to Europe and the United States.

Kenn Ariga is Professor at the Institute of Economic Research, Kyoto University.

Giorgio Brunello is Professor at the Department of Economics, University of Padua.

Yasushi Ohkusa is Associate Professor at the Institute of Social and Economic Research, Osaka University.

Internal Labor Markets in Japan

Internal Labor Markets in Japan

KENN ARIGA, GIORGIO BRUNELLO AND
YASUSHI OHKUSA

CAMBRIDGE
UNIVERSITY PRESS

CAMBRIDGE UNIVERSITY PRESS
Cambridge, New York, Melbourne, Madrid, Cape Town, Singapore,
São Paulo, Delhi, Dubai, Tokyo

Cambridge University Press
The Edinburgh Building, Cambridge CB2 8RU, UK

Published in the United States of America by Cambridge University Press, New York

www.cambridge.org
Information on this title: www.cambridge.org/9780521142748

First published 2000
This digitally printed version 2010

A catalogue record for this publication is available from the British Library

ISBN 978-0-521-64240-8 Hardback
ISBN 978-0-521-14274-8 Paperback

To our families

Contents

Figures

Tables

Preface

In the past few years, economists have shown an increased interest in the theoretical and empirical analysis of the organization of labor within (mainly large) firms, and in the working of internal labor markets. Advances in the theory of contracts and in agency theory on the one hand, and the increased access to personnel data on the other, have been instrumental to these new developments.

At the same time, the emergence of a dominant Japanese economy on the international economic scene during the 1980s and its relatively good performance in the wake of the two oil shocks attracted considerable interest about the working of the Japanese labor market, both because of Japan's innovative human resource management (HRM) practices and because of the persistently low unemployment rate.

This book tries to bring together these two research threads by focusing on Japanese internal labor market (ILM). Japan is an interesting case, because a well known stylized feature of the Japanese way of organizing labor, especially but not exclusively in large firms, is the importance of long-term employment relationships, steep earnings profiles, and substantial investment in (firm-specific) human capital. All these features are typical of internal labor markets.

Part I of this book (chapters 1–6) looks at important features of Japanese internal labor markets (promotion, earnings profiles, rent-sharing) and tries to relate them to macroeconomic developments such as the slowdown in the rate of economic growth of the Japanese economy and the progressive ageing of its labor force.

Internal labor markets are not immutable organizations, and are sensitive to long-run economic changes. With the burst of the asset-prices bubble in the early 1990s, the Japanese economy entered a period of prolonged stagnation and approach the new millennium with increasing unemployment and slow or even negative economic growth. What are the implications of these dramatic changes in economic performance for the organization of Japanese internal labor markets? Part II of this book (chapters 7–10) tries to answer this question by combining a qualitative analysis of case studies with an empirical investigation of the evolution of the wage and employment structures in large and medium-sized Japanese firms.

This book is the outcome of almost 10 years of joint work by the three authors. Our venture started when Professor Masahiko Aoki at Stanford University introduced Brunello to Ariga in Kyoto. On top of our intellectual debt, we owe a great deal to Professor Aoki for pushing us in the right direction. Ohkusa joined our project within a few years, first as a graduate student, and rapidly became an indispensable member. Part of this research has been published in *Economica, Industrial Relations, The Journal of Economic Behavior and Organization, Labour Economics, The International Journal of Industrial Organization*, and *The Journal of the Japanese and International Economies*. The chapters that draw from published research have been substantially rewritten and updated, and may be considered as almost completely new.

During the span of this research we have benefitted from comments and suggestions from many people, including Yukiko Abe, Masahiko Aoki, Bruce Chapman, Hiroyuki Chuma, Ronald Dore, Mary Gregory, Bertil Holmlund, Hideshi Itoh, Takao Kato, Kazuo Koike, Claudio Lucifora, David Marsden, Alan Manning, Michael McAleer, Paul Milgrom, Naoki Mitani, Yoshifumi Nakata, Iwao Nakatani, Steve Nickell, Yoshihiko Nishiyama, Hiroyuki Odagiri, Konosuke Odaka, Isao Ohashi, Soichi Ohta, Fumio Ohtake, Keijiro Otsuka, Canice Prendergast, Marcus Rebick, Takehiro Ryoji, Ronald Schettkat, Paul Sheard, David Soskice, Haruo Shimada, Hideo Suehiro, Toshiaki Tachibanaki, Tsuyoshi Tsuru, and Guglielmo Weber. We are also grateful to Noriko Kinoshita for her excellent secretarial help.

A special thought goes to Tsuneo Ishikawa, a teacher and a friend, who inspired and encouraged us during this research project. Unfortunately, he passed away in June 1998, but his memory is very strong in our hearts.

Almost all the material covered in the book has been presented at seminars or conferences in Japan, the United States, Europe, and Australia. We are grateful to audiences at these events for helpful criticism and suggestions.

The idea to write this book started in the Italian Alps. We were able to get together in the same country at different stages of the research and we are grateful to IGIER Bocconi, ISER Osaka, and The Nissan Institute of Japanese Studies in Oxford for hospitality. We also acknowledge the financial support of the Italian Ministry of Universities and Research, the Italian National Research Foundation, the University of Udine, the Inamori Foundation, the Japanese Ministry of Education, and the Nihon Shoken Shorei Zaidan.

Last but not least, we are grateful to Ashwin Rattan of Cambridge University Press for his help throughout this venture.

Introduction

Before the burst of the economic bubble in the early 1990s, the Japanese way of organizing labor within firms attracted considerable attention outside Japan. This interest was driven by two facts. First, the Japanese labor market emerged from the two oil shocks of the 1970s with a remarkably low unemployment rate, partly because of its allegedly flexible wage system.[1] Second, Japanese human resource management (HRM) practices were considered as a key comparative advantage in the remarkable performance of many export oriented Japanese industries (automobiles, electric appliances).[2]

With the prolonged economic downturn following the burst of the bubble, not only economic growth but also academic interest on Japan waned to some extent, and new questions started to emerge. Perhaps the most obvious is whether the Japanese way of organizing labor will survive the prolonged economic slowdown that is taking place, together with the rapid ageing of the Japanese labor force, or will Japan experience a rather dramatic structural change?[3]

The purpose of this book is to contribute to answering this question by looking at internal labor market (ILM), the typical way of organizing labor in large and medium-sized Japanese firms, and at their evolution during the past 20 years. Briefly, internal labor markets are employment systems characterized by four key features: (a) long-term employment relationships; (b) new hirings occurring at designated ports of entry; (c) allocation of labor after entry based mainly on internal promotion; (d) individual pay influenced by administrative rules and only partially affected by market forces.[4]

---

[1] See Ito (1992); Freeman and Weitzman (1987).
[2] See Womack, Jones and Roos (1991).
[3] See Nakatani (1996) for a view in favor of this latter hypothesis.
[4] See Doeringer and Piore (1970); Baker and Holmstrom (1995).

Our focus is on such issues as promotion, recruitment, earnings profiles, and the evolution of wage and employment structures in large and medium-sized firms belonging to different industries. By so doing, we do not consider important topics and areas of research, including the large secondary sector composed mainly of small firms. Since the primary labor market that we analyze in this book is mainly a market for male labor suppliers, we also leave out the female labor market. Needless to say, a complete picture of recent developments in the Japanese aggregate labor market cannot ignore these important topics. Apart from the obvious reasons of space, one justification of our choice is that there is already important research that covers the ground not explored in this book (see for instance, Ito, 1992; Osawa, 1993; Ishikawa and Dejima, 1994; Yoshikawa, 1995; Tachibanaki, 1996).

Our approach is both theoretical and empirical, and the tools we use are those typical of modern economic analysis. This is not to say, the institutional context is not important. We do not subscribe, however, to the view, often heard in Japan, that the analysis of Japanese economic behavior requires the development of special analytical tools. Our approach has been much influenced by the important and path-breaking work on Japan by Masahiko Aoki and Kazuo Koike.

The book is organized in two parts. Part I (chapters 1–6) deals with different aspects of Japanese internal labor markets, including measurement issues, internal promotion, earnings profiles, and rent-sharing. Part II (chapters 7–10), focuses on recent changes and studies how the wage and employment structures of large and medium-sized Japanese firms have been affected by the slowdown in economic growth and by the ageing of the labor force. These important and long-lasting macroeconomic changes suggest that Japanese internal labor markets are also changing and that we may currently be observing the transition from the traditional to a new mode of organizing labor within large and medium-sized Japanese firms.

Part I includes two theoretical and four empirical chapters. In the introductory chapter (chapter 1), we use a very simple job-search environment, in the tradition of Diamond and Pissarides, to nest the concept of internal labor markets in a general equilibrium setup and to explore the relationship between productivity growth, labor turnover, unemployment, and the relative importance of internal labor markets. The model is built on a simple idea. In the presence of significant labor market frictions, firms can choose to fill skilled vacancies either by costly recruiting or by training and upgrading unskilled incumbents (internal promotion). This choice is influenced both by (exogenous) labor turnover and by (exogenous) productivity growth. For instance, when an economy grows faster, it is increasingly difficult to fill skilled vacancies from the market and internal upgrading becomes more important. When the economy slows down, training becomes an increasingly costly option, because of the higher number of skilled unemployed workers available in the market.

The predictions of the model are broadly consistent with a stylized characterization of the Japanese economy, featuring relatively high productivity growth, low turnover, low unemployment, and the widespread presence of internal labor markets. The model also implies that the slowdown in the rate of productivity growth experienced by the Japanese economy should over time reduce the relative importance of internal labor markets.

In chapter 1, we identify internal labor markets with the practice of internal training and promotion. In chapter 2, we look more closely at promotion, and develop a model of job allocation and investment in heterogeneous human capital in a two-layer corporate hierarchy. The model highlights the critical role played by the proximity of skills and by training in shaping the promotion policy and the hierarchical structure of firms. The higher the degree of proximity of skills, the higher the human capital complementarity among different jobs within a hierarchy. The degree of proximity depends not only upon technological conditions, but also upon the way jobs and training systems are designed.

We show that, depending on the degree of skill proximity, there can be two types of firm. In one type, skill proximity is relatively high, skill formation is predominantly internal, and involves a long, continuous accumulation process along promotion ladders where jobs with closely related skills are lined up in a progression. Experience within the hierarchy and along these promotion ladders is the most important determinant of promotion decisions. Promotion timing can be delayed substantially for some employees, hiring decisions are based upon stringent standards, and income distribution within the firm is fairly equal. Not surprisingly, these characteristics fit almost exactly the stylized facts about large Japanese firms, viewed as having a well developed system of internal labor markets.

In the other type of firm, skill proximity across tasks is relatively low, internal training is less common, and inter-firm mobility is higher than intra-firm mobility. Because of the relative independence of jobs, qualifications and innate talents at the start of the career largely determine job assignments. Internal promotions, if they occur at all, are concentrated in the early stages of a career and workers are highly specialized. The demarcation between upper and lower ranks in the hierarchy is also more clear-cut. Experience in lower ranks may be helpful to increase

productivity in lower-ranked jobs but is not helpful to increase productivity in upper-ranked jobs. There are multiple ports of entry, with less
demanding hiring standards and larger earnings differentials between
upper- and lower-ranked jobs. All these characteristics are more commonly found among UK and US firms.

Chapter 3 inaugurates the empirical section by asking how can we
measure the relative importance of internal labor markets in an economy.
The distinction between internal and occupational labor markets (OLM)
can be implemented empirically only with the development of informative indicators, that go beyond vague standard measures such as firm size
and average seniority. In chapter 3 we develop an alternative indicator,
based on the comparison between firm-specific and occupation-specific
tenure, and apply it to Japanese occupational data. This measure is
derived from human capital theory and is based on a very simple idea:
if skills are developed mainly within firms, as suggested by internal labor
market theory, firm-specific tenure (seniority) should be at least as important as occupation-specific tenure. On the other hand, if skills are developed mainly in the market, occupation-specific tenure should be more
important than firm-specific tenure.

We find that a classification of the top and of the bottom 20 occupations based on the value taken by our indicator is in line with common
economic sense. We also find that our measure is positively correlated
with both average seniority and average firm size, but that these variables
explain only about one-third of its total variation. Next, we test whether
our measure of the degree of labor market internalization has information content by estimating Japanese wage–seniority profiles. It turns out
that the slope of these profiles is positively correlated with our indicator.
In particular, occupations with a higher degree of internalization have
steeper earnings profiles, independently of firm size. Interestingly, we also
find that the impact of a high value of internalization on the slope of
wage–seniority profiles is larger among small and medium-sized firms.
We consider this result as suggestive of the fact that internal labor markets extend beyond large firms. Apparently, it is not firm size alone that
identifies the presence of these markets, but also the type of occupation.
When an occupation is organized in internal labor markets, pay and
HRM practices are affected both in large and in small and medium-
sized firms.

Chapter 4 looks at earnings profiles, a key feature of internal labor
markets. We start by noticing that standard estimates of earnings profiles
ignore that, with unobserved heterogeneity, cross-section evidence need
not reflect the "true" relationship between earnings and tenure. We then
argue that the observation of the position filled by an employee in the

firm hierarchy is informative both of her quality and of the quality of her match. Under some additional assumptions, this information can be used to construct an unbiased estimator of the effects of tenure on earnings growth.

We apply this simple idea to Japanese and British data, and find that tenure effects are less important than the effects estimated with the traditional approach used by Hashimoto and Raisian (1985). The difference, however, is small. Conditional effects, obtained by conditioning earnings on the hierarchical position or rank, make up a substantial part of the overall impact of tenure on earnings, especially for short–medium tenure spells and in large firms. While within-rank earnings growth is important earlier on in a career, between-rank earnings growth becomes more important as tenure increases, especially among small and medium-sized firms.

Interestingly, we find that both conditional and unconditional seniority premia are smaller in the United Kingdom than in Japan, and that the ratio of unconditional to conditional premia, measuring the importance of between-rank earnings growth, is higher in the former. This difference is particularly significant in the manufacturing sector, and confirms the common view that internal labor markets are less widespread in the United Kingdom than in Japan.

Chapter 5 presents the analysis of case studies illustrating the recruitment and promotion practices of large Japanese firms. In the absence of aggregate data, especially on promotion, personnel data trade off the advantage of being a detailed representation of HRM policies with the disadvantage of not being representative of the universe of large Japanese firms. Our analysis partly confirms, and partly casts some doubts, on the well known stylized facts about career development in large Japanese firms, including late selection in promotion and a strong preference for regular recruits. In one firm where we have data, we find both that irregular recruits are important and that there are multiple ports of entry and exits for such recruits.

In most of the firms studied in this chapter, firm-specific tenure matters for promotion. Merit, however, is also important, and in one case it is the key determinant. Importantly, the relevance of seniority in the promotion decision does not imply that the speed of promotion is equal. Conditional on tenure and education, our evidence suggests that "fast flyers" in lower ranks are more likely to fly faster to higher ranks. The presence of fast promotion tracks suggests that individual performance, given seniority and other individual characteristics, is likely also to play a decisive role in promotion in large Japanese firms operating internal labor markets.

Chapter 6 investigates the interaction between competition within the firm and competition among firms in the labor market. This interaction is important because most of the arrangements discussed in this book cannot be implemented unless firms and employees are to some extent insulated from the discipline of the external labor market. Take, for example, the late selection approach to promotion investigated in chapter 5. Unless firms have an information advantage with respect to other firms over the quality of their employees, or there are frictions preventing employees from freely seeking their best employers, such a policy is clearly untenable. Given the fact that the large majority of white-collar workers in large Japanese firms tends to stay with one firm for an extended period of time, there is little doubt that firms do have at least some room to choose and design their employment and wage policy in order to meet specific needs and conditions. An important question is therefore to what extent these firms are insulated from the external labor market.

Our empirical analysis, based upon micro data, finds evidence that major Japanese firms and their employees are insulated from the pressure of the external labor market. In particular, workers of firms with higher price markups have both longer average tenure and higher average wages. At the same time, however, we find no evidence that the wage policy of firms, measured either by the slope of the wage–tenure profile or by the initial wage, significantly affects productivity, that is influenced instead negatively by price markups and positively by the presence of a main bank relationship. These results underline the importance of external monitoring and discipline mechanisms that induce firms to maintain production efficiency.

Part II of the book, focusing on changes in Japanese internal labor markets, begins with chapter 7, presenting a qualitative analysis of changes in the Japanese employment system. After describing the main changes underway, we argue that these changes differ in important ways from previous episodes, mainly because the management of major firms is hard pressed by the need to make organizations leaner, cost efficient, and more flexible. At the same time, however, there is also strong inertia in the current system, especially in the ranking system (*Shokuno Shikaku Seido*) that remains the basis of the employment relationship in most of these firms.

Chapter 8 turns to the data and looks at the evolution of wages and employment in large and medium-sized firms belonging to manufacturing, trade and distribution, and finance during the period 1976–96. To highlight the changes taking place in internal labor markets, we use data that distinguish employees by rank, or the position filled in the vertical hierarchy, and look both at relative wages (by rank) and at relative employment (spans of control). The main findings of the chapter can be summarized as follows:

(1) With the deceleration of output and employment growth, there is evidence of a long-term decline in both relative wages and spans of control. Hence, there are relatively more individuals in higher ranks, but their relative wages are lower.

(2) There is evidence of convergence in the wage and employment structure of large and medium-sized firms, indicating that these firms are becoming increasingly similar in terms of hierarchical structures and compensation systems.

(3) Average age and tenure have increased over time, especially among medium-sized firms.

(4) Both promotion rates and promotion premia declined in the 1990s, and average promotion age slightly increased.

(5) Fluctuations in average promotion rates are positively correlated to fluctuations in five-year real sectoral output growth.

Slower growth has affected the career opportunities of young workers in large and medium-sized firms, but has not affected the average length of the employment relationship, which has actually increased, because also of the reduced intake of young workers and the limited turnover of older workers.

An important question is whether the slowdown in the rate of growth and the ageing of the labor force has affected the slope of earnings profiles and the (expected) returns to tenure. In chapter 9, we compare earnings profiles ten years apart, during 1980–4 and 1990–4, and show that (1) average tenure has increased more than average age: with small changes in educational attainment, previous labor market experience has declined, especially among medium-sized firms; (2) the returns to tenure, both conditional and unconditional, have declined in both large and medium-sized firms: the reduction has been sizeable, especially for longer tenure spells; (3) the returns to previous labor market experience have increased.

We argue in chapter 1 that sustained economic growth is key to the development of internal labor markets. By increasing the ratio of vacancies to unemployment, higher growth makes labor market matching relatively more difficult and encourages firms both to use internal upgrading and to establish long-term employment relationships by rewarding tenure. When growth slows down, however, the required skills can be more easily obtained from the labor market, and internal labor markets are partly replaced by occupational labor markets. At the same time, the progressive ageing of the labor force reduces the pool of young labor market entrants, who are expected to fill the lower rungs of promotion hierarchies in internal labor markets, thus increasing the relative wage of new entrants and making internal upgrading more costly compared to the market procurement of skilled employees.

As shown in chapter 2, labor market experience matters more in occupational labor markets, and tenure is more important in internal labor markets. The observed decline in the returns to tenure and the increase in the returns to labor market experience can thus be taken as indicating the increased importance of occupational labor markets among large and medium-sized firms, induced by the slowdown in the rate of economic growth and by the ageing of the Japanese labor force.

In chapter 10, the last chapter of this book, we explicitly relate the observed changes in the wage and employment structures of large and medium-sized firms with both long-run and short-run changes in the rate of economic growth. We start the chapter with a simple theoretical model that clarifies the interactions between economic growth and the structure of wages and employment in firms that organize labor in internal labor markets. Compared to the models in chapters 1 and 2, this model brings into the picture the important role of promotion in modern organizations, to provide incentives to employees when there is limited information about individual actions. The model predicts that a slowdown in the rate of growth that reduces employment growth in corporate hierarchies should also reduce rank-specific relative wages, promotion rates, and spans of control. These predictions are supported by our empirical analysis. We also show that alternative stories, such as skill-biased technical progress, cannot explain the observed joint occurrence of lower relative wages, lower spans of control and lower promotion rates.

We next look at the relationship between rank-specific relative wages and business cycle fluctuations, and find limited support in our data for the view that wages paid to workers in lower ranks or with shorter seniority spells are more responsive to short-term variations in output per head. Hence, there is no clear evidence that workers near the ports of entry of internal labor markets are less sheltered from business fluctuations. One possible explanation of this result is that we consider only regular workers, who belong to the employment core of large and medium-sized firms, and ignore both temporary workers and employees of small firms, who belong to the employment periphery and are more exposed to the consequences of business fluctuations. We find instead interesting differences among industries. In the manufacturing industry, real wages are pro-cyclical but the wage structure is a-cyclical. In the finance industry, wage differentials by rank vary with the ups and downs of the sectoral cycle; in this industry, it is the wages of employees with higher ranks that are more responsive to business fluctuations.

Going back to the question raised at the beginning of this introduction, this book has identified important features of Japanese internal labor markets and produced evidence that substantial changes involving all these features are taking place under the pressure of lower growth and of an ageing labor force. On the other hand, we also find evidence that the employment structure of medium-sized firms is converging towards that of large firms.

At the risk of simplifying things, the future of the Japanese employment relationship in the primary sector of the economy faces two rather distinct options. One is to more or less completely abandon the current employment system and move towards the more market oriented Anglo-Saxon system. The other is to minimize the costs of the current system – for instance, by eliminating age-related elements in individual pay and by reducing promotion probabilities for incumbent employees – and to maintain it in an important segment of large and medium-sized firms. Our evidence suggests that this second option represents the most likely scenario, and we come back to this in the epilog of the book.

Part I
Features of Japan's internal labor markets

1 Internal labor markets in search equilibrium

Overview[1]

A distinctive feature of most modern economies is that many job vacancies are filled from within, with firms often upgrading their incumbent employees rather than hiring new workers for the vacant position. This practice is typical of internal labor markets. In firms with internal labor markets (ILM) "new workers are used principally to fill specially designated entry jobs, which exist at various levels of the organizational structure. Other jobs are linked to entry jobs through promotion ladders and, hence, are filled from within" (Taubman and Watcher, 1986, p. 1189).

The emergence of internal labor markets in modern economies is usually justified by a number of reasons, ranging from the need to provide proper incentives to employees to the importance of human capital, from union behavior to bounded rationality and the reduction of transaction costs. The key feature of internal labor markets that we focus on in this chapter and chapter 2 is *internal training*, which in turn generates skill upgrading and internal promotion. In this chapter, we consider mainly training and skill upgrading. In chapter 2, we concentrate more upon *internal promotion* and *hierarchical design*.

The extent of internal labor markets in modern economies is difficult to gauge, as discussed in detail in chapter 3. Based on indicators such as tenure in the firm and earnings profiles, however, there is a wide consensus that internal labor markets are particularly developed in Japan, especially but not exclusively among large firms (see Aoki, 1988; Koike, 1988; Siebert and Addison, 1991). In this chapter, we associate this stylized fact with other facts, including relatively high productivity growth, low turnover rates, and very low unemployment rate experienced on average by the post-war Japanese economy.

---

[1] This chapter draws from Brunello (1996).

Japanese productivity grew during the postwar years faster than in the United States and in Europe. The average rate of growth was close to 9 percent a year during 1961–70 but fell to 3.9 percent a year during 1971–80 and to 3.2 percent a year during 1981–90.[2] Labor turnover in Japan is low, at least compared to the United States. Ito (1992) shows that retention probabilities in a job after 15 years of tenure are higher than 70 percent in Japan and lower than 50 percent in the United States.[3] Data on job creation and job destruction confirm that gross job turnover is relatively low in Japan (see Genda, 1998; Contini and Filippi, 1995). Finally, the Japanese unemployment rate has been less than 3 percent for the whole postwar period, with the exception of the late 1990s (Ito, 1992).

The model presented in this chapter creates a stylized characterization of internal labor markets in a simple general equilibrium setup and associates the diffusion of internal labor markets with economic factors such as productivity growth and labor turnover. We start from the observation that, if jobs are heterogeneous and can be organized into career ladders, openings do not necessarily require that firms post vacancies in the market. Hence, an important part of job matches need not be regulated by the matching function relating job matches to the market stock of vacancies and unemployed job searchers,[4] and trade can occur both within and without the firm, so that the market is not the sole allocator of workers to jobs.

Our key idea is simple. Consider an economy with two types of workers, skilled and unskilled. Skills can be accumulated either in vocational schools or in the workplace. While graduates of vocational schools are skilled and can be employed by firms without additional training costs, individuals with no vocational skill can be employed in skilled jobs only after undergoing workplace training.[5] Skills are general, and can be freely transferred from firm to firm. Firms have both skilled and unskilled job slots. While profitable unskilled job slots are filled by searching and matching in the labor market, skilled vacancies can be filled either by matching in the market or by training and upgrading an unskilled incumbent worker. In an economy with frictions, matching saves training costs but requires matching costs. Training, on the other hand, saves matching

---

[2] Eurostat, *The European Economy* (various issues). Japanese real GDP per head grew on average by 5.4% a year during 1961–90, compared to 1.23% a year in the United States and to 3.1% a year in the European Community.

[3] See also Blinder and Krueger (1992).

[4] See Blanchard and Diamond (1992) for a discussion of the matching function.

[5] In this chapter, we do not model explicitly the decision to invest in (vocational) education. An informal discussion of the relationship between education and training is contained on p. 31.

costs but requires firms to sink training costs. Since training is an option that saves on recruitment costs, firms are willing to bear the training cost.[6]

Given an exogenous distribution of firms, that differ in their training costs, and market-determined matching costs, firms can select either to train and upgrade or to recruit workers from outside by posting vacancies in the labor market. In the model developed below, while ILM (internal labor market) firms use both internal training and external recruitment to fill their skilled vacancies, OLM (occupational labor market) firms rely exclusively on external hirings.[7]

In the steady-state equilibrium, the labor force and productivity growth are constant and each firm has selected its most profitable recruitment mode. An interior equilibrium is an equilibrium allocation in which both types of firm coexist. After describing the equilibrium, we show how the distribution of firms between ILM and OLM types is affected by changes in exogenous variables. Our key result is that the steady-state proportion of firms choosing the ILM mode increases with the rate of (exogenous) productivity growth and decreases with the (exogenous) turnover rate.

Compared to the Anglo-Saxon economies, postwar Japan experienced high productivity growth and limited job turnover. These factors help to explain why internal labor markets appear to be relatively more widespread in Japan than in these economies. Our simple model also predicts that the substantial slowdown in the rate of productivity growth experienced by Japan since the early 1970s should reduce the relative importance of internal labor markets in the Japanese economy.

The chapter is organized as follows. We first present the model and then discuss the results and two extensions. The first extension considers training externalities. The second is devoted to the interaction between education and training. A brief summary concludes the chapter.

The model

Consider a stylized economy populated by a continuum of firms, each operating with two types of job. The first type is unskilled and the second requires a general transferable skill. For both types of firms, we assume that output Y is given by

---

[6] See Demougin and Siow (1994); Brunello and Medio (1996); Acemoglu and Pischke (1997) for reasons why firms are willing to pay for general training.
[7] The stark contrasts of the two types of firms in our model is meant to highlight the crucial difference. See the appendix (p. 32) for some generalizations of the model.

$$Y = y_1 e_1 + y_2 e_2 \tag{1.1}$$

$$y_2 > y_1$$

where y_1 (y_2) is the exogenous productivity of unskilled (skilled) workers and e_1 (e_2) is the number of unskilled (skilled) employees.[8] Throughout the chapter, we use subscript 1 (2) to denote unskilled (skilled) jobs and workers. Naturally, we assume that skilled workers are more productive than unskilled workers. Skills can be acquired either with formal off-the-job training (vocational schooling) or with enterprise training. While enterprise training is decided by the firm, the decision to invest in off-the-job training is taken by the individual, and is akin to the decision to invest in education.

Training an unskilled employee does not take time but requires that firms incur the training cost, τ.[9] This cost varies across firms according to the distribution G, and this is the only heterogeneity we allow for firms in this model. The assumption that training costs are carried by firms even when skills are transferable does not require that workers are credit-constrained. As shown by Acemoglu and Pischke (1999), the presence of labor market imperfections and frictions is sufficient.

Because of exogenous separations by individuals who retire from the labor force, firms in this economy recruit to fill vacancies in both types of jobs.[10] Denote by v_i the vacancies held by a firm, with $i = 1, 2$, and by $\phi^i(v_i)$ the cost (per unit of time) of filling these vacancies. Letting q_i be the ratio of matches to vacant jobs, $v_i q_i$ is the number of filled vacancies per unit of time.

The ratio q_i is a function of the aggregate skill-specific vacancy–unemployment ratio

$$q_i = \frac{x_i}{v_i} = \delta^i \left(\frac{U_i}{V_i} \right) \qquad 0 < \frac{\partial \delta^i}{\delta^i} \frac{V_i}{U_i} < 1 \tag{1.2}$$

where x_i is the number of matches and $U_i(V_i)$ is aggregate unemployment (vacancies) for each type. We assume that δ^i is strictly increasing in its argument and with an elasticity less than one.[11] Since firms face the same matching conditions in the market for skilled and unskilled jobs,

---

[8] In this specification, skilled and unskilled workers are perfect substitutes in production at the rate y_2/y_1. The model can be extended to incorporate a more general setting with finite substitution between the two types of workers, without changing the key qualitative results. See the appendix (p. 32).
[9] This is a useful simplification. Adding time to the training process complicates the setup without any substantially new insight.
[10] An alternative assumption is that exogenous separations flow into the unemployment pool.
[11] See Pissarides (1990).

$$q_i = \frac{x_i}{v_i} = \frac{X_i}{V_i}$$

where X are aggregate matches. With a linear homogeneous aggregate matching function, the number of matches in each firm is given by[12]

$$x_i = x_i(U_i, V_i) \equiv v_i q_i = v_i \delta^i \left(\frac{U_i}{V_i}\right) \tag{1.3}$$

Since each firm is small with respect to the market, changes in the individual supply of vacancies, v_i, do not affect aggregate vacancies V_i. Therefore, the ratio q_i does not depend on the behavior of individual firms.

We assume that the cost of posting a vacancy is a strictly increasing and convex function of the number of vacancies, given by

$$\phi^i(v_i) \equiv \frac{1}{2c_i} v_i^2 \tag{1.4}$$

where c_i is a positive constant, common to all firms. Notice that the quadratic form has the property that the marginal cost is zero at zero vacancies. This is a convenient property that greatly simplifies the subsequent analysis.

While skilled vacancies are filled either from the market or by internal upgrading, unskilled vacancies are filled exclusively from the external labor market. We denote by p the number of promoted individuals, who are trained and upgraded from an unskilled to a skilled job in each period of time. Since the training cost per employee, τ, is constant, the total training cost faced by each firm per period is simply $p\tau$. The assumption of linear training costs is ad hoc but has two advantages: first, it considerably simplifies the algebra; second, it sharpens the contrast between ILM and OLM firms discussed below. Notice that, in the current setup, we need at least convex recruiting costs to obtain a mixed equilibrium where both ILM and OLM coexist.[13]

With the possibility of internal upgrading, employment changes in each firm are given by

$$\frac{de_1}{dt} = v_1 q_1 - p - s e_1 \tag{1.5}$$

---

[12] Linear homogeneity in the matching function is used for analytical convenience.
[13] See Bertola and Caballero (1994).

$$\frac{de_2}{dt} = v_2 q_2 + p - se_2 \tag{1.6}$$

where s is the exogenous retirement rate from the labor force.

In the baseline model discussed below, firms and employees jointly maximize the net surplus from the match. With perfect information, this assumption is reasonable if the parties can commit not to recontract after matching or training costs have been sunk.[14] Using (1.1) and (1.4), and assuming that output prices are constant and equal to one, the net surplus for each firm in this economy is given by

$$\pi = y_1 e_1 + y_2 e_2 - p\tau - \frac{1}{2c_1} v_1^2 - \frac{1}{2c_2} v_2^2 \tag{1.7}$$

The choice of vacancies and promotions

The parties maximize the present discounted value of the net surplus stream subject to (1.5) and (1.6)

$$\max_{v_1, v_2, p} \Pi \equiv \int_0^\infty \exp(-rt)\pi dt \tag{1.8}$$

$$s.t. \quad \frac{de_1}{dt} = v_1 q_1 - p - se_1$$

$$\frac{de_2}{dt} = v_2 q_2 + p - se_2$$

Assuming a constant real rate of interest (r), this problem can be solved using the Maximum Principle. Hence, the current valued Hamiltonian corresponding to (1.8) is

$$H \equiv y_1 e_1 + y_2 e_2 - p\tau - \frac{1}{2c_1} v_1^2 - \frac{1}{2c_2} v_2^2 + J_1(v_1 q_1 - p - se_1)$$
$$+ J_2(v_2 q_2 + p - se_2) + \lambda_1 e_1 + \lambda_2 e_2$$

where J_i are the *costate* variables for e_i and λ_i is the Lagrangian multiplier for the non-negativity constraint on e_i. The necessary conditions for an optimum are

$$\frac{dJ_i}{dt} = rJ_i - \frac{\partial H}{\partial e_i} = (r+s)J_i - (y_i + \lambda_i) \tag{1.9}$$

for the state variables e_i and

$$\frac{\partial H}{\partial v_i} = 0 \rightarrow v_i = c_i J_i q_i \tag{1.10}$$

[14] See p. 23 and the appendix (p. 33) for a discussion of this important point.

$$\frac{\partial H}{\partial p} = J_2 - J_1 - \tau \leq 0 \; ; p \geq 0 \text{ and } p\frac{\partial H}{\partial p} = 0 \tag{1.11}$$

for the control variables. Given that employment, e_i, is weakly positive, the corresponding Kuhn–Tucker conditions are:

$$\lambda_i e_i = 0 \tag{1.12}$$

In what follows, we focus on the steady-state equilibrium. At the steady state, employment, e_i, and the corresponding costate variables are constant. Using this in (1.9), we have that

$$J_i = (r + s)^{-1}(y_i + \lambda_i) \tag{1.13}$$

The costate variable J_i can also be interpreted as the steady-state asset value of a filled vacancy, consisting of the current dividend, y_i, *plus* the capital gain or loss associated with a change of state, that occurs with probability s, and consists of the vacancy turning unfilled.

Finally, in the steady state and using (1.10), (1.5) and (1.6) can be rewritten as

$$c_1 J_1 q_1^2 = se_1 + p \tag{1.14}$$

$$c_2 J_2 q_2^2 = se_2 - p \tag{1.15}$$

The allocation of firms to internal and occupational labor markets

Equation (1.11) states that internal upgrading is used by firms whenever the difference in the shadow value of the two types of vacancies is at least as large as the idiosyncratic training cost. At the same time, (1.10) suggests that internal upgrading does not exclude external recruitment of skilled workers, occurring whenever v_2 and q_2 are non-zero. Since training costs are linear in the number of trained workers, (1.11) holds independently of the number of promoted individuals, p. Hence, this equation cannot determine the optimal level of training; to do so, we need to use the non-negativity condition on unskilled employment, e_1.

To see why, consider a firm that is initially endowed with a strictly positive level of unskilled employment – that is, $\bar{e}_1 > 0$. Suppose also that the training cost for this firm is such that (1.11) holds as a strict equality. In this case, the optimal policy is to train immediately and upgrade all incumbent unskilled employees, thus immediately depleting the available pool. From this point onwards, the maximum number of upgraded employees per unit of time is given by

$$v_1 q_1 - p - se_1 = v_1 q_1 - p \geq 0 \tag{1.16}$$

because $e_1 = 0$ in the steady state. Hence, in the steady state, firms that use training to fill their skilled vacancies can train and upgrade only the unskilled workers hired during the period.

When firms prefer to use external recruitment to fill skilled vacancies, unskilled employment, e_1, is positive if the matching probability, q_1, is strictly positive. This must be the case in an interior steady-state equilibrium.

Next, consider the non-negativity constraint on the employment of skilled workers, e_2. When firms use internal upgrading to fill skilled vacancies, e_2 is strictly positive because p is positive. When external recruitment is used because training costs are relatively high, e_2 is obviously positive. We conclude from this that the non-negativity constraint is never binding for skilled workers.

The threshold value of the training cost τ, τ^*, that divides ILM from OLM firms, is that value that makes firms indifferent between internal upgrading and external recruitment. To obtain this critical value, we set

$$J_2 - J_1 = \tau; \quad \lambda_1 = 0$$

and obtain

$$\tau^* = \frac{y_2 - y_1}{r + s} \tag{1.17}$$

Firms with $\tau > \tau^*$ belong to the OLM sector and firms with $\tau \leq \tau^*$ belong to the ILM sector.

OLM firms do not use internal upgrading ($p = 0$), the non-negativity constraint on employment, e_1, is not binding and (1.11) is satisfied as a strict inequality. For these firms, the marginal return from filling a skilled vacancy from within (J_2) is less than the marginal cost ($J_1 + \tau$). Hence, (1.13) can be rewritten as

$$J_i = (r + s)^{-1} y_i$$

ILM firms have training costs smaller than τ^* and can increase their surplus by training and upgrading as many unskilled workers as possible. These firms use both external recruitment and internal upgrading ($p > 0$) and the non-negativity constraint on unskilled employment is binding. Hence, for these firms we have

$$J_2 - J_1 = \tau; \quad \lambda_1 > 0$$

Using (1.13) we obtain

$$\lambda_1 = y_2 - y_1 - (r + s)\tau = (r + s)(\tau^* - \tau)$$
$$J_1 = (r + s)^{-1}(y_1 + \lambda_1) = (r + s)^{-1} y_2 - \tau$$

In this simple model, the contrast between ILM and OLM firms is sharp: in ILM firms, all hired unskilled workers are trained and upgraded. Skilled vacancies are filled both by internal upgrading and by external recruitment and, in the steady state, firms employ only skilled workers. In OLM firms, skilled vacancies are filled exclusively by external recruitment. The firm endowed with the training cost, τ^*, is just indifferent between the ILM and the OLM type and the percentage of firms using internal promotion (ILM firms) is given by $G(\tau^*) = \mathrm{Prob}(\tau \leq \tau^*)$.

Equation (1.17) can be slightly modified by reinterpreting the discount rate. Suppose that this economy experiences steady and constant productivity growth at the rate g, with output, training, and recruiting costs all growing at the same rate. Since the effective discount rate in this case is equal to $r - g$,[15] we obtain

$$\tau^* = \frac{y_2 - y_1}{r + s - g} \tag{1.18}$$

We can now state the following

> **Remark 1.1** *The share of ILM firms in the economy increases in equilibrium when the exogenous turnover rate s decreases.*

The intuitive explanation is that a decrease in the separation rate stimulates firms to open up more vacancies because it increases the surplus from matching. The consequent increase in vacancy–unemployment ratios reduces the probability of matching from the market, q_i, for both skilled and unskilled jobs. Since the opportunity cost of leaving a vacancy unfilled is higher for skilled than for unskilled vacancies, the share of ILM firms increases.

> **Remark 1.2** *An increase in the rate of productivity growth, g, increases the equilibrium value of τ^*, thus increasing the share of ILM firms in the economy.*

---

[15] To see this, rewrite the Hamiltonian using

$\hat{f} \equiv e^{gt} f$

$\hat{\tau} = e^{gt} \tau$

$\hat{c}_j = e^{-gt} c_j$

The new Hamiltonian has a common discount rate equal to $\hat{r} = r - g$.

An increase in productivity growth is equivalent to a reduction in the effective discount factor, and has effects similar to those already discussed in the case of a lower separation rate.

> **Remark 1.3** *A reduction in the mean of the exogenous distribution of training costs, $G(\tau)$, increases the relative share of ILM firms in the economy.*

It is often argued that (academic) education is socially valuable because it improves learning skills and facilitates workplace training. The remark suggests that the diffusion of internal labor markets in Japan can be associated with the presence of a well educated labor force.

OLM firms

Using the fact that OLM firms do not train and inserting (1.13) into (1.14) and (1.15), we obtain

$$e_i^{OLM} = \frac{c_i y_i}{s(r+s)} q_i^2 \tag{1.19}$$

Skilled and unskilled vacancies in OLM firms are given by

$$v_i^{OLM} = \frac{c_i y_i}{(r+s)} q_i \tag{1.20}$$

ILM firms

In ILM firms, unskilled workers recruited from the external labor market are trained and promoted to skilled workers. Hence, steady-state employment in these firms is given by

$$e_1^{ILM} = 0 \tag{1.21}$$

$$e_2^{ILM} = s^{-1}(p + v_2 q_2) = s^{-1}(v_1 q_1 + v_2 q_2) \tag{1.22}$$
$$= [s(r+s)]^{-1}\left[\{c_1 q_1^2 (y_2 - (r+s)\tau)\} + c_2 q_2^2 y_2\right]$$

and steady-state vacancies are defined by

$$v_1^{ILM} = \frac{c_1 \{y_2 - (r+s)\tau\}}{(r+s)} q_1 \tag{1.23}$$

$$v_2^{ILM} = \frac{c_2 y_2}{(r+s)} q_2 \tag{1.24}$$

where we have used the value of J_1 for ILM firms. Employment and vacancies in ILM and OLM firms both depend on the ratio of matches to vacancies, q_i, determined by the equilibrium conditions in the market for skilled and unskilled labor.

Wage bargaining and returns from search for unemployed workers

In this chapter, we have assumed that firms and employees jointly maximize the net surplus from the match. As long as wage bargaining is consistent with this assumption, the precise outcome of the bargain is irrelevant except for the fact that the resulting wage affects the expected returns from search for unemployed workers.

As shown by Malcomson (1997), when information is perfect and agents are risk-neutral, as happens in our setup, the bargain between the parties involved in the match yields an efficient outcome when: (a) it takes place before the investment in the specific relationship is sunk; (b) both agents can commit not to renegotiate after the investment has been sunk. As discussed in the appendix (p. 32), when the parties cannot commit to the sharing rules decided before matching and/or training occurs, there can be inefficient training and recruitment.

Before moving on to analyze labor market equilibrium, we close the model by describing the behavior of unemployed workers. We assume that each new entrant into the labor force, either skilled or unskilled, flows into the unemployment pool and receives no income while unemployed. Job search is costless, except for the time discount. An unemployed worker also retires at rate s. Hence the asset value, Γ_i, of an unemployed worker is given by

$$r\Gamma_1 = q_1^U [W_1 - \Gamma_1] - s\Gamma_1 \tag{1.25}$$

$$r\Gamma_2 = q_2^U (W_2 - \Gamma_2) - s\Gamma_2 \tag{1.26}$$

where W_i is the expected asset value from employment in a skilled or in an unskilled job[16] and q_i^U is the probability that a type i unemployed worker finds a job vacancy of her type

$$q_i^U = \frac{V_i q_i}{U_i} = \frac{q_i}{\delta_i^{-1}(q_i)} = \theta_i(q_i); \quad \frac{d\theta_i}{dq_i} < 0 \tag{1.27}$$

---

[16] Since we have not specified in detail the outcome of the wage bargain, we do not explicitly analyze how the asset values, W_i, vary among firms as functions of the training cost, τ.

All the matched vacancies result in employment if the asset value of employment exceeds the asset value of unemployment. We assume this to be the case.

Search market equilibrium

Aggregate vacancies

In the previous section, we established the optimal recruitment policy of firms as a function of q_1, q_2, τ, and other parameters. Aggregating individual decisions over the distribution of training costs, we obtain aggregate vacancies for each type of job. Using (1.20) and (1.23), we get

$$V_1 \equiv \int_{\tau^{\min}}^{\tau^{\max}} v_1 dG(\tau) \tag{1.28}$$

$$= \int_{\tau^{\min}}^{\tau^*} \frac{c_1\{y_2 - (r+s)\tau\}q_1}{(r+s)} dG(\tau) + \{1 - G(\tau^*)\} \frac{c_1 y_1 q_1}{(r+s)}$$

$$= \frac{c_1 \tilde{y}_1 q_1}{(r+s)}$$

where $\tilde{y}_1$ is given by

$$\tilde{y}_1 \equiv \int_{\tau^{\min}}^{\tau^*} \{y_2 - (r+s)\tau\} dG(\tau) + \{1 - G(\tau^*)\} y_1$$

$$y_1 < \tilde{y}_1 < y_2$$

$$\frac{d\tilde{y}_1}{d\tau^*} = \{(y_2 - y_1) - (r+s)\tau^*\} dG(\tau^*) = 0$$

Similarly, from (1.20) and (1.24), we obtain aggregate skilled vacancies as

$$V_2 = \frac{c_2 y_2 q_2}{(r+s)} \tag{1.29}$$

Labor market equilibrium

We are now ready to define and analyze the steady-state equilibrium in the markets for skilled and unskilled jobs. Recall that, in the steady state, employment changes are zero so that

$$v_1 q_1 = s e_1 + p$$

$$v_2 q_2 = s e_2 - p$$

Since these equalities hold for each firm, we can aggregate over firms simply by replacing small letters with capital letters, and write

$$V_1 q_1 \equiv sE_1 + P \tag{1.30}$$

$$V_2 q_2 \equiv sE_2 - P \tag{1.31}$$

where E_i and P are, respectively, aggregate employment and the aggregate promotion flow.

This economy has two types of worker, the skilled and the unskilled. Recall that we have assumed a common and exogenous outflow rate, s, from the labor force. Since some unskilled workers are internally promoted and become skilled workers after receiving workplace training, labor market inflows cannot be the same for both types of workers in the steady-state equilibrium.

Denoting by σ_i the exogenous inflows into the labor force, and normalizing the size of total labor force to unity $(L \equiv L_1 + L_2 \equiv 1)$, labor force dynamics are given by

$$\frac{dL_1}{dt} = \sigma_1 - P - sL_1$$

$$\frac{dL_2}{dt} = \sigma_2 + P - sL_2$$

In the steady-state equilibrium, L_1 and L_2 must be constant. Hence,

$$s(U_1 + E_1) = \sigma_1 - P$$

$$s(U_2 + E_2) = s - \sigma_1 + P$$

where U_i is unemployment and we have used both the identity $L_i = E_i + U_i$ and the requirement $\sigma_1 + \sigma_2 = s(L_1 + L_2) = s$. Equations (1.30) and (1.31) allow us to substitute out P in these expressions, and rearrange to get

$$sU_1 + V_1 q_1 = \sigma_1 \tag{1.32}$$

$$sU_2 + V_2 q_2 = s - \sigma_1 \tag{1.33}$$

To close the model, we rewrite (1.2) as follows

$$U_i = V_i \delta_i^{-1}(q_i) \tag{1.34}$$

Equations (1.32) and (1.33) can also be rewritten by using (1.28), (1.29), and (1.34) to obtain

$$\frac{c_1 \tilde{y}_1}{(r+s)} q_1 [s \delta_1^{-1}(q_1) + q_1] = \sigma_1 \tag{1.35}$$

$$\frac{c_2 y_2}{(r+s)} q_2 [s \delta_2^{-1}(q_2) + q_2] = \sigma_2 \equiv s - \sigma_1 \tag{1.36}$$

These two equations determine the equilibrium ratios of matches to vacancies, q_i. Notice that, since the elasticity of δ_i with respect to the unemployment–vacancy ratio is less than one, a 1 percent increase in q_i increases δ_i^{-1} by more than 1 percent. This implies that the elasticity of $q_i [s \delta_i^{-1}(q_i) + q_i]$ with respect to q_i is greater than two. Thus we get

$$q_i = \psi_i(M_i) \tag{1.37}$$

$$M_i = \sigma_i \left\{ \frac{c_i x_i}{(r+s)} \right\}^{-1} ; \ x_1 \equiv \tilde{y}_1; \ x_2 \equiv y_2$$

$$0 < \frac{d\psi_i}{dM_i} \cdot \frac{M_i}{\psi_i} < \frac{1}{2}$$

The equilibrium ratio of matches to vacancies, q_i, is increasing in the inflow rate, σ_i, and in the recruitment cost, $1/c_i$, and decreasing in the asset value, J_i. The higher the cost of recruiting from the market, the smaller the supply of vacancies for a given number of matches. The higher the asset value of a filled vacancy, the larger the number of vacancies on supply, and the lower the probability of recruiting from the market.

We can plug (1.37) back into (1.28), (1.29), and (1.34) to get aggregate unemployment, aggregate vacancies, and the aggregate number of matches for each type of job

$$V_i = \frac{\sigma_i [\psi_i(M_i)]}{M_i}; \quad \frac{d(V_i)}{dM_i} < 0; \ \frac{d(V_i)}{d\sigma_i} > 0 \tag{1.38}$$

$$V_i q_i = \frac{\sigma_i [\psi_i(M_i)]^2}{M_i}; \quad \frac{d(V_i q_i)}{dM_i} < 0; \ \frac{d(V_i q_i)}{d\sigma_i} > 0 \tag{1.39}$$

$$U_j = \frac{\sigma_j \psi_j(M_j) \delta_j^{-1} [\psi_j(M_j)]}{M_j}, \quad \frac{d(U_j)}{dM_j} > 0, \ \frac{d(U_j)}{d\sigma_j} > 0 \tag{1.40}$$

Similarly, aggregate employment and the aggregate flow of upgraded workers can be written as functions of M_i

$$E_1 = E_1^{OLM} = \{1 - G(\tau^*)\}s^{-1}V_1^{OLM}q_1 \qquad (1.41)$$
$$= \{1 - G(\tau^*)\}[s(r+s)]^{-1}c_1y_1q_1^2$$
$$= \frac{\sigma_1[\psi_1(M_1)]^2}{sM_1}\frac{\{1 - G(\tau^*)\}y_1}{\widetilde{y}_1}$$

$$E_2^{OLM} = s^{-1}\{1 - G(\tau^*)\}V_2q_2 = \{1 - G(\tau^*)\}\frac{\sigma_2[\psi_2(M_2)]^2}{sM_2} \qquad (1.42)$$

$$E_1^{ILM} = 0 \qquad (1.43)$$

$$E_2^{ILM} = \int_{\tau^{\min}}^{\tau^*} s^{-1}[v_1q_1 + v_2q_2]dG(\tau) \qquad (1.44)$$
$$= \frac{\sigma_1[\psi_1(M_1)]^2}{sM_1}\int_{\tau^{\min}}^{\tau^*}\frac{y_2 - (r+s)\tau}{\widetilde{y}_1}dG(\tau)$$
$$+ G(\tau^*)\frac{\sigma_2[\psi_2(M_2)]^2}{sM_2}$$

$$P = \int_{\tau^{\min}}^{\tau^*} v_1q_1 dG(\tau) = \frac{\sigma_1[\psi_1(M_1)]^2}{M_1}\int_{\tau^{\min}}^{\tau^*}\frac{y_2 - (r+s)\tau}{\widetilde{y}_1}dG(\tau)$$
$$\qquad (1.45)$$

$$E_2 \equiv E_2^{OLM} + E_2^{ILM} \qquad (1.46)$$
$$= \frac{\sigma_1[\psi_1(M_1)]^2}{sM_1}\int_{\tau^{\min}}^{\tau^*}\frac{y_2 - (r+s)\tau}{\widetilde{y}_1}dG(\tau) + \frac{\sigma_2[\psi_2(M_2)]^2}{sM_2}$$

The comparative statics analysis discussed below is based upon (1.38)–(1.46). The key results are summarized in table 1.1.

Comparative statics

We describe the comparative statics results by looking at the effects on aggregate matches, employment, unemployment, and promotion flows of changes in the discount rate, $r - g$, the separation rate, s, and output per head, y_j. These variables affect matches and unemployment because they change the asset value of filled vacancies, J_i, which is also the shadow price of each type of job. We also consider the effects of changes in the inflow rate, σ_i, and in the recruitment cost $1/c_i$.

The ratio of matches to vacancies, q_i, is a decreasing function of the shadow price, J_i. When the shadow price increases, firms open up new

Table 1.1 *Comparative statics*

	g	s	y_1	y_2	c_1	c_2	σ_1	$\sigma_2{}^a$
V_1q_1	+	−	+	+	+	0	+	0
V_1	+	−	+	+	+	0	+	0
U_1	−	+	−	−	−	0	+	0
V_2q_2	+	−	0	+	0	+	0	+
V_2	+	−	0	+	0	+	0	+
U_2	−	+	0	−	0	−	0	+
P	+	−	−	+	+	0	+	+
τ^*	+	−	−	+	0	0	0	0
E_1	?	?	+	−	+	0	+	0
E_2	+	−	−	+	+	+	+	+
$U(\sum U_j)$	−	+	−	−	−	−	+	+

Note: We use +, −, and 0 when an increase in the variable heading each column leads, respectively, to an increase, a decline, and no change in the variable heading each row. A question mark is used when the direction of the effect cannot be signed.
^{a}The result in this column shows the effects of an exogenous change in σ_2, although σ_2 cannot be changed independently, because $\sigma_2 = s - \sigma_1$.

vacancies, and the aggregate number of vacancies, V_i, increases for each level of aggregate unemployment. Hence, the ratio of matches to vacancies, q_i, falls. Since the elasticity of the ratio, q_i, with respect to M_i is less than $\frac{1}{2}$, the total number of matches, V_iq_i, also increases, both with J_i and with σ_i. Unemployment is increasing, too, in the inflow rate, σ_i, but declines when the asset value of filled jobs, J_i, increases.

Total internal upgrading (P) depends positively on the ratio q_1. The relationship between P and q_1 reflects the fact that upgrading fills a skilled vacancy but creates at the same time an unskilled vacancy. The easier it is to fill such a vacancy from the market, the higher the promotion flows. Somewhat surprisingly, the upgrading flow turns out to be independent of both the cost of recruiting skilled workers, $1/c_2$, and the ratio of skilled matches to skilled vacancies, q_2. This result is the consequence of our simplifying assumption that relative productivities are exogenously given, with infinite substitution between the two types of labor.

In the steady-state equilibrium and with no promotion, unskilled employment in OLM firms, which is equal to total unskilled employment, is given by the ratio of total matches to the exogenous separation rate,

$V_1 q_1/s$, and it varies in the same direction of total matches. The effects of r and s on employment cannot be signed because changes in these variables increase the share of OLM firms but reduce the matching rate, thus reducing employment in each OLM firm. On the other hand, skilled employment depends upon the recruiting rate of both types of labor.

A reduction in the cost of recruitment parameters, $1/c_i$, increases both matches and employment, but reduces the ratio of matches to vacancies, q_i. While a higher value of c_2 has no effect on upgrading, an increase of c_1 induces further reliance on internal upgrading, as it becomes less costly to fill the skilled vacancies by promoting recruited unskilled workers.

Finally, consider the effects of an increase in the inflow rate σ_1 (which in turn implies a corresponding decrease in σ_2) on aggregate unemployment, U, defined by

$$U = U_1 + U_2 = \sum_{i=1}^{2} \frac{\sigma_i \psi_i(M_i) \delta_i^{-1} [\psi_i(M_i)]}{M_i} \tag{1.47}$$

A higher inflow rate, σ_1, increases both unemployment and employment of unskilled workers but has ambiguous effects on total unemployment. As (1.47) shows, there exists a critical value of σ_1 that minimizes total unemployment. Moreover, total unemployment is decreasing in σ_1 when σ_1 is small (U_1 is small relative to U_2) and increasing in σ_1 when σ_1 is beyond a critical level.

Discussion and extensions

Our comparative statics results imply the following.

> **Remark 1.4** *An increase in productivity growth, g, reduces unemployment for both types of worker. An increase in efficiency in recruiting of either types (c_i) also reduces unemployment and increases skilled employment. Moreover, internal upgrading increases as c_1 increases.*

An increase in productivity growth raises the asset value, J_i. As a consequence, both q_i and U_i fall but V_i increases. An interesting implication of Remarks 1.1, 1.2, and 1.4 is that economies with higher rates of productivity growth and lower turnover rates have both a higher share of ILM firms and a lower aggregate unemployment rate. Two distinctive features of the Japanese labor market are the importance of internal labor markets and the low aggregate unemployment rate. Our model explains both these two features in a simple way by relating them to the relatively high productivity growth and the relatively low turnover rate experienced by the Japanese economy in the postwar period. Moreover, the analysis indicates that employment of skilled workers benefits from the ease of recruiting *unskilled workers*, $1/c_1$. This occurs because with smaller value of $1/c_1$, ILM firms find it easier to recruit unskilled workers and train them internally. Hence one implication of Remark 1.4 is that the share of ILM employment is large in an economy with a well developed labor market for unskilled workers (large $1/c_1$) and a less developed one for skilled workers (small $1/c_2$). Experience of the postwar Japanese economy seems to fit well with such a characterization.

An important implication of the model presented in this chapter is that the substantial slowdown of productivity growth experienced by Japan since the early 1970s – and especially during the 1990s, after the burst of the bubble – should increase the (natural) rate of unemployment and reduce the relative importance of internal labor markets.

Training externalities

We have characterized internal training as an alternative to external recruitment of skilled workers, and treated the inflow of skilled workers in the labor market as exogenous. In the long run, however, the decision to invest in off-the-job training is influenced by the costs and benefits, and it is likely to respond to wage differentials across different types of skill.

Since firms that train internally do not usually take into account the indirect effect of their decisions either on the schooling decision taken by workers or on the recruitment decision taken by other firms, workplace training can generate externalities. To see this point, notice that an increase in the frequency of workplace training reduces the expected earnings differential between skilled and unskilled jobs. The reason is that, by providing career opportunities to unskilled labor, workplace training makes unskilled jobs relatively more attractive.

An increase in the frequency of internal training can thus discourage vocational schooling. If the matching technology exhibits a thin market externality (ruled out in this chapter[17]), a reduction in skilled job

---

[17] Note, however, that a thin market externality can arise even if the aggregate matching technology is linear homogeneous as long as jobs and workers are heterogeneous, and some offers are rejected. For example, skilled workers in our model may not accept unskilled job offers. If the external labor market does not effectively sort out heterogeneous types of vacancies and workers *ex ante*, the thin market externality will be present even if the matching technology is linear homogeneous.

searchers can further discourage the recruitment of skilled workers from the market and encourage internal training. The cumulative effect of these feedback effects could be that some markets for skilled jobs cease to exist.

This chain of effects may have played an important role in the process of internalization of training in the postwar Japanese labor market. As we show in chapters 5 and 7, Japanese firms have a strong tendency to train their employees internally, rather than to search for suitable workers in the external market. In the high-growth era, the shortage of skilled workers was particularly acute in rapidly growing manufacturing industries. As a result, many firms invested heavily in internal training, which in turn severely limited the labor market opportunities available to skilled workers.

The complementarity between education and workplace training

In this chapter, we have treated off-the-job training and workplace training as alternative ways of endowing workers with the necessary labor market skills. Workers who have received vocational training need no additional training and firms that wish to save matching costs can do so only by training and upgrading unskilled workers.

We have deliberately ignored both the decision to invest in off-the-job training and, more generally, the decision to invest in education. (Academic) education and training are often considered as complements, and there is evidence that individuals with better education usually face a better prospect of additional (workplace) training (OECD, 1991). As stressed in the comments concerning Remark 1.3, one reason why education matters is because it improves learning skills, thus reducing the training costs faced by firms.[18]

There is also a wide consensus concerning the view that enterprise training is more widespread in Germany and Japan than in other developed economies (Lynch, 1993). According to Richard Freeman, "the US has a weak in-firm training system, with much of the training concentrated on high level workers rather than on raising the skills of the low paid. The experience of Germany and Japan, the exemplars of in-firm training, show that considerable institutional structure is needed to induce firms to provide training to workers" (1995, p. 7).

The relative success of these two countries in the development of industrial skills has been closely linked to their educational system, that per-

---

[18] See Brunello and Medio (1996); Brunello and Ishikawa (1999).

forms better than other countries in terms of both quantity and quality.[19] As remarked by Prais in his international comparison of education systems, "Japan's industrial success is strongly based on foundations laid during compulsory schooling, till the age of 15, by way of substantially higher attainments in mathematics by average pupils than in Britain . . . these higher standards make possible more advanced preparation" (Prais, 1990, p. 210).

During the years of rapid economic growth, when skilled workers were in relative short supply, workplace training had an important role to play in the Japanese economy. The presence of a well educated labor force was certainly a key factor in the development of internal labor markets, with their emphasis on skill development within firms. This heavy reliance upon internal training[20] could have had important side effects in the Japanese labor market, the most notable perhaps being the limited development of external labor markets for some skills.

Summary

In this introductory chapter, we have used a very simple job-search environment, in the tradition of Diamond and Pissarides, to explore the relationship between productivity growth, labor turnover, unemployment, and internal labor markets. The predictions obtained from the model are broadly consistent with the stylized view of the Japanese economy, which includes high productivity growth, low turnover, low unemployment, and the importance of internal labor markets. Our characterization of internal labor markets has focused exclusively on training and on internal promotion, and we have paid little attention to incentives and assignment problems. We will come back to these issues in chapter 2 and later on in the book.

Appendix

Inefficient bargaining

In the main text, we have assumed that the bargain between firms and employees is efficient because it maximizes the joint net surplus. This assumption greatly simplifies the analytical structure of the model but

---

[19] These remarks exclude top university education, where the United Kingdom and the United States perform better than Germany and Japan, but with a substantially higher dropout rate. See Lynch (1993).

[20] See, for example, the lucid description and analysis of enterprise training in Odaka (1993).

is open to question. In this appendix, we sketch alternative specifications of the bargain, and consider their consequences.

Consider first the hold-up problem.[21] For the bargain to yield efficient outcomes, employees must be willing to share the surplus net of the recruitment (training) cost. After recruitment (training) has taken place, however, bygones are bygones and employees have an incentive to renegotiate their pay on the basis of the surplus gross of sunk costs. Inefficient recruitment (training) arises if employees cannot commit not to recontract. To the extent that the firm bears the full cost of recruiting (training) but fails to capture all the surplus, there is under-investment in hiring (training).

Another possible source of inefficiency is when firms treat the negotiated wage as given, thus maximizing profits rather than the net surplus. In this case the maximization problem becomes

$$\pi = y_1 e_1 + y_2 e_2 - w_1 e_1 - w_2 e_2 - p\tau - \frac{1}{2c_1} v_1^2 - \frac{1}{2c_2} v_2^2 \qquad (1A.1)$$

Suppose that the wage, w_i, is determined as a share β of the surplus, but assume that firms treat wage payments as costs rather than as rent-sharing devices. In this specific case, the maximization of the profit stream associated with (1A.1) yields:

$$J_i = (r+s)^{-1}(y_i - w_i) \qquad (1A.2)$$

$$W_2 = (r+s)^{-1} w_2 \qquad (1A.3)$$

$$W_1 = [(r+s)(r+s+\varepsilon)]^{-1}\{(r+s)w_1 + \varepsilon W_2\} \qquad (1A.4)$$

where ε is the probability that an unskilled worker is trained and upgraded, and the sharing scheme is such that

$$(1-\beta)W_i = \beta J_i \qquad (1A.5)$$

Eliminating wages from (1A.2–1A.4) we obtain

$$J_1 = [(r+s)(r+s+\beta\varepsilon)]^{-1}(1-\beta)\{(r+s)y_1 + \beta\varepsilon y_2\} \qquad (1A.6)$$

$$J_2 = (r+s)^{-1}(1-\beta)y_2 \qquad (1A.7)$$

$$W_1 = [(r+s)(r+s+\beta\varepsilon)]^{-1}\beta\{(r+s)y_1 + \beta\varepsilon y_2\} \qquad (1A.8)$$

$$W_2 = (r+s)^{-1}y_2 \qquad (1A.9)$$

[21] See Malcomson (1997) for a detailed review.

In this case, the threshold value of the training cost, τ^*, that divides firms into OLM and ILM types is given by

$$J_2 - J_1 = \frac{(1 - \beta)(y_2 - y_1)}{r + s + \beta\varepsilon} = \tau^* \tag{1A.10}$$

This equation coincides with (1.17) in the text when β is equal to zero. As β increases from zero, the critical training cost, τ^*, falls below the level determined by (1.17) and the share of ILM firms in the economy shrinks. The economic mechanism at work is that firms incur the full cost of internal training but split the benefit with employees in terms of higher wages. As in the previous case, we obtain under-investment in training. The important point, however, is that Remarks 1.1–1.4 continue to hold even in the presence of this inefficiency.

Finite substitution between the two types of labor

In the main text, we have assumed that the marginal product of each type of labor is exogenously given and independent of the ratio of the two types of employees. If we assume a conventional linear homogeneous production function with the two types of labor as inputs, the Hamiltonian can be rewritten as

$$H^F \equiv e_2 f(k) - p\tau - \frac{1}{2c_1}v_1^2 - \frac{1}{2c_2}v_2^2 \tag{1A.11}$$
$$+ J_1(v_1 q_1 - p - se_1) + J_2(v_2 q_2 + p - se_2)$$

where $k \equiv e_1/e_2$ is the ratio of two inputs. In this case, the corresponding shadow prices are

$$J_1 = (r + s)^{-1} f'(k) \tag{1A.12}$$

$$J_2 = (r + s)^{-1}[f(k) - kf'(k)] \tag{1A.13}$$

and the threshold value of training satisfies the following condition

$$(r + s)^{-1}[f(k) - (k + 1)f'(k)] = \tau^* \tag{1A.14}$$

Since the LHS is increasing in k, it follows that ILM firms have lower k than OLM firms. Given the optimal input mix, the rest of the analysis is qualitatively similar to that described in the main text.

2 Demand and supply of skills in a corporate hierarchy

Overview[1]

Hierarchies are ubiquitous modes of organization, that appear in a great variety of forms and sizes. Modern large corporations are no exception. Corporate hierarchies share a set of common characteristics with hierarchies in other types of organization and consist of a large number of participants with diverse responsibilities, technical expertise, personal traits, and, among other things, their own interests and goals.

Corporate hierarchies perform multiple functions. First of all, a hierarchy is a way of *organizing tasks and activities efficiently* within a firm. Second, a hierarchy is a system for *decision-making and information processing*. Last but not the least, a hierarchy is a *personnel* (human resource) *management system*, organizing careers as vertical progressions along promotion ladders.

More often than not, these goals are not perfectly aligned and designers of corporate hierarchies must find a compromise among them. Consider, for example, the Peter Principle: a person who performs superbly at a lower rank may not be the best candidate for an upper-ranked job. If promotion to a high-ranked job is used as an incentive device to elicit individual effort, the firm could have to compromise the first goal (to allocate workers to tasks according to their comparative advantage) in order to achieve the second (to maintain incentives among junior workers).

In chapter 1 we focused on internal upgrading versus external procurement to characterize in a simple but effective way the allocation of firms among internal and occupational labor markets. In this chapter, we deepen the analysis by looking at the interactions between skill formation and production efficiency (allocation of workers to their most suitable

---

[1] This chapter builds on Ariga, Brunello and Ohkusa (1997).

jobs). We do this by building a model of human capital accumulation that includes multiple skills and jobs.

Such a model has two purposes. First, we provide a rigorous and coherent framework to describe key features of internal and occupational labor markets in the context of human capital accumulation. While the institutional features of these two modes of organizing labor within firms have received considerable attention in the empirical literature, the underlying economic factors and the complex interactions that generate the observed stylized differences have remained rather elusive. Second, we present a set of mutually consistent and empirically testable predictions about internal and occupational labor markets that set the stage for the empirical analysis in chapters 3–5 of this book.

We analyze the dynamic optimization problem involving both the investment in more than one type of human capital and the job assignment of workers to tasks over time. The key parameter in the analysis is the proximity of different jobs within a hierarchy in terms of the required skills (human capital). This degree of proximity depends not only upon various technological conditions related to tasks but also upon the way in which jobs and training system are designed. We show that the solution to this dynamic optimization problem offers a rich menu of covariations among various facets of internal labor markets, including recruitment and promotion policies, skill formation and training, earnings profiles, income distribution, and spans of control. In particular, two contrasting types of hierarchy emerge from the analysis, depending upon the degree of proximity in the required skills.

In one class of firms, skill proximity is relatively high and we find a set of characteristics common to jobs (firms) with internal labor markets (hereafter, ILM firms). Skill formation in these firms is predominantly internal and involves a long, continuous accumulation process along promotion ladders where jobs with closely related skills are lined up in a progression. Experience within the hierarchy and along these promotion ladders is the most important determinant of promotion decisions. Innate talent or comparative advantage at the start of a career matters less. As a result, even the less talented are promoted, albeit at a later stage of their career.

Promotion timing can be delayed substantially for some employees. Since a relatively large percentage of employees are promoted to upper ranks, both the span of control and the differential between marginal products of lower- and upper-ranked employees are smaller. Hiring decisions in this type of firm are based upon stringent standards. Because of the skill proximity of jobs in lower and upper ranks, individuals who are unlikely to be promoted to upper ranks may not be employable even at lower ranks. This, together with a relatively small earnings differential between lower- and upper-rank jobs, gives rise to a fairly equal income distribution within the firm. Not surprisingly, these characteristics correspond almost exactly to the stylized description of human resource management (HRM) in large Japanese firms, viewed as having a well developed system of internal labor markets.[2]

In the other type of firms, skill proximity across tasks is relatively low and we find a set of characteristics typical of occupational labor markets (hereafter, OLM firms). Skill requirements to perform tasks in these firms are determined mainly in the labor market and, most typically, each occupation is clearly defined by a (portable) license. Internal training is less common and inter-firm mobility is relatively higher than intra-firm mobility. Because of the relative independence of jobs, qualifications and innate talents at the start of a career largely determine job assignments. Internal promotions, if they occur at all, are concentrated in the early stages of a career and workers are highly specialized.

The demarcation between upper and lower ranks in the hierarchy is also more clear-cut. Experience in lower ranks may be helpful to increase productivity in lower-ranked jobs but is not helpful to increase productivity in upper-ranked jobs. The span of control and inter-rank earnings differentials are both larger in OLM than in ILM firms. Furthermore, OLM firms are likely to employ multiple ports of entry, depending upon the comparative advantages of applicants. Consequently, hiring standards are less demanding. Because of the diversity of talents and of the larger earnings differentials between upper- and lower-ranked jobs, income distribution within this type of firm is highly skewed and the overall earnings differential is larger.

Compared to chapter 1, where the existence of internal promotion was taken as an exogenous feature of ILM firms, in this chapter we show that the key features of ILM and OLM firms briefly summarized above emerge endogenously from the solution to a dynamic optimization problem that involves both investment in human capital and job assignment. The analysis in this chapter shares its basic thrust with a relatively small but growing literature that extends traditional human capital theory to incorporate the demand side of the market.[3] While our model explicitly

[2] See Koike (1988); Aoki (1988).
[3] Perhaps the earliest work in this area is Stern (1987). Our model is closest to that developed by Demougin and Siow (1994), who investigate career dynamics in corporate hierarchies by building upon human capital theory. Our model differs from theirs in two important ways. First of all, training in their paper is purely on-the-job and they do not explicitly consider different types of accumulated human capital. Second, workers in their model live two (discrete) periods and the timing of promotion is exogenously fixed.

treats heterogeneous human capital accumulation in the context of the design of a corporate hierarchy, we do abstract from the issues associated with information asymmetry, that have been investigated intensively in the recent literature on career dynamics.[4]

The remainder of the chapter is organized as follows. In the next section, we develop and analyze a partial equilibrium model of human capital accumulation in a corporate hierarchy. We then extend the model to full market equilibrium, and relate the major predictions of the model to some empirical regularities reported in the literature. A brief summary concludes the chapter.

A model of human capital accumulation

In this section, we develop a model of job assignment and investment in human capital for the two types of firm discussed in the Introduction. Our principal purpose is to show that much of the stylized features of ILM and OLM firms can be explained in terms of their training systems. In particular, we believe that the critical difference is the degree to which the training system is integrated with the promotion ladder in a hierarchy.

In this section, we model this difference by focusing on the degree of proximity in the types of human capital necessary for upper- and lower-ranked jobs. In ILM firms, these jobs are closely related to each other (their proximity is high). Hence, the productivity loss of employing individuals in tasks other than the most suitable ones is relatively small. In OLM firms, skills needed in lower- and upper-ranked tasks are quite different, and the productivity loss of employing individuals in the wrong position is large.

To illustrate and explain verbally the key assumptions of the model below, consider as an example a hospital providing medical care to patients.[5] In designing work organization, this hospital has two alternatives, type I and type O.

In the type O mode, the hospital divides the set of tasks into two groups, one performed by nurses and the other by doctors. The job demarcation between these two occupations is determined in external occupational labor markets. In type O organizations, nurses accumulate

---

[4] See Gibbons (1996) and Gibbons and Waldman (1998) for recent reviews.
[5] The characterization of ILM and OLM firms in this chapter is based on a highly stylized interpretation of a large body of empirical research in the field of industrial relations. See Marsden (1990) for an international comparison of ILM and OLM labor markets, and Dore and Sako (1988) for a comparison of training systems in the United Kingdom and Japan.

the skills required to perform better the group of tasks assigned to them. Hence skilled nurses perform better than less skilled, but they never perform the group of tasks assigned to doctors.

On the other hand, the type I mode has two jobs, called nursedoc A and nursedoc B. The guiding principle of job demarcations at type I organizations is the accumulation of skills along the promotion ladder, with nursedoc A being less skilled than nursedoc B. In type I hospitals, nursedoc A often perform the tasks assigned to doctors in type O hospitals. For example, nursedoc A can be fully responsible for the daily treatment of patients whose illness is well diagnosed and stable. Nursedoc A can even perform relatively simple operations under the supervision of nursedoc B. At the same time, nursedoc B perform some of the tasks normally assigned to highly experienced nurses in type O hospitals.

As a rule, type O hospitals are very similar and doctors and nurses move relatively easily from one (type O) hospital to the other because job demarcations, and hence skill requirements, are more or less the same. Type I hospitals, on the other hand, differ not only from type O hospitals but also from other type I hospitals. This makes sense because job demarcations in each hospital are designed to accommodate the idiosyncrasies these hospitals have to cope with. For example, nursedoc A in a large inner city hospital could be highly skilled in treating emergency patients from traffic accidents.

There are clear advantages and disadvantages in both types of work organizations. In type I organizations, the flexibility of work design enhances productivity. In the longer run, continuity of skills across jobs and ranks makes skill formation more efficient. Obviously, there are also disadvantages. For example, workers are mobile within the hospital but the idiosyncrasy of work organization hinders worker mobility between hospitals.

Hiring standards also differ between the two types of organization. Clearly, type I organizations prefer to hire relatively young, inexperienced workers in lower-ranked jobs. Workers in type I organizations are expected to perform a wide range of tasks during the course of a long career in the hospital. Those who are judged to be not suitable for upper-ranked jobs are not hired in lower-ranked jobs because type I organizations invest heavily in the training of junior workers to increase their productivity when they are promoted to upper-rank jobs. Type O organizations have different recruitment policies and, because of the differences in skill requirements, nurses and doctors are hired according to their own standards and qualifications. Applicants for nurse (doctor) vacancies will not be turned down even if they are not fit for doctor (nurse) jobs.

In a nutshell, the key differences in the two modes of organization are: (a) job demarcations and (b) training. In type I firms, training is provided internally because of the idiosyncrasies of work organization. Interactions and work-sharing across jobs and ranks are frequent and workers accumulate a wide range of skills as they progress along the promotion ladder. In type O firms, job demarcations are clear and stable. The relationship between upper-rank and lower-rank workers is mainly in terms of supervision and monitoring. Relatively little work-sharing across ranks makes it practical to train workers externally or to offer off-the-job training.

In sum, the example has focused, on one hand, on the homogeneity/ idiosyncrasy of work organization, and, on the other, on the continuity/ discontinuity of skill formation across tasks within organizations. In what follows, we model these key properties and demonstrate analytically that the observations made above can be derived as properties of a model of optimal human accumulation in a corporate hierarchy.

The model

Consider a firm consisting of a large number of similar production units. Each unit is a simple two-layer hierarchy, headed by a supervisor who oversees and organizes activities. Supervisors can have different numbers of subordinates, depending on their own and their subordinates' productivities.[6]

All the employees work for T years, and then retire. Without loss of generality, we normalize $T = 1$. We also conveniently set the age of entry in the labor force at zero. Workers differ in their age, τ, and in an innate ability vector (u_s, u_n) randomly drawn from the joint symmetric probability distribution, G. As we shall see shortly, a natural interpretation of vector (u_s, u_n) is the initial endowment of the two types of human capital, (k_s, k_n), where s is for upper-rank (supervisors) and n is for lower-rank (subordinates), except from the fact that we allow u_s to take negative values.

A cohort of workers is therefore defined by age and by the value of innate ability. Innate ability, by definition, remains constant throughout employees' life. Until the next section, we use a partial equilibrium model and define the value of outside employment opportunities available to

---

[6] See Rosen (1982) for a similar setup.

workers as $\bar{V} \geq 0,$[7] where V is lifetime earnings net of the disutility of investment in human capital that workers can earn in the labor market. As shown below, this reservation value is non-negative since no investment and no earnings yield zero lifetime utility. In the next section, we endogenously determine the market equilibrium value of offers for each cohort of workers. Until then, we simply assume that the only outside opportunity available to each worker is to remain idle. Thus we set $\bar{V} = 0$. The number of new entrants is assumed constant so that the size and age distribution of employees are also constant.

Utility (disutility) is assumed to be transferable between workers and the firm. For the sake of simplicity, the discount rate is zero and we abstract from information imperfections (symmetric or not). Hence the optimal contract between workers and firms achieves the first best, and the efficient solution is independent of the distribution of the net surplus. Under these assumptions, employees and the firm maximize the steady-state joint net surplus from production.[8]

Two types of human capital (skills) are needed for production. Denote by k_s (k_n) the human capital needed to perform tasks in upper-ranked (lower-ranked) jobs. Examples of upper- and lower-ranked jobs are, respectively, supervision and production. The productivity of each type of human capital is highest when skills are matched to their most suitable jobs. Hence, skills k_s and k_n are more productive when used respectively in upper- and lower-ranked jobs.

We denote by v ($0 \leqslant v \leqslant 1$) the productivity of each type of human capital when employed in less suitable jobs relative to the productivity of the same capital employed in its most suitable job. Following the informal discussion in the previous section, it is natural to associate ILM firms with a relatively high value of v and OLM firms with a low value of v. In other words, the parameter v measures the proximity of skills (human capital) between supervisors and subordinates.

We measure productivities in terms of the labor services generated per unit of time. Denote by e_s and e_n, respectively, the labor services provided by each worker in order to perform tasks in either a supervisory or in a subordinate position. A worker with accumulated human capital (k_s, k_n) and with innate ability (u_s, u_n), when employed as a supervisor, generates

$$e_s = k_s + u_s + v(k_n + u_n) - \bar{c} \tag{2.1}$$

---

[7] As we shall see later (p. 50), the outside employment opportunity in a full market equilibrium model is a function of innate ability, rather than a constant. The substance of the analysis (especially lemmas 2.1, 2.2, and 2.4 in this section) carries over to the case of general market equilibrium.

[8] See the discussion in chapter 1 (p. 18).

units of labor services, where $\bar{c}$ is the non-negative cost of setting up a production unit, measured as a reduction in the input of labor services. Similarly, when employed as a subordinate, she generates

$$e_n = k_n + u_n + v(k_s + u_s) \qquad (2.2)$$

To simplify the analysis, we assume that workers are homogeneous in terms of u_n and set $u_n = \bar{u} \geq 0$.[9] Hence, innate ability matters only in terms of initial endowment of human capital suitable for supervisors, u_s. Moreover, until we get to the numerical example in the next section, we set $\bar{c} = 0$.

Output of a representative productive unit, headed by a supervisor, is given by

$$Q = F(e_s, D_n) = e_s f\left(\frac{D_n}{e_s}\right) \qquad (2.3)$$

where D_n are the labor services provided by all the subordinates in the unit. The latter equality follows from the linear homogeneity of function F.

Job assignment of each cohort of workers is denoted by h, where h is the share of the workers in the cohort who are assigned to supervisory positions. Obviously, $(1 - h)$ is the share of subordinates. As we shall see shortly, optimal assignment rules always involve a corner solution: either all or none of the workers within a cohort are supervisors. As a subordinate, a worker supplies subordinate labor services, e_n. As a supervisor, the worker supplies e_s and commands D_n units of subordinate labor services. Since total supply and demand for subordinate labor services must exactly match, the following condition must hold

$$\int_{-\infty}^{\infty} \int_0^1 [\{1 - h(u_s, \tau)\}e_n(u_s, \tau) - h(u_s, \tau)D_n(u_s, \tau)]d\tau dG(u_s) = 0$$

$$(2.4)$$

where the first term within the square bracket is the supply of subordinate labor services, the second term is the demand, and we aggregate over cohorts and innate ability. Equation (2.4) simply states that supply and demand for subordinate labor must match within a firm.[10] If (2.4) is

---

[9] This simplification is innocuous as far as lemmas 2.1, 2.2 and 2.4 are concerned. When we allow workers to differ also in terms of u_n, lemma 2.3 no longer holds. On the other hand, much of the analysis in the next sections carries over to this general case, in particular, proposition 2.1 holds.
[10] Because of linear homogeneity, neither the firm size nor the size of each unit within the firm is determinate. The assumption that the firm has many (and similar) units is used here only to avoid integer problems and to appeal to the law of large numbers.

satisfied, the adding-up condition ensures the balance between supply of and demand for supervisory services, e_s.

Accumulation of human capital yields disutility to workers. Measured in units of output, disutility per unit of time is given by

$$C = \tfrac{1}{2}(i_s + i_n)^2 \tag{2.5}$$

where i_s (i_n) is the investment in k_s (k_n). To emphasize the demand side of human capital, we assume that k_s and k_n are perfect substitutes in terms of investment costs. In this case, individual investment will fall on the type of human capital that yields the highest rate of return. For simplicity, we also assume zero depreciation of human capital. Hence we have

$$k_j(t) = \int_0^t i_j(\tau)d\tau \tag{2.6}$$

where $j = s, n$.

The optimal allocation of workers to tasks and the optimal investment policy are obtained by maximizing net output

$$\int_{-\infty}^{\infty} \int_0^1 \left\{ h e_s f\left(\frac{D_n}{e_s}\right) - C(i_s, i_n) \right\} d\tau dG(u_s) \tag{2.7}$$

subject to (2.1)–(2.6). To solve the problem, we use (2.1) and (2.2) to substitute out e_s and e_n, and replace C in the maximand with (2.5). The Hamiltonian associated with (2.7) is then given by

$$H \equiv \int_{-\infty}^{\infty} \int_0^1 \left[h(k_s + u_s + vk_n + v\bar{u})f\left(\frac{D_n}{k_s + u_s + vk_n + v\bar{u}}\right) \right.$$

$$\left. - \frac{1}{2}(i_s + i_n)^2 \right] d\tau dG(u_s)$$

$$+ \lambda \left[\int_{-\infty}^{\infty} \int_0^1 \{(1 - h)(k_n + vu_s + vk_s + \bar{u}) - hD_n\}d\tau dG(u_s) \right]$$

$$+ \int_{-\infty}^{\infty} \int_0^1 \mu_s \left\{ \int_0^\tau i_s d\tau - k_s \right\} d\tau dG(u_s)$$

$$+ \int_{-\infty}^{\infty} \int_0^1 \mu_n \left\{ \int_0^\tau i_n d\tau - k_n \right\} d\tau dG(u_s) \tag{2.8}$$

where μ_s and μ_n are the Lagrange multipliers associated with (2.5) and λ is the Lagrange multiplier associated with the adding-up constraint (2.4).

Maximization of the lifetime net utility of each employee

It is convenient to divide the maximization problem into two stages. In the first, we solve the investment and job assignment problem for a given value of λ, without taking explicit account of the adding-up constraint (2.4). In the second, we obtain the full solution by equating the demand and the supply for subordinate labor services as functions of λ. As it turns out, most of the key findings can be obtained in the first stage.

Let us start with this first stage and ignore until the next section the role of the adding-up constraint (2.4). The first-order condition for D_n is

$$h\left\{f'\left(\frac{D_n}{e_s}\right) - \lambda\right\} = 0 \tag{2.9}$$

When $h = 0$ we get

$$f'\left(\frac{D_n}{e_s}\right) \equiv \lambda$$

$$\frac{D_n}{e_s} = \psi(\lambda), \ \psi'(\lambda) < 0, \ f'(\psi(\lambda)) = \lambda$$

where $\psi(\lambda)$ is the effective span of control measured in efficiency units, a decreasing function of λ, the shadow price of subordinate labor services. Hence, measured in efficiency units, all the units in the firm have exactly the same span of control.

Similarly, the first-order conditions for k_s and k_n yield:

$$\mu_s = hg(\lambda) + (1 - h)v\lambda \tag{2.10}$$

$$\mu_n = hvg(\lambda) + (1 - h)\lambda \tag{2.11}$$

where $g(\lambda)$ is defined as

$$g(\lambda) \equiv f(\psi(\lambda)) - \psi(\lambda)\lambda, \ g(\lambda) > 0, \ g'(\lambda) = -\psi(\lambda) < 0$$

The interpretation of $g(\lambda)$ and λ is simple: they are the implicit wage rates for the two ranks – i.e. shadow prices of e_s and e_n.

In the first stage, the maximization problem can be solved for each cohort independently. That is, for a given value of λ (and $g(\lambda)$) and for each cohort of workers, the optimal investment and job assignment policy are given by solving the following maximization problem

$$\max_{i_s, i_n, h} V = \max\left[\int_0^1 \{hg(\lambda)e_s + (1 - h)\lambda e_n - C(i_s, i_n)\}dt, 0\right] \tag{2.12}$$

subject to (2.5) and (2.6).

Differentiation of V with respect to i_s and i_n yields:

$$i_k = \delta[\Delta_{km}]\sigma_k, \quad \Delta_{km} = \sigma_k - \sigma_m, \quad k = s, n; \quad m = s, n; \quad m \neq k$$

$$(2.13)$$

where

$$\sigma_k = \int_\tau^1 \mu_k(t)dt, \quad k = n, s$$

and $\delta(\cdot)$ is a sign function equal to one if the argument is non-negative, and to zero otherwise. Hence, the investment decision at each point in time depends upon the sign of Δ_{km}. Since accumulated invested capital never depreciates, the return from investment is the sum of the flow of marginal products until retirement. If a worker invests one unit in k_s, this unit yields g units of output per time if she is a supervisor and $v\lambda$ units of output if she is a subordinate. Similarly, investment in k_n yields vg and λ units of output, respectively, in a supervisory and in a subordinate position. The optimal investment policy has a "bang-bang" type of solution. At each point in time, all the investment is concentrated in the type of human capital that yields the highest returns. When the flow of returns from investing in k_s is higher than the returns from investing in k_n, $\Delta_{sn} = \sigma_s - \sigma_n$ is positive and $i_n = 0$. When the opposite occurs, Δ_{sn} is negative, $i_s = 0$ and $i_n = \sigma_n$.

Next, we differentiate H with respect to h and obtain

$$h = 1 \text{ iff } P(k_s, k_n) \geq -P(u_s, \bar{u}) \equiv -\bar{P},$$

$$h = 0 \text{ otherwise} \qquad (2.14)$$

where $P(x_1, x_2) \equiv (g(\lambda) - v\lambda)x_1 + (vg(\lambda) - \lambda)x_2$. This condition shows that the allocation of each cohort to supervisory and subordinate jobs is such that either all are supervisors or all are subordinates.

We close this subsection by introducing a critical assumption on the relative size of the marginal product of labor in the two positions.

Assumption 2.1 $g(\lambda) > \lambda$: the configuration of exogenous variables, production technology, investment cost functions, etc. is such that the marginal product of human capital is always higher in a supervisory position. This condition is not at all restrictive. If it is violated, we could rename all variables and identify supervisory positions as lower-ranked jobs and subordinate positions as the upper-ranked jobs.

Career paths and investment policy

Define a career path as a job allocation sequence involving both lower-and upper-ranked jobs. Given assumption 1, we can prove lemma 2.1.

Lemma 2.1 *There are no demotions in any optimal career path.*

Proof: See the appendix (p. 60).

Once demotions are ruled out[11] efficient allocations of workers to jobs can be organized into three possible career paths, as detailed below. The analytical conditions determining each career path are derived in the appendix.

Path A This path applies to workers with a clear advantage in supervisory jobs. Along this path, a worker is a supervisor from the beginning to the end of a career. Naturally, she invests only in k_s.

Path B In this path, the worker is a subordinate until age $\hat{\tau}$ and is promoted to a supervisory position afterwards. The investment policy depends upon the sign of Δ_{sn} at $t = 0$. Using (2.8), (2.11) and (2.13), we get $\Delta_{sn}|_{t=0} = g(\lambda)(1 - \hat{\tau}) - \lambda\hat{\tau}$. Since Δ_{sn} is increasing over time and is positive when promotion occurs at age $\hat{\tau}$, there are two possibilities, depending upon the sign of Δ_{sn} at $t = 0$. If the sign is positive, the optimal policy is to invest in k_s from the start. We call this path B1. If it is negative, the optimal policy calls for investment in k_n until $\bar{\tau}$, when Δ_{sn} turns positive, and for investment in k_s afterwards. We call this second path B2. In general, both $\hat{\tau}$ and $\bar{\tau}$ are decreasing in u_s. Path B applies when $-\bar{P}$ lies between the values taken in paths A and C and investment decisions balance the trade off between immediate and future returns. Since a worker in this path is a subordinate at the earlier stage of her career, k_n is more productive than k_s as long as she remains in a subordinate position. After promotion, the relative efficiency is reversed. Under path B2 workers invest in k_n and stay longer in a subordinate position than workers in path B1.

Path C If $-\bar{P}$ is sufficiently large, the optimal policy is that the worker remains in a subordinate position until retirement. Obviously, she invests only in k_n.

---

[11] Demotions in ILM firms are rare. See the evidence in Baker, Gibbs and Holmstrom (1994a) and in chapter 5 below.

Career paths and investment policies in ILM and OLM firms

We use the optimal investment plan for each path to evaluate V in (2.12). The technical details are in the appendix (p. 61). As we have noted above, the optimal investment and job assignment policy for the firm is the collection of the corresponding optimal policies for individual workers. Each cohort of workers chooses a career path by maximizing

$$V(u_s) = \max[V_A, V_{B1}, V_{B2}, V_C, 0] \qquad (2.15)$$

where V_A, V_{B1}, V_{B2}, and V_C are the expected net outputs associated with each career path. Assuming that firms differ in the value of v, the degree of skill proximity, lemmas 2.2–2.4 characterize the optimal selection of career paths and the optimal investment policy.

Lemma 2.2 *If v is sufficiently close to zero, then path B2 is never part of the optimal policy. If v is sufficiently close to one, path B2 can be part of the optimal policy.*

Proof: See the appendix (p. 63).

When v is close to zero, the productivity loss of employing a worker in the wrong position is large because the proximity of skills in term of productivity is low. To put it differently, the investment in k_n in the early stages of a career adds little or nothing to the productivity potential in a supervisory position. Recall that the only reason why path B2 is chosen instead of path B1 is that a worker needs to accumulate enough skills before promotion to overcome the comparative disadvantage generated by a small value of u_s. Hence, path B2 is clearly suboptimal at $v = 0$. By continuity, it is suboptimal also when v is small but positive.

On the other hand, when v is equal to one, the two types of capital are perfect substitutes and investment is equally productive in either type of human capital. When v is very close to one, investing in k_n increases one-to-one the productivity potential after promotion to supervisor. At the same time, switching from path C to path B2 yields a first-order gain because the same human capital is more productive in a supervisory position (see assumption 2.1).

Lemma 2.3 *If v is close to one, the firm employs only those workers with innate ability, u_s, higher than a critical value. If v is zero, workers are employed independently of their innate ability. When employees are drawn randomly from the common distribu-*

tion, G, the share of employees promoted to upper-ranked jobs (supervisors) increases in the degree of proximity of skills, v.

Proof: See the appendix (p. 64).

The interpretation of lemma 2.3 is also straightforward. If v is equal to one, the only advantage of employing a worker in a subordinate position is that employing her as a supervisor involves a large cost if innate ability, u_s, takes a large negative value. Employing this worker as a subordinate only makes the size of the negative net surplus small in absolute value. Hence, those workers who cannot be employed in paths A and B1 cannot be profitably employed in path C either. By continuity, this argument applies to the case when v is close to one.

If v is zero, the worker's draw of u_s has no effect in the subordinate position. Since the net surplus from the match between the worker and the firm under path C is positive when $v = 0$, all workers yield a positive net surplus and can thus be employed, independently of their innate ability.

As a result, firms where v is close to or equal to one employ workers who are either assigned to supervisory tasks from the start or are promoted to supervisors at a later stage. Hence, this type of firm has a relatively low span of control, defined as the ratio of subordinates to supervisors.

Lemma 2.4   *The distribution of lifetime earnings (net surplus) within a firm becomes more skewed to the left as the value of v declines.*

Proof: See the appendix (p. 66).

To summarize the findings so far, we have shown that workers in OLM firms, where v is low, fully specialize in one type of human capital, because career path B2 is precluded. Workers in these firms can nevertheless start their career in a subordinate position before promotion to supervisor. To the extent that their human capital, k_s, is ill suited for the subordinate position, the time spent before promotion to supervisor is shorter in an OLM than in an ILM firm, where v is high. Workers with innate ability, u_s, below a given cut-off level remain in the subordinate position until retirement.

In ILM firms, there are three career paths that eventually lead to a supervisory position. If the worker is extremely well suited for the job, she starts off as a supervisor; if she is less talented, she is assigned to a subordinate position and invests in k_n at the start of her career. Later on, before promotion occurs, she switches to investing in k_s. Finally, workers with limited talent remain in the subordinate position until retirement. These career paths are illustrated in figure 2.1.

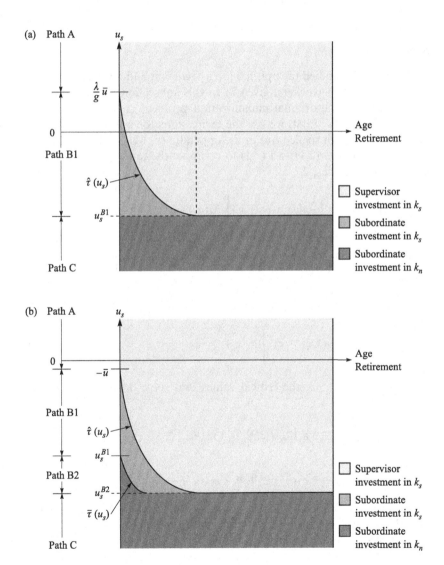

Figure 2.1 Alternative career paths, OLM and ILM firms

Apart from the differences in career paths, the two types of firm also differ in their spans of control, lower in ILM firms where promotion to a supervisory position is more likely than in OLM firms. Last but not least, the distribution of the net surplus is highly skewed to the left in OLM firms because job assignment based upon innate ability tends to magnify the effects of ability on productivity.[12]

General equilibrium

So far, we have studied the optimal job assignment and investment policy for each cohort of workers, given λ. In this subsection, we describe the full solution to the original maximization problem, given by (2.8). We proceed as follows. First, we use the expressions for optimal investment in each career path spelled out in the appendix (p. 61) and the definition of labor services in (2.1) and (2.2) to compute the total supply of supervisory labor services, E_s, as

$$
\begin{aligned}
E_s = & \int_{\frac{\lambda - g\nu}{g - \lambda\nu}\overline{u}}^{\infty} \left\{ \frac{1}{3}g(\lambda) + u_s + v\overline{u} \right\} dG(u_s) \\
& + \int_{u_s^{B1}}^{\frac{\lambda - g\nu}{g - \lambda\nu}\overline{u}} \left[\frac{\lambda(1 - \nu^2)}{g(\lambda) - \nu\lambda}\overline{u}(1 - \hat{\tau}) + \frac{1}{3}g(\lambda)(1 - \hat{\tau})^3 \right] dG(u_s) \\
& \int_{u_s^{B2}}^{u_s^{B1}} \left[\frac{\lambda(1 - \nu^2)}{g(\lambda) - \nu\lambda}(1 - \hat{\tau})\left(\overline{u} + H\overline{\tau} - \frac{1}{2}\lambda\overline{\tau}^2\right) \right. \\
& \left. + \frac{1}{3}g(\lambda)(1 - \hat{\tau})^3 \right] dG(u_s) \quad (2.16)
\end{aligned}
$$

where u_s^{B1} and u_s^{B2} are the critical values that solve the following equations

$$
V_{B1}\left(u_s^{B1}\right) = V_{B2}\left(u_s^{B2}\right) \geq 0 \text{ or } V_{B1}\left(u_s^{B1}\right) = 0
$$

$$
V_{B2}\left(u_s^{B2}\right) = V_C\left(u_s^{B2}\right) \geq 0 \text{ or } V_{B2}\left(u_s^{B2}\right) = 0
$$

The demand for subordinates is equal to $\psi(\lambda)E_s$, total labor inputs supplied by supervisors multiplied by the effective span of control, ψ.

Next, we compute the supply of labor services by subordinates, E_n, as

---

[12] See Rosen (1982).

$$E_n = \int_{u_s^{B1}}^{\frac{\lambda - g v \bar{u}}{g - \lambda v \bar{u}}} \left\{ \frac{1}{2} v \Lambda \hat{\tau} - \frac{1}{6} v^2 \lambda \hat{\tau} + v u_s + \bar{u} \right\} dG(u_s)$$

$$+ \int_{u_s^{B2}}^{u_s^{B1}} \left[\hat{\tau}(v u_s + \bar{u}) + \frac{1}{2} H \bar{\tau}^2 - \frac{1}{6} \lambda \bar{\tau}^3 + (\hat{\tau} - \bar{\tau})(H \bar{\tau} \right.$$

$$\left. - \frac{1}{2} \lambda \bar{\tau}^2) + \frac{1}{2} v \wedge (\hat{\tau} - \bar{\tau}^2) - \frac{1}{6} v^2 \lambda (\hat{\tau}^3 - \bar{\tau}^3) + (\hat{\tau} - \bar{\tau})(-v \wedge \bar{\tau} \right.$$

$$\left. + \frac{1}{2} \bar{\tau}^2) \right] dG(u_s) + \int_{u_s^C}^{u_s^{B2}} \left[\frac{\lambda}{3} + v u_s + \bar{u} \right] dG(u_s) \tag{2.17}$$

where u_s^C solves

$$V_C\!\left(u_s^C\right) = 0$$

If $V_C\!\left(u_s^C\right) \geq 0$ for any u_s, we set $u_s^C = -\infty$. After tedious but straight-forward differentiation, we obtain

$$E_s = \phi(\lambda, v \mid G) \text{ where } \frac{\partial \phi}{\partial \lambda} < 0 \text{ and } \frac{\partial \phi}{\partial v} < 0 \tag{2.18}$$

$$E_n = \rho(\lambda, v \mid G) \text{ where } \frac{\partial \rho}{\partial \lambda} > 0 \text{ and } \frac{\partial \rho}{\partial v} > 0 \tag{2.19}$$

Using (2.18) and (2.19), the full solution to the original maximization problem is obtained by noticing that the demand for subordinates is

$$D_n = \psi(\lambda) E_s = \psi(\lambda) \phi(\lambda, v)$$

and the supply of subordinates is

$$S_n = E_n = \rho(\lambda, v)$$

Since the original adding-up constraint (2.4) can be rewritten in terms of demand equal to supply, we obtain

$$\psi(\lambda) = \frac{\rho(\lambda, v)}{\phi(\lambda, v)} \tag{2.20}$$

From this equation we can derive the equilibrium value of λ as

$$\lambda = \Sigma(v \mid G) \qquad \text{where } \frac{\partial \Sigma}{\partial v} > 0$$

We can now fully integrate the analysis in this and the previous sections by replacing λ with its equilibrium value. It can easily be confirmed that the lemmas 2.2–2.4 not only remain valid, but are actually reinforced. In particular, we can show that

$$\frac{\partial \psi[\Sigma(v \mid G)]}{\partial v} < 0$$

so that the effective span of control declines as the degree of proximity v increases.

Market equilibrium with ILM and OLM firms

Up to now, our analysis has been strictly partial equilibrium. In this section, we extend it to cover general equilibrium. To do so, we introduce assumption 2.2.

> *Assumption 2.2*   The labor market is populated by a large number of firms that differ only in the value of v. Each firm acts in a competitive way and competes for workers by bidding on their lifetime earnings. For simplicity, we assume that v can take only two values, zero and one, and that firms choose either value.

Under assumption 2.2, the steady-state market equilibrium is characterized as follows. Start by noticing that the two types of firm (ILM for $v = 1$ and OLM for $v = 0$) use a different set of policies in recruitment, human capital investment, and promotion. Hence, the net surplus generated by employment in each type of firm generally differs. Since all firms make zero profit in equilibrium, net surpluses are equivalent to net wage offers.

In order to make explicit the relationship between the maximization problem in (2.8) and the distribution of workers among firms, we define

$$\Omega(u_s, v \mid G) = \max[V_A(u_s, v \mid G), V_{B1}(u_s, v \mid G), V_{B2}(u_s, v \mid G),$$
$$V_C(u_s, v \mid G), 0]$$

where $\Omega(x, y \mid G)$ is the offer by a firm with $v = y$ to an employee with innate ability, $u_s = x$, drawn from the distribution G. With only two types of firm, the market-best offer to an individual with ability u_s is

$$V(u_s) = \max[\Omega(u_s, 1 \mid G), \Omega(u_s, 0 \mid G)]$$

At equilibrium, the full set of possible realizations of innate ability is divided into the following two subsets

$$R^{ILM} = \{r \mid \Omega(r, 1 \mid G) \geq \Omega(r, 0 \mid G)\}$$

$$R^{OLM} = \{r \mid \Omega(r, 0 \mid G) > \Omega(r, 1 \mid G)\}$$

To solve for the equilibrium allocation, consider the following algorithm: start with an arbitrary pair of values of λ, one for each type of firm and plug these numbers into into the value functions (2A.5a)–(2A.5c) in the appendix to generate $V^{ILM} = \Omega(u_s, 1 \mid G)$ and $V^{OLM} = \Omega(u_s, 0 \mid G)$. These values in turn determine R^{ILM} and R^{OLM}. Define next

$$G^k(u_s) = \frac{\displaystyle\int_{u \in R^k}^{u_s} u dG(u)}{\displaystyle\int_{u \in R^k} u dG(u)} \text{ for } k = ILM, OLM$$

In words, G^{ILM} $\left(G^{OLM}\right)$ is the distribution of workers employed in ILM (OLM) firms. Next, compute the full equilibrium for each type of firm by replacing G with $G^{ILM}\left(G^{OLM}\right)$, and obtain the equilibrium value of λ. Reiterate the procedure if λ is different from the initial value of λ. A market equilibrium is a fixed point of the mapping generated by this algorithm.

Next, we state the following:

Lemma 2.5 *Suppose that the ability distribution of workers is sufficiently dispersed so that all the available career paths (A, B, and C) are used at least in one type of firm. Assume further that both types of firm hire a strictly positive number of workers. Then $\lambda_{ILM} > \lambda_{OLM}$ at the market equilibrium.*

Proof: See the appendix (p. 67).

This lemma can be used to show that the proposition 2.1 holds.

Proposition 2.1   Consider a market equilibrium where both types of firm employ a strictly positive number of workers. If such an equilibrium exists, OLM firms hire workers with innate ability at both ends of the ability distribution and ILM firms employ workers with ability in the middle range of the same distribution.

Proposition 2.1 can be interpreted as follows. Since $\lambda_{ILM} > \lambda_{OLM}$, $g(\lambda_{ILM}) < g(\lambda_{OLM})$. Inspection of the V functions reveals that $V_{OLM} > V_{ILM}$ when u_s is drawn from both tails of the ability distribution. Therefore, if a market equilibrium exists and if both types of firm hire a positive number of workers, the wage offers by ILM firms (equal to the net surpluses) must dominate the offers by OLM firms to individuals with values of u_s in the middle range of the distribution. Consequently, if such a market equilibrium exists, OLM firms hire workers who differ greatly in their ability, while ILM firms employ only workers whose ability is included in a relatively narrow band. Figure 2.2 illustrates such an equilibrium.

A numerical example

A numerical example of general equilibrium with two types of firm is illustrated in table 2.1. The example is based upon the following assumptions: (a) $\bar{u} = \bar{c} = 1$; (b) the production function at the firm level is a CES, given by $F(E_s, E_n) = \left[0.75E_s^{-0.5} + 0.25E_n^{-0.5}\right]^{-2}$; (c) innate ability, u_s, is drawn from a uniform distribution with range $[-20, 5]$. The results in table 2.1 confirm proposition 2.1 and show that while ILM firms employ workers with medium ability, OLM firms hire workers from both tails of the ability distribution. As a result, OLM firms do not use path B for their employees, who all remain in the job they were assigned upon entrance. The large majority of workers in OLM firms are subordinates, whereas more than half of the employees in ILM firms are hired as, or promoted to, supervisors.

Earnings profiles, seniority, talents, and jobs

Since employees capture all the surplus from the employment relationship, their lifetime wages are equal to the surplus *plus* the cost of investing

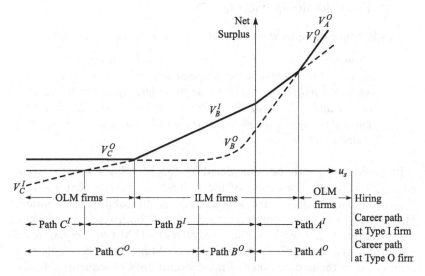

Figure 2.2 Allocation of workers, OLM and ILM firms

Table 2.1 *Numerical example of market equilibrium*

	ILM firms	OLM firms
λ	0.316	0.205
$g(\lambda)$	0.629	1.002
$\psi(\lambda)$	0.440	2.637
Ability range in Path A	[1.03, 2.43]	[2.43, 5.00]
Ability range in Path B	[0.63, 1.03]	None
Ability range in Path C	[−0.38, 0.63]	[−20.00, −0.38]
Percentage employed in Path C	48.6	87.9

in human capital – i.e. to gross output attributable to each individual. Assuming that the wage rate at each point in time is equal to current gross output, this rate is given by[13]

$$w = hg(\lambda)e_s + (1 - h)\lambda e_n \qquad (2.21)$$

Using the optimal job assignment condition (2.14), we have that

$$g(\lambda)e_s - \lambda e_n = P(e_s, e_n) + \overline{P}$$

and promotion occurs ($h = 1$) precisely when gross outputs in the upper and lower rank jobs are equal. Therefore, (2.21) is continuous over time as far as e_s and e_n are continuous, which is indeed the case, as shown in the appendix (p. 60). This implies that individual wages do not jump upon promotion to upper-rank jobs in mid-career. While wages do not jump, wage growth does.[14] To see this, we differentiate (2.21) with respect to time and get

$$\frac{\partial w}{\partial t} = v\lambda i_s + \lambda i_n \quad \text{if } h = 1$$

---

[13] When both firms and workers can commit to long-term contracts, any lifetime wage profile is consistent with the rest of our model as long as the overall offer is worth exactly the size of the net surplus. Without commitment, however, any deviation of wages from current productivity is policed by counter-offers and the equilibrium wage offer must be equal to current output.

[14] These properties are consistent with a growing body of empirical literature investigating individual wage growth and promotions. A typical finding is that wage increases during the years of promotion are larger than wage increases in the years without promotion. The difference, however, is small when compared to average wage differentials between job levels and ranks. See Baker, Gibbs and Holmstrom (1994b).

Table 2.2 *Simulated wages*

	ILM firms	OLM firms
Mean	0.758	0.505
Standard deviation	0.393	0.858
Minimum	0.196	0.196
Maximum	1.553	4.099
Skewness	0.405	2.780
Nobs[a]	28,381	46,056

[a] In all tables in this chapter: number of observations.

$$\frac{\partial w}{\partial t} = g(\lambda)(i_s + vi_n) \quad \text{if } h = 0$$

Although the investment rate in human capital does not jump upon promotion, the marginal product jumps up from λ to $g(\lambda)$. It should also be noted that wage growth is the same for all supervisors, irrespective of the timing of promotion or of the career path taken. Hence, wage differentials among supervisors cannot be explained by the wage rate at the time of promotion.[15]

Wage differentials are larger in OLM firms than in ILM firms. In ILM firms, not only do wages differ less across the ability distribution, but the distribution of ability of employees is also contained within a relatively narrow band. As a result, excluding the large effect of seniority on earnings, wage differentials are relatively small. In OLM firms, not only does innate ability matter more in upper-rank jobs, but OLM employees are drawn from a wider ability range. As a consequence, the wage distribution in OLM firms is highly skewed. Low-ability workers are allocated to career path C, where they earn relatively low wages. As shown in table 2.1, middle-ability workers are hired away by ILM firms. In the right tail of the earnings distribution in OLM firms, workers are scattered over a relatively wide range of wages because they have been either promoted to, or employed from the start in, upper-ranked jobs where talent makes the difference.

Table 2.2 reports the descriptive statistics of the simulated wage distribution when we use the values specified for the simulation in table 2.1. The contrast between wages in the two types of firm is easily seen. Compared to wages in ILM firms, wages in OLM firms have a much larger variance and positive skewness, while the mean wage is about

[15] See the appendix (p. 60) for details.

Table 2.3 *Regression using simulated log wages; dependent variable: log wages*

	ILM firms	OLM firms
Age	0.276	0.198
Age^2	−0.144	−0.101
h	0.017	2.539
$h*Age$	0.088	0.175
$h*Age^2$	−0.039	−0.093
Nobs	28,381	46,056

three-quarters of the mean wage in ILM firms. As shown by table 2.1, our simulation implies that most employees in OLM firms are subordinates and receive exactly the same wage at the same age, irrespective of their innate ability. At the same time, a minority of about 10 percent of all employees are supervisors, and their mean earnings is way above the mean earnings of subordinates.

Table 2.3 reports the results from regressing the log of simulated wages in each type of firm on age (seniority), age squared, position or rank, and the interaction between position and age. Simulated wages are obtained by random draws from the uniform distribution of u_s over a given number of periods constituting a career path. The qualitative differences in estimated earnings profiles are in line with the stylized differences between ILM and OLM firms. First, we find that the effect of age on earnings is larger in ILM firms, although both wage–age profiles are positively sloped and concave. Second, we find that the effects both of the rank dummy, h, and of the interactions of h with age on wages are much more important in OLM firms.

In our example, between-rank earnings differentials are fairly large in OLM firms, and employees in these firms are sharply divided into two different groups. In ILM firms, wage profiles are smoother and more egalitarian and there exist no clear-cut divisions of employees in two separate groups. Ranks are less important a determinant of pay, age (seniority) matters more for earnings, and an important share of subordinates achieve promotion to higher ranks.

Experience, earnings profile, and promotions

In previous sections, we have showed that contrasting patterns of promotion, investment in human capital, and hierarchical structures can emerge in ILM and OLM firms. In this section, we try to briefly relate these predictions to the empirical findings in the literature.

First of all, we have shown that OLM firms select promotion candidates at a relatively early stage of their career, and that employees specialize in one type of human capital to fully exploit their comparative advantage. In contrast, promotion decisions in ILM firms are delayed for an important subset of workers. Furthermore, some of the workers employed in these firms accumulate two types of human capital that are close substitutes.

The importance of late selection in promotion has been emphasized by Koike (1988) and Aoki (1988) in their discussions of the Japanese firm. While their evidence is based on case studies and cannot be easily generalized, as discussed at length in chapter 5, late promotion remains a distinguishing feature of HRM in large Japanese firms.[16]

The proximity of skills across ranks within a corporate hierarchy plays a critical role in our model. In comparison with the United States and European countries, Koike and others find that training and job assignment in large Japanese firms encompass a wider spectrum of skills (multiskilling).[17] Using a large set of data on lateral and vertical job changes within firms, Matsushige (1995b) finds that workers experiencing lateral moves to jobs completely unrelated to previous jobs have a lower promotion probability. This can be interpreted as evidence in support of our emphasis on the proximity of skills as a necessary condition for the frequent use of internal promotion.

The differences in promotion and investment in human capital between the two types of firm in our model also generate differences in earnings profiles and in the pattern of correlations both with seniority and with innate ability. First, we find that the distribution of workers' productivity is more skewed in OLM than in ILM firms. If we could measure productivity, seniority, and ranks in the two types of firm, we expect to find the following: (a) promotion probabilities in ILM firms are positively correlated with tenure, at least up to a certain point, because promotion standards decline over seniority as workers accumulate more human capital; (b) promotions in OLM firms are concentrated in the early stages of a career so that the correlation with seniority is likely to be negative. The promotion standard in OLM firms becomes more stringent as workers in the lower ranks accumulate human capital and shift their comparative advantage further away from upper-rank jobs.

---

[16] See the evidence in Prendergast (1990); Hatvany and Pucik (1981); Sato (1997).
[17] Multiskilling in Japanese firms is discussed by Carmichael and McLeod (1993); Aoki (1988).

The evidence on promotion standards is rather scanty and international comparisons are even more difficult to come by. Yoshino (1968), Dore (1973), and Lincoln, Hanada and McBride (1986) are three studies that document how spans of control are lower in Japan than in the United States or the United Kingdom. Other studies that focus on the relationship between seniority and promotion probabilities are reviewed in some detail in chapter 5.

If we approximate earnings profiles with productivity profiles, as is done in most of the empirical literature on human capital, we expect to find that earnings depend more on seniority in ILM firms and more on rank allocation in OLM firms. We look at this issue in chapters 3 and 4. In chapter 3, we show that earnings profiles in ILM-type jobs are steeper than earnings profiles in OLM-type jobs. In chapter 4, we compare earnings profiles in a typical ILM setup (Japan) and in a typical OLM economy (the United Kingdom), and find evidence that between-ranks earnings growth matters more in Britain, especially in the manufacturing industry, while seniority matters relatively more in Japan.

Our model also predicts a distinct pattern in the relationship between wage growth and promotion. First, we have shown that wage growth accelerates after promotion without any discrete jump at the moment of promotion. Empirical studies have found that wage growth after promotion is larger than wage growth in the absence of promotion, but that the difference between the two is typically not very large. Baker, Gibbs and Holmstrom (1994b), in particular, find that wage increases upon promotion are larger than wage increases without promotion but smaller than the difference in average wages between the two levels. They find substantial overlap in the distribution of earnings between ranks: in spite of the large differences in average wages between ranks (positions), a substantial percentage of workers in lower ranks earns more than some workers assigned to upper ranks. This finding is consistent with our model but inconsistent with "tournament" models that explain vertical mobility (promotion) and earnings growth.[18]

All in all, the correspondence between empirical regularities and the predictions drawn from the model presented in this chapter is surprisingly good, especially when we take into account the fact that the sharp contrast between ILM and OLM firms described above depends upon a single parameter, the degree of proximity among different types of skill.

---

[18] See the discussion in Gibbons (1996).

Summary

In this chapter, we have developed a model of job allocation and investment in heterogeneous human capital in a two-layer corporate hierarchy. By incorporating the demand side in a human capital model we have obtained predictions that are consistent with well known stylized facts about internal labor markets. In particular, our model has highlighted the critical role played by the proximity of skills and by training in shaping the promotion policy and the hierarchical structure of firms.

The model distinguishes between two types of firms. In one type, skill proximity is relatively high and skill formation is predominantly internal and involves a long, continuous accumulation process along promotion ladders where jobs with closely related skills are lined up in a progression. Experience within the hierarchy and along these promotion ladders is the most important determinant of promotion decisions. Promotion timing can be delayed substantially for some employees, hiring decisions are based upon stringent standards, and income distribution within the firm is fairly equal. Not surprisingly, these characteristics correspond almost exactly to the stylized facts about large Japanese firms, that are viewed as having a well developed system of internal labor markets.

In the other type of firm, skill proximity across tasks is relatively low, internal training is less common, and inter-firm mobility is relatively higher than intra-firm mobility. Because of the relative independence of jobs, qualifications and innate talents at the start of the career largely determine job assignments. Internal promotions, if they occur at all, are concentrated in the early stages of a career, and workers are highly specialized. The demarcation between upper and lower ranks in the hierarchy is also more clear-cut. Experience in lower ranks may be helpful to increase productivity in lower-ranked jobs but is not helpful to increase productivity in upper-ranked jobs. Furthermore, this type of firm is likely to employ multiple ports of entry, depending upon the comparative advantages of applicants. Consequently, hiring standards are less demanding and there are larger earnings differentials between upper- and lower-ranked jobs.

Appendix

Proof of lemma 2.1

Suppose that a worker who has been a supervisor until age τ is demoted to a subordinate position. This implies that $P(k_s(t), k_n(t))$ is positive until τ and negative afterwards as a result of her investment in k_n. This is clearly suboptimal under assumption 2.1. Suppose that this worker invests in k_s instead than in k_n until τ, at exactly the same rate as in the hypothetical investment policy that implies demotion. Clearly, this alternative investment policy yields a higher return and demotions are ruled out. ∎

The V functions

We use the optimal investment plan for each career path to evaluate the maximand, V. First, we determine the investment policy under each career path.

Path A This case obtains if $\overline{P} \leqslant 0$ or if $(g(\lambda) - \nu\lambda)u_s + (\nu g(\lambda) - \lambda)\bar{u} \geqslant 0$. Setting $h = 1$ in (2.10)–(2.13), we obtain the following equations

$$i_s = g(\lambda)(1 - t), k_s = \tfrac{1}{2}g(\lambda)(2 - t)t \text{ for } 0 \leqslant t \leqslant 1$$
$$i_n = k_n = 0 \text{ for } 0 \leqslant t \leqslant 1 \tag{2A.1a}$$

Path B In this path, the worker is a subordinate until age $\hat{\tau}$ and is then promoted to supervisor. In this case, the investment policy depends upon the sign of Δ_{sn} at $t = 0$. Since Δ_{sn} is increasing over time and is positive at the time of promotion, $\hat{\tau}$, there are two subcases, depending upon the sign of Δ_{sn} at $t = 0$. If the sign is positive, the optimal policy is to invest in k_s from the beginning. We call this path B1. If the sign is negative, the optimal policy calls for investment in k_n until $\bar{\tau}$ when Δ_{sn} turns positive. We call this second path B2. Which of these subcases applies depends upon the sign of Δ_{sn} at age zero:

$$\Delta_{sn} |_{t=0} = g(\lambda)(1 - \hat{\tau}) - \lambda\hat{\tau}$$

The set of equations governing path B1 is:

$$i_s = g(\lambda)(1 - \hat{\tau}) + \nu\lambda(t - \hat{\tau}), k_s(t) = \Lambda t - \tfrac{1}{2}\nu\lambda t^2 \text{ for } 0 \leqslant t \leqslant \hat{\tau}$$
$$i_s = g(\lambda)(1 - t), k_s(t) = \Lambda\hat{\tau} - \tfrac{1}{2}\nu\lambda\hat{\tau}^2 + \tfrac{1}{2}g(\lambda)(2 - t - \hat{\tau})(t - \hat{\tau})$$
$$\text{for } \hat{\tau} \leqslant t \leqslant 1$$
$$i_n = k_n = 0 \text{ for } 0 \leqslant t \leqslant 1$$
$$\Lambda \equiv g(\lambda)(1 - \hat{\tau}) + \nu\lambda\hat{\tau} \tag{2A.1b1}$$

The critical value $\hat{\tau}$ must satisfy $P(k_s(\hat{\tau}), 0) = -\overline{P}$, or

$$[g(\lambda) - \nu\lambda]\left(\Lambda\hat{\tau} - \frac{1}{2}\nu\lambda\hat{\tau}^2\right) = -\overline{P} \tag{2A.2}$$

On the other hand, path B2 is characterized by

$$i_s = g(\lambda)(1 - \tau), k_s = \Lambda(t - \bar\tau) - \tfrac{1}{2}v\lambda(t^2 - \bar\tau^2) \text{ for } \bar\tau \leqslant t \leqslant \hat\tau$$
$$k_s = k_s(\hat\tau) + \tfrac{1}{2}\lambda(2 - t - \tau)(t - \tau) \text{ for } \hat\tau \leqslant t \leqslant 1$$
$$i_n = H - \lambda t, k_n = Ht - \tfrac{1}{2}\lambda t^2 \text{ for } 0 \leqslant t \leqslant \bar\tau$$
$$i_n = 0, k_n = H\bar\tau - \tfrac{1}{2}\lambda\bar\tau^2 \text{ for } \bar\tau \leqslant t \leqslant 1$$
$$H \equiv vg(\lambda)(1 - \hat\tau) + \lambda\hat\tau$$

$$(2A.1b2)$$

with $\hat\tau$ and $\bar\tau$ that must jointly satisfy

$$P[k_s(\hat\tau), k_n(\hat\tau)] = (g(\lambda) - v\lambda)\frac{g(\lambda)(1 - \hat\tau)}{\lambda}\left\{\Lambda - \frac{1}{2}v\lambda(1 - \hat\tau)\right\}$$
$$+ (vg(\lambda) - \lambda)\frac{[g(\lambda) + \lambda]\hat\tau - g(\lambda)}{\lambda}\left\{H - \frac{[g(\lambda) + \lambda]\hat\tau - g(\lambda)}{2}\right\} = -\bar P \quad (2A.3)$$

$$\bar\tau = \frac{(g(\lambda) + \lambda)\hat\tau - g(\lambda)}{g(\lambda)} < \hat\tau \qquad (2A.4)$$

Path C If $-\bar P$ is sufficiently large, the optimal policy is such that the worker remains in a subordinate position until retirement. Obviously, she invests in k_n. The following conditions summarize path C:

$$i_n = \lambda(1 - t), k_n(t) = \frac{1}{2}\lambda(2 - t)t \text{ for } 0 \leqslant t \leqslant 1$$
$$i_s = k_s = 0 \text{ for } 0 \leqslant t \leqslant 1$$

$$(2A.1c)$$

Next, we use the optimal investment policy given in (2A.1a) through (2A.1c) to integrate the maximand V along each career path. The results are shown below

$$V_A = g(\lambda)u_s + \tfrac{1}{6}g(\lambda)^2 \qquad (2A.5a)$$

$$V_{B1} = \lambda(u_s + v\bar u)\hat\tau + \tfrac{1}{6}g(\lambda)^2(1 - \hat\tau)^3 + \frac{g(\lambda)\lambda(1 - v)^2}{g(\lambda) - v\lambda}\bar u(1 - \hat\tau)$$
$$+ \hat\tau(-\tfrac{1}{3}v^2\lambda^2\hat\tau^2 + \lambda\Lambda v\hat\tau - \tfrac{1}{2}\Lambda^2) \qquad (2A.5b1)$$

$$V_{B2} = \lambda\bar{\tau}(vu_s + \bar{u}) + \bar{\tau}\{-\tfrac{1}{3}v^2\lambda^2\hat{\tau}^2 + \lambda H\hat{\tau} - \tfrac{1}{2}H^2\}$$
$$+ g(\lambda)(\hat{\tau} - \bar{\tau})\{u_s + v\bar{u} + v(H\bar{\tau} - \tfrac{1}{2}\lambda\bar{\tau}^2)\}$$
$$- \tfrac{1}{6}\{g(\lambda) + v\lambda\}v\lambda(\hat{\tau}^3 - \bar{\tau}^3) + \tfrac{1}{2}\Lambda\{g(\lambda) + v\lambda\}(\hat{\tau}^2 - \bar{\tau}^2)$$
$$+ (\hat{\tau} - \bar{\tau})\{-g(\lambda)\Lambda\bar{\tau} + \tfrac{1}{2}g(\lambda)v\lambda\bar{\tau}^2 - \tfrac{1}{2}\Lambda^2\}$$
$$+ (1 - \hat{\tau})\frac{g(\lambda)\lambda(1 - v^2)}{g(\lambda) - v\lambda}(\bar{u} + H\bar{\tau} - \tfrac{1}{2}\lambda\bar{\tau}^2)$$
$$+ \tfrac{1}{6}g(\lambda)^2(1 - \hat{\tau})^3 \tag{2A.5b2}$$

$$V_C = \frac{\lambda^2}{6} + \lambda(\bar{u} + vu_s) \tag{2A.5c}$$

Using these results, it can be shown that $V(u_s) = \max[V_A, V_{B1}, V_{B2}, V_C, 0]$ is a weakly increasing, continuous and convex function of u_s.

Proof of lemma 2.2

In order to prove lemma 2.2, we check feasibility for each of the four paths, A, B1, B2, and C. Path A is chosen if:

$$P(0, 0) = -\overline{P} = -(g(\lambda) - v\lambda)u_s - (vg(\lambda) - \lambda)\bar{u} \leqslant 0$$

or if

$$u_s \geq \frac{\lambda - vg(\lambda)}{g(\lambda) - v\lambda}\bar{u} \tag{2A.6}$$

Comparing (2A.5a) with (2A.5b1) and (2A.5b2), it is also optimal to choose path A if (2A.6) is satisfied. Under path B1, $\hat{\tau}$ is the smaller root of

$$\{g(\lambda) - v\lambda\}\{\Lambda\hat{\tau} - \tfrac{1}{2}v\lambda\hat{\tau}^2\} = -\overline{P} \tag{2A.7}$$

Similarly, under path B2, $\hat{\tau}$ is the smaller root of

$$\{g(\lambda) - v\lambda\}\lambda^{-1}g(\lambda)(1 - \hat{\tau})\{\Lambda - \tfrac{1}{2}v\lambda(1 - \hat{\tau})\}$$
$$+ \{vg(\lambda) - \lambda\}\lambda^{-1}[\{g(\lambda) + \lambda\}\hat{\tau} - \lambda] \times$$
$$[H - \tfrac{1}{2}[\{g(\lambda) + \lambda\}\hat{\tau} - \lambda]] = -\overline{P} \tag{2A.8}$$

The LHS of (2A.7) and (2A.8) are both second-degree polynomials in $\hat{\tau}$ and their maximum values are:

$$\bar{P}_1 \equiv \max_{\hat{\tau}} P[k_s(\hat{\tau}), k_n(\hat{\tau})] \mid_{Path\ B1}$$

$$= [2\{2g(\lambda) - \lambda\}]^{-1}\{g(\lambda)\}^2(g(\lambda) - \nu\lambda)$$

$$\bar{P}_2 \equiv \max_{\hat{\tau}} P[k_s(\hat{\tau}), k_n(\hat{\tau})] \mid_{Path\ B2} =$$

$$\frac{g(\lambda)^2}{2\lambda} \left[\frac{\{2(\nu^2 + \nu - 1)g(\lambda)^2 - (1 - \nu)g(\lambda)\lambda - \nu(1 + \nu)\lambda^2\}^2}{2(\nu^2 + \nu - 1)g(\lambda)^3 + (\nu^2 + 2\nu - 1)g(\lambda)^2\lambda - \nu(2\nu + 3)g(\lambda)\lambda^2 + \lambda^3} \right]$$

$$+ 2(\wedge - \nu - \nu^2)g(\lambda) + (\wedge + \nu^2)\lambda$$

By direct comparison, it can be confirmed that

$$\bar{P}_2 > \bar{P}_1$$

if ν is equal to or close to unity. Consider the case when ν is small. Recall that for B2 to be chosen instead of B1, we need

$$\Delta_{sn=0} = (1 - \nu)\{g(\lambda)(1 - \hat{\tau}) - \lambda\hat{\tau}\}$$

$$\Rightarrow \hat{\tau} > \frac{g(\lambda)}{g(\lambda) + \lambda} > \frac{1}{2}$$

After tedious computations, it can be shown that

$$\bar{P}_1 > \bar{P}_2$$

if ν is close to zero. Since $P[k_s(\hat{\tau}), k_n(\hat{\tau})]$ is continuous at $\hat{\tau} = g(\lambda)/g(\lambda) + \lambda$, it is also necessary that $P[k_s(\hat{\tau}), k_n(\hat{\tau})]$ be increasing in $\hat{\tau}$ at $\hat{\tau} = g(\lambda)/g(\lambda) + \lambda$. We get

$$\frac{\partial P}{\partial \hat{\tau}} \mid_{\hat{\tau} = \frac{g(\lambda)}{g(\lambda)+\lambda}} \propto \{g(\lambda) - \nu\lambda\}\{\nu\lambda - 2g(\lambda)\}$$

$$+ \{\nu g(\lambda) - \lambda\}\{g(\lambda) + \lambda\}(1 + \nu) \qquad (2A.9)$$

Hence $\partial P/\partial \hat{\tau}$ is clearly positive at $\hat{\tau} = g(\lambda)/g(\lambda) + \lambda$ when $\nu = 1$, whereas it is negative if $\nu < \lambda/g(\lambda)$. Consequently, we have shown that path B1 is chosen at or around $\nu = 1$ as $-\bar{P}$ increases beyond $\bar{P}_1(< \bar{P}_2)$, whereas path B2 is never chosen when $\nu < \lambda g(\lambda)$. ∎

Proof of lemma 2.3

Suppose that $\nu = 1$. In this case k_s and k_n are perfect substitutes and paths B1 and B2 are identical. Solving for $V_B = V_C$, we get

$$\hat{\tau} = \frac{g(\lambda) + \lambda}{2(2g(\lambda) - \lambda)}$$

and solving (2A.7) we get

$$u_s = \frac{\{g(\lambda) - \lambda\}^2 - 4\{g(\lambda)\}^2}{8\{2g(\lambda) - \lambda\}} - \bar{u}$$

at $V_B = V_C$. Inserting this value in (2A.1c), we obtain

$$V_B = V_C = \frac{1}{6}\lambda^2 + \lambda(u_s + \bar{u}) = \frac{-\{g(\lambda) - \lambda\}^2 - 8\{g(\lambda)\}^2}{8\{2g(\lambda) - \lambda\}} < 0$$

$$(2A.10)$$

Hence, at $v = 1$, workers assigned to path C cannot generate positive surplus. Clearly, the cut-off value of u_s is greater than (2A.10) and no workers will be hired for path C when $v = 1$. By continuity, this property holds when v is close to unity. On the other hand, if $v = 0$, we get

$$V_C \mid_{v=0} = \frac{1}{6}\lambda^2 + \lambda\bar{u} > 0$$

Thus all the workers are employable if $v = 0$ as they generate positive net surplus.

Next, to prove the latter half of lemma 2.3, differentiate (2A.7) with respect to v to get:

$$\frac{d\hat{\tau}}{dv} = \frac{-\lambda\hat{\tau}^2 - [g(\lambda)^2 - \lambda^2 g(\lambda) - v\lambda]}{2[g(\lambda) - \{2g(\lambda) - v\lambda\}\hat{\tau}]} < 0 \qquad (2A.11)$$

Hence, we know that workers with a given value of u_s are promoted earlier as v is increased. Next, define $\tilde{u}_s$ as the solution to

$$V_{B1} = V_C$$

This is equivalent to:

$$\lambda(vu_s + \bar{u})\hat{\tau} + \hat{\tau}\{-\frac{1}{3}v^2\lambda^2\hat{\tau}^2 + v\lambda\Lambda\hat{\tau} - \frac{1}{2}\Lambda^2\} + \frac{g(\lambda)\lambda(1 - v^2)}{g(\lambda) - v\lambda} \times$$

$$\bar{u}(1 - \hat{\tau}) + \frac{1}{6}\{g(\lambda)\}^2(1 - \hat{\tau})^3 = \frac{1}{6}\lambda^2 + \lambda(v\tilde{u}_s + \bar{u})$$

After lengthy computations, it can be shown that

$$\frac{d\tilde{u}_s}{dv} < 0 \qquad (2A.12)$$

From (2A.11) and (2A.12), we know that the cut-off value dividing path B and C is lower and $\hat{\tau}$ is smaller if v is increased. Therefore, more workers are employed in either path A or B, and promotions take place earlier for a given value of u_s. ∎

Proof of lemma 2.4

Using (2A.5a)–(2A.5c), we can differentiate the V functions under paths A, B, and C and obtain:

$$\frac{\partial V_A}{\partial u_s} = g(\lambda)$$

$$\frac{\partial V_{B1}}{\partial u_s} = \frac{\partial V_{B2}}{\partial u_s} = \nu\lambda\hat{\tau} + g(\lambda)(1 - \hat{\tau})$$

$$\frac{\partial V_C}{\partial u_s} = \nu\lambda$$

These equations show that the V functions become increasingly convex as the value of ν declines. Consequently, the distribution of the values of V spanned by the common ability distribution, G, is more skewed to the left if ν declines. ∎

Wage profiles

Using (2.21), it is straightforward to compute the earnings profile. For each career path, we have:

$$w_A = g(\lambda)\left\{\frac{g(\lambda)(2 - t)t}{2} + u_s + \nu\bar{u}\right\}$$

$$w_{B1} = \begin{cases} \lambda\{\nu\Lambda t - \frac{1}{2}\nu^2\lambda t^2 + \nu u_s + \bar{u}\} & \text{for } 0 \leqslant t \leqslant \hat{\tau} \\ g(\lambda)\{\Lambda\hat{\tau} - \frac{1}{2}\nu\lambda\hat{\tau}^2 + \frac{1}{2}g(\lambda)(2 - t - \hat{\tau})(t - \hat{\tau}) + u_s + \nu\bar{u}\} & \text{for } \hat{\tau} \leqslant t \leqslant 1 \end{cases}$$

$$w_{B2} = \begin{cases} \lambda[Ht - \frac{1}{2}\lambda t^2 + \nu u_s + \bar{u}] & \text{for } 0 \leqslant t \leqslant \bar{\tau} \\ \lambda[H\bar{\tau} - \frac{1}{2}\lambda\bar{\tau}^2 + \nu\Lambda(t - \bar{\tau}) - \frac{1}{2}\nu^2\lambda(t^2 - \bar{\tau}^2) + \nu u_s + \bar{u}] & \text{for } \bar{\tau} \leqslant t \leqslant \hat{\tau} \\ g(\lambda)\left[\nu H\bar{\tau} - \frac{1}{2}\lambda\bar{\tau}^2 + \nu\Lambda(\hat{\tau} - \bar{\tau}) - \frac{1}{2}\nu\lambda\left(\hat{\tau}^2 - \bar{\tau}^2\right)\right] \\ \quad + \frac{1}{2}g(\lambda)(2 - t - \hat{\tau})(t - \hat{\tau}) + u_s + \nu\bar{u} & \text{for } \hat{\tau} \leqslant t \leqslant 1 \end{cases}$$

$$w_C = \lambda[\frac{1}{2}\lambda(2 - t)t + \nu u_s + \bar{u}]$$

Next, differentiate the above expressions with respect to time to get:

$$\frac{\partial w_A}{\partial t} = g(\lambda)^2(1-t)$$

$$\frac{\partial w_{B1}}{\partial t} = \left\{ \begin{array}{l} v\lambda\{g(1-\hat{\tau}) + v\lambda(\hat{\tau}-t)\} \text{ for } 0 \leqslant t \leqslant \hat{\tau} \\ \{g(\lambda)\}^2(1-t) \text{ for } \hat{\tau} < t \leqslant 1 \end{array} \right\}$$

$$\frac{\partial w_{B2}}{\partial t} = \left\{ \begin{array}{l} \lambda\{vg(\lambda)(1-\hat{\tau}) + \lambda(\hat{\tau}-t)\} \text{ for } 0 \leqslant t \leqslant \bar{\tau} \\ v\lambda\{g(1-\hat{\tau}) + v\lambda(\hat{\tau}-t)\} \text{ for } \bar{\tau} < t \leqslant \hat{\tau} \\ g(\lambda)^2(1-t) \text{ for } \hat{\tau} < t \leqslant 1 \end{array} \right\}$$

$$\frac{\partial w_C}{\partial t} = \lambda^2(1-t)$$

Proof of lemma 2.5

Suppose that $\lambda_{ILM} < \lambda_{OLM}$ at equilibrium. From (2A.1a), we know that

$$V_A(u_s, \lambda_{ILM}) > V_A(u_s, \lambda_{OLM})$$

Thus all the workers in the career path A are hired by type I firms. From lemma 2.3, we also know that only OLM firms hire workers for path C. Consequently, OLM firms hire workers for path C and possibly some workers for path B1, but none for path A. On the other hand, ILM firms employ workers for paths A and B1, but none for path C. Moreover, for the same value of u_s, a worker is promoted earlier in ILM than in OLM firms, thus making the effective span of control smaller at ILM firms, even if both types recruit from the identical distribution of innate ability. Therefore we know that the span of control is smaller in ILM than in OLM firms. This, however, contradicts our assumption that $\lambda_{ILM} < \lambda_{OLM}$. ∎

3 Measuring occupational and internal labor markets

Overview[1]

This chapter and chapters 4 and 5 follow up the theoretical insights of chapters 1 and 2 and focus on relevant empirical aspects of Japanese internal and occupational labor markets, including the classification of firms and occupations into different modes of organizing labor, earnings profiles, and internal promotion.

In this chapter we look at *criteria for classifying occupations* into internal (ILM) and occupational (OLM). After developing an operational measure of the degree of internalization of an occupation, we apply it to the analysis of earnings profiles and test whether these profiles are steeper in ILM occupations, as implied by the theory developed in chapter 2. A brief summary concludes the chapter.

Review of the literature

Key features of internal labor markets are that

employees enter the firm at a limited number of ports of entry and progress along well defined job ladders. Wage setting is administered via a series of bureaucratic procedures which, at the minimum, delay and diffuse market forces. Well defined procedures and company norms govern job security rules. Training typically is on-the-job and firm-specific. This plus limited ports of entry makes inter-firm mobility difficult. (Osterman, 1982, p. 350)

ILM employment systems usually coexist within a single firm and industry with alternative, and often complementary, ways of organizing labor, including occupational and secondary labor markets. Occupational, or craft, systems are often characterized by greater mobility and more loyalty to the skill or profession than to the firm. Secondary

---

[1] This chapter draws on Ohkusa, Brunello and Ariga (1997).

systems contain jobs with low skill content, limited earnings growth, and little job security.[2]

The composition of national labor markets into internal, occupational, and secondary employment systems tends to differ across countries. In a comparative perspective, most economists would agree on a broad classification that places Japan as the country where ILM are more widespread (Osterman, 1994). The rich sociological literature on Japanese work attitudes and organization also stresses the importance of internal labor markets in Japan as commitment maximizing organizations. Lincoln and Kalleberg, for instance, study Japanese internal labor markets and argue that a

facet of firm internal labor market organization with strong implications for control and commitment is a stress on firm-specific skills and knowledge, which have value in a particular employer but are not readily transferable to jobs with other companies. Organization designs that stress job rotation and team production, coupled with strong corporate cultures and intensive on-the-job training, represent a formula for the creation of enterprise specific skills at the expense of easily portable occupation specific skills. (Lincoln and Kalleberg, 1990, pp. 15–16)

The comparative research carried out by Ronald Dore (1973) and Robert Cole (1979) also emphasizes the importance of internal labor markets in Japan and associates them with the broader concepts of welfare corporatism and corporate paternalism, both with deep cultural and historical roots. Finally, Lincoln, Hanada and McBride (1986) illustrate the main features of Japanese internal labor markets by using the results of a survey of American and Japanese manufacturing plants.

Each employment system influences both the type of human resource management (HRM) practices and economic performance. Scholars of Japan, for instance, emphasize the merits of the ILM "task oriented, highly flexible and adaptive system, that maximizes the interchangeability of job occupants in accordance with needs" (Cole, 1979, p. 119). On the other hand, ILM systems are often viewed as less suitable than OLM systems, both for the development of new skills in an environment characterized by rapid technological change and for the adequate utilization of the full scope of individual talents.

Given the different implications of alternative employment systems, the allocation of firms, industries, and occupations to each of these systems is important. This allocation is, however, fairly complicated, both

[2] Saint Paul (1997) is a theoretical analysis of dual labor markets based on efficiency wages. Ishikawa and Dejima (1994) review the literature on Japanese dual labor markets and present important new empirical evidence.

because different employment systems can coexist within the same firm or industry and because of the fuzziness of some of the allocating criteria. It is common in this literature to identify the ILM employment system with large and unionized firms. For instance, Siebert and Addison argue that "some idea of the extent of internal labor markets can be gauged from the distribution of employment by firm size. Only the larger firms can (or need) develop their own enterprise markets" (Siebert and Addison, 1991, p. 77).

The focus on firm size, however, presents some problems. First of all, there is the question of the dividing line – that is, of the critical size that allocates larger firms to ILM markets and smaller firms either to secondary or to occupational labor markets. Second, and more importantly, large ILM firms, especially in Japan, are often composed of a core of occupations organized as ILM employment systems, with long-term employment contracts, fairly steep earnings profiles and career opportunities based on internal promotion, and a periphery of secondary and occupational labor markets that are organized in a different way. Typical examples of jobs organized as secondary labor markets are clerical workers, mailroom staff, and messengers. Typical examples of occupational systems are programmers and sales personnel.[3] Because of their general skills, these occupations are not organized into lengthy job ladders and mobility is not penalized but rewarded.

Firm size is thus a useful but incomplete measure of ILM employment systems, because it focuses on firms rather than on occupations. The purpose of this chapter is to develop a complementary measure of ILM systems based on occupations. Our empirical measure is derived from human capital theory and can be summarized with the following very simple idea: if skills are developed mainly within firms, as suggested by ILM theory, firm-specific tenure (seniority) should be at least as long as occupation-specific tenure. On the other hand, if skills are developed mainly in the market, occupation-specific tenure should be longer than firm-specific tenure.

To evaluate whether this measure provides additional information on ILM systems that is not contained in firm size, the chapter presents an application based on Japanese data and investigates the relationship between the degree of internalization of an occupation and the slope of the associated earnings profile. The consolidated empirical evidence is that earnings profiles are steeper in large Japanese firms (see Hashimoto and Raisian, 1985). If our measure simply replicates the

---

[3] See Osterman (1987).

information already incorporated in firm size, we should find that, after controlling for firm size, it does not affect the relationship between earnings and seniority. On the other hand, if the contrary is true, the adoption of such a measure is likely to improve our ability to describe ILM and OLM employment systems.

A measure of the degree of internalization

The organization of labor into internal and occupational (or craft) labor markets is likely to vary with occupation and skill. In occupations with portable skills, workers move fairly often from firm to firm and accumulate over time substantial occupation-specific tenure. Typical examples of this type of occupation are computer programmers and system engineers. On the other hand, several blue-collar and managerial occupations are characterized by fairly long firm-specific tenure spells, substantial in-house training, few quits, and elaborate job ladders. In these jobs, occupation-specific tenure tends to coincide with firm-specific tenure, as skills are developed mainly within firms.

This relationship between occupation-specific and firm-specific tenure (seniority) suggests a simple measure of the degree of internalization of labor transactions, that allows us in principle to classify occupations into ILM (internal labor market) and OLM (occupational labor market) employment systems. If skills are developed mainly within a single firm, firm-specific tenure is at least as large as occupation-specific tenure, and the occupation is typically ILM. In this case, workers may even change occupation in the same firm, receive internal training, and move along the internal job ladder. On the other hand, if skills are general, workers can increase their occupational tenure by moving from firm to firm, with little firm-specific tenure.[4]

Define T_{ij} and E_{ij}, respectively, as firm-specific tenure and occupation-specific tenure of an individual, i, employed in occupation j. Next, define N_{ij} as the number of workers in occupation j, and the function $\Lambda[\cdot]$ as a function taking the value of one when its argument is weakly positive and the value of zero when its argument is strictly negative. A measure of the degree of internalization of occupation j is

$$\phi_j = \frac{1}{N_j} \sum_{i=1}^{N_j} \Lambda[T_{ij} \geq E_{ij}] \tag{3.1}$$

---

[4] Chapter 2 contains a theoretical discussion of the relationship between skill formation and alternative employment systems.

where $N_j = \sum_i N_{ij}$. The indicator ϕ ranges from zero to one and increases when the number of employees in the same occupation with mainly firm-specific tenure increases. The higher the value of ϕ for occupation j, the closer the occupation to the ILM type.[5] An alternative measure of internalization is

$$\xi_j = \frac{1}{N_j} \sum_{i=1}^{N_j} \Lambda\left[T_{ij} - E_{ij}\right] \tag{3.2}$$

Compared to ϕ, this indicator can take negative values and does not vary within the range of zero to one. Moreover, because it weights each individual with the difference between her seniority and her occupational tenure, it gives a considerably higher importance either to long seniority spells with little occupational tenure or to long occupational spells with little seniority. For our purposes, however, it does not matter whether a seniority spell is five or 10 years longer than an occupational spell. In both cases the individual is developing her skills within the firm rather than in the market. Similarly, it is not important whether an occupational spell is five or 10 years longer than a seniority spell. In both cases, we can argue that the market has played an important role in skill development. For these reasons, we focus hereafter on the indicator ϕ.

Our conceptually simple measure captures a key aspect of ILM versus OLM employment systems and can be easily implemented when statistical information on both firm-specific and on occupation-specific tenure is available. We hasten to stress that firm-specific tenure has often been considered in the literature as an indicator of ILM versus OLM employment systems at least as relevant as firm size. An example is the review of internal labor markets by Osterman (1994), where he uses the frequency of long-term employment relationships as the key indicator of the current importance of ILM employment systems. Firm-specific tenure *per se*, however, is not fully informative of skill development within firms, because the same (average) tenure spell can be consistent with substantially different occupation-specific spells in other firms. The bottom line of this chapter is that information on firm-specific tenure is even more valuable when it can be matched with information on occupation-specific tenure.

Conditional on occupation-specific experience, the indicator ϕ is correlated by construction with seniority in the firm. If this correlation is high in the data, perhaps because occupational tenure exhibits little variation among occupations, one could argue that using ϕ is equivalent to

---

[5] As in the case of firm size, this measure does not automatically provide a dividing line between ILM and OLM systems.

using average seniority in the occupation. For this reason, we also consider an adjusted version of ϕ, $\hat{\phi}$, obtained as follows. First, we use the data on occupations to compute average seniority in each occupation, T_j,[6] and to run an ordinary least squares regression of ϕ_j on a constant and on average seniority, T_j, for the full set of available occupations. Second, we obtain $\hat{\phi}$ as the estimated constant *plus* the residuals from the regression. By construction, this adjusted measure is orthogonal to average seniority, T_j.

The empirical implementation of the measures discussed above is based on the 1990 wave of the Survey on the Wage Structure (*Chingin Kouzou Kihon Chousa*), providing detailed information on earnings and employment on an occupational basis. In particular, table 3 in volume 3 of the survey contains cell means of tenure, age, earnings, hours, and employment for 141 occupations,[7] 12 age groups and three firm sizes. Information in this table can be matched with information contained in table 4 in the same volume, including cell means of earnings, hours, and employment by four ranges of occupation-specific tenure, 141 occupations and 12 age groups. The key advantage of these data is that information on both firm- and occupation-specific tenure is available for a number of occupations. This information comes at the price of an incomplete list of occupations. First of all, the survey includes only the most representative occupations, covering a relevant number of employees. Second, the survey design is likely to be biased toward excluding ILM occupations, because jobs that can be fitted into a rank hierarchy are ruled out.[8] These are mainly white-collar and managerial jobs, usually organized into ILM employment systems. Overall, our data cover at least 51 percent of full-time males in the establishments surveyed by the Survey on the Wage Structure.[9] Needless to say, these limitations are serious, and should be kept in mind when drawing any implications from the current exercise for the aggregate Japanese labor market.

---

[6] We define T_j in the following way

$$T_j = \frac{1}{N_j} \sum_j T_{ij}$$

[7] The full list of the occupations used below may be found in the appendix (p. 93).
[8] Standard ranks are subsection director, division director, and department director.
[9] In 1990, full-time male workers in the survey could be classified as follows: 4,708,000 in the included occupations, 1,845,000 in ranked jobs, and 2,652,000 either in jobs without a specific rank or in excluded occupations. Since an explicit breakdown of the last group is impossible, the percentage in the text is obtained by assuming that all workers in this group are without a specific rank. One reason why this percentage is fairly low is that many Japanese firms treat their employees as "generalists" rather than as "specialists."

Since the published data include only cell means, we need to adapt our indicator as follows. Let T_{mj} and E_{mj} denote, respectively, average firm-specific tenure and average occupational tenure of a group, m, of homogeneous workers employed in occupation j. Next, define N_{mj} as the number of workers in the m group (cell). With M groups of workers in each occupation, the indicator ϕ can be redefined as follows

$$\phi_j = \frac{\sum_{m=1}^{M} \Lambda \left[T_{mj} \geq E_{mj} \right] N_{mj}}{\sum_{m=1}^{M} N_{mj}} \qquad (3.3)$$

We focus on male employees younger than 60.[10] Since our purpose is to develop a measure that orders occupations depending on their closeness to ILM and OLM systems, we need to purge the data of obvious candidates for SLM (secondary labor markets) systems. A key feature of occupations organized into secondary labor markets is that they have very limited earnings growth. In this chapter, we use the ratio of hourly earnings by workers in the 40–44 age range to hourly earnings by workers aged 20–24 and purge from the sample all occupations with a ratio lower than 1:30. It turns out that nine occupations are excluded (mine pit-men, iron-making workers, crane men, taxi drivers, large and small truck drivers, private police guards, amusement arcade receptionists, and janitors), so we end up with 92 occupations and 10 age groups.[11]

Since occupation-specific tenure comes in five ranges ([0], [1–4], [5–9], [10–14] and [15–]) rather than on a continuous basis, average measured tenure, E_{ij}, is likely to depend on the selection of values for each range, especially for the last, which is open ended. We choose mid-points for the second, third, and fourth range and experiment with two alternative values for the last range, 20 and 22.5. These values correspond, respectively, to a maximum of 25 and 30 years of occupation-specific tenure, and are used to compute the indicators ϕ_{20} and $\phi_{22.5}$. Table 3.1 presents the average values and the correlation between the two alternative measures of ϕ, both adjusted and unadjusted for average seniority in the occupation. Table 3.1 shows two things. First, both adjusted and unadjusted measures exhibit substantial positive correlation. In particular, while the correlation between the unadjusted indicators, ϕ_{20} and $\phi_{22.5}$, is equal to 0.895, the correlation between the adjusted indicators, $\hat{\phi}_{20}$ and $\hat{\phi}_{22.5}$, is equal to 0.854. Furthermore, if we rank occupations by the value of ϕ and compare alternative rankings of the top and the bottom 20 occupations, we find that measures ϕ_{20} and $\phi_{22.5}$ share 14 out of 20

[10] We exclude workers older than 60 because of the mandatory retirement system. After retirement, many workers typically fill SLM jobs.
[11] 40 occupations were lost because they employ female labor.

Table 3.1 *Means and correlation matrix for two alternative measures of*
ϕ, *both adjusted and unadjusted, 92 occupations*
(a) Means

	ϕ_{20}	$\phi_{22.5}$	$\hat{\phi}_{20}$	$\hat{\phi}_{22.5}$
Mean	0.614	0.485	0.474	0.372
Standard Deviation	0.294	0.283	0.213	0.231

(b) Correlation matrix

	ϕ_{20}	$\phi_{22.5}$	$\hat{\phi}_{20}$	$\hat{\phi}_{22.5}$
ϕ_{20}	1			
$\phi_{22.5}$	0.895	1		
$\hat{\phi}_{20}$	0.794	0.731	1	
$\hat{\phi}_{22.5}$	0.678	0.856	0.854	1

occupations in the list of top 20 occupations and 16 out of 20 in the list of
bottom 20 occupations. Second, the correlation between adjusted and
unadjusted measures is also fairly high. For instance, indicators $\phi_{22.5}$
and $\hat{\phi}_{22.5}$ have a correlation coefficient equal to 0.856. This finding suggests that controlling for average seniority in an occupation does not
change in a substantial way the information content of the selected measure of internalization, and points to the presence of relevant between-
occupations variation in occupation-specific tenure. Overall, the table
shows that the information content of the four measures is fairly similar.
Because of this, in the rest of the chapter we shall focus mainly on $\phi_{22.5}$ as
an estimate of ϕ. The cumulative distribution of $\phi_{22.5}$ in the sample of 92
occupations is presented in table 3.2.

As mentioned in the introduction, internal labor markets are often
characterized in the literature as typical of large and unionized firms.
Moreover, firms operating these markets are considered as more likely
to offer long-term employment and steep earnings profiles. Table 3.3
presents information on average age, seniority, occupational tenure,
firm size (defined as the employment share of firms with more than
1,000 employees), and relative earnings (measured as the earnings of
workers aged 40–44 relative to the earnings of workers aged 20–24),
both for the whole sample and for three subsamples the top 20 occupations (typically ILM, with a value of $\phi_{22.5}$ larger than or equal to 0.75),
the bottom 20 occupations (typically OLM, with a value of $\phi_{22.5}$ lower

Table 3.2 *Cumulative distribution of*
$\phi_{22.5}$, *92 occupations*

Values of $\phi_{22.5}$	Cumulative distribution
0–0.10	0.087
0.11–0.20	0.174
0.21–0.30	0.337
0.31–0.40	0.413
0.41–0.50	0.522
0.51–0.60	0.608
0.61–0.70	0.717
0.71–0.80	0.880
0.81–0.90	0.913
0.91–1.00	1.000

than or equal to 0.23), and the rest of the sample. In more detail, tables 3.4 and 3.5 present the same information for each of the top 20 and of the bottom 20 occupations.

Interestingly, many OLM occupations listed in table 3.5 do actually carry an official license. System engineers and computer programmers, truck drivers, cooks, pilots, medical doctors, pharmacists, clinical X-ray technicians, and clinical examination technicians do so. With the exception of the former two, in all of these cases failure to hold a license precludes entry into the occupation. On the other hand, only computer operators and motormen in private railways among the top 20 occupations hold a license, and this license does not preclude entry into the occupation.[12]

On average, firm size is larger among ILM occupations (see figure 3.1). There are, however, a few exceptions. For instance, car salesmen are listed among the top 20 occupations, even though the employment share of large firms in the occupation is less than 20 percent. On the other hand, insurance canvassers are listed among the bottom 20 occupations, even though large firms employ more than 85 percent of workers in the occupation. A regression fitting firm size on a constant and on $\phi_{22.5}$ explains less than 20 percent of the total variance and yields an estimate of the slope parameter equal to 0.366, with a T-ratio equal to 3.99.[13]

---

[12] Licenses for motormen are not portable, because they are specific to the railway that issues them.
[13] If we use the adjusted measure $\hat{\phi}_{22.5}$, the estimated slope parameter is equal to 0.274, with a T-ratio of 2.35, and explained variance is only 6% of total variance.

Table 3.3 *Average age, seniority, occupational tenure, firm size, and relative earnings for different ranges of $\phi_{22.5}$, 92 occupations*

Values of $\phi_{22.5}$	$\phi_{22.5}$	Age	Seniority	Occ. tenure	Firm size	Rel. ear.[a]
All values of $\phi_{22.5}$	0.485	38.5	12.1	12.1	0.32	1.75
$\phi_{22.5} \geq 0.75$ (top 20)	0.870	38.9	14.8	12.7	0.52	1.79
$0.23 < \phi_{22.5} < 0.75$	0.483	38.6	12.0	12.0	0.28	1.70
$\phi_{22.5} \leq 0.23$ (bottom 20)	0.110	37.8	9.4	11.4	0.23	1.82

[a]Relative earnings (Rel. ear.) are earnings of workers in the age bracket [40–44] relative to earnings of workers in the bracket [20–24].

Average seniority is significantly higher among occupations with higher value of $\phi_{22.5}$ (see figure 3.2). In particular, steel workers as well as private railway operators have on average more than 20 years of firm-specific tenure. This compares, for instance, with less than five years of tenure for computer programmers and medical doctors. A regression fitting average seniority on a constant and on $\phi_{22.5}$ explains about 26 percent of total variance and attracts a positive and significant slope coefficient.

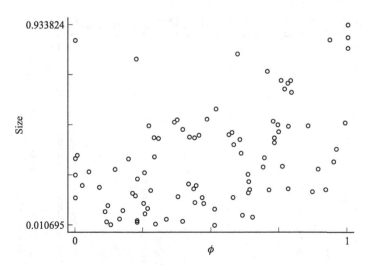

Figure 3.1 Firm size and ϕ

Table 3.4 Average age, seniority, occupational tenure, share of large firms, and relative earnings, top 20 occupations, ranked by value of $\phi_{22.5}$.

Occupation	$\phi_{22.5}$	Age	Seniority	Occ. tenure	% L firms[a]	Rel. ear.[b]
Computer operator	0.95	29.3	6.9	5.7	30.4	2.18
Watchman	0.99	51.9	14.2	10.8	48.2	1.61
Paper-making worker	0.75	38.7	14.3	13.1	44.1	1.64
Relief printer	0.76	38.1	14.5	13.3	28.2	2.15
Chemical analyst	0.85	35.9	13.9	11.9	46.9	2.11
Chemical fiber spinner	0.77	41.1	17.9	16.0	63.8	1.67
Steel worker	0.78	42.0	19.4	17.4	66.6	1.80
Metal-fusing worker	0.78	44.7	16.4	14.1	46.6	1.62
Furnace worker	0.79	41.6	22.2	19.0	67.5	1.99
Metal molder	0.96	39.3	14.0	12.9	36.1	1.42
Pattern-forging worker	0.89	39.8	14.6	12.8	27.0	1.67
Steel rolling-millworker	0.75	41.3	18.8	17.1	67.8	1.68
Electroplating worker	0.92	39.4	12.6	11.2	17.4	1.66
Machine inspector	0.79	36.2	13.3	12.3	62.3	1.71
Autom. assembler	0.93	35.2	11.6	10.6	86.5	1.59
Plastic mold worker	0.78	36.9	9.5	9.2	17.8	1.43
Car salesman	0.87	32.6	9.1	8.4	16.4	2.03
Motorman – priv. railways	1.00	39.6	20.1	14.0	87.5	1.88
Conductor – priv. railways	1.00	36.4	17.1	11.9	82.6	1.94
Ticket seller – priv. railways	1.00	35.4	15.6	12.2	93.3	2.03

Notes: [a] L = large. [b] Relative earnings (Rel. ear.) are earnings of workers in the age bracket [40–44] relative to earnings of workers in the bracket [20–24].

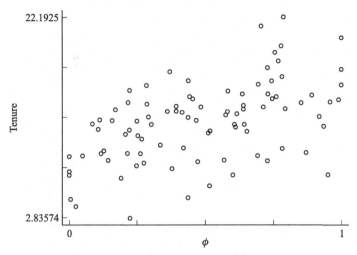

Figure 3.2 Tenure and ϕ

Turning to relative pay, figure 3.3 illustrates the relationship between relative pay and ϕ in the 92 occupations and tables 3.4 and 3.5 present, for each occupation, the ratio of annual earnings by the 40–44 age group to earnings by the 20–24 age group. A quick inspection suggests that there is no clear evidence that relative pay is higher in ILM occupations. Medical doctors, computer programmers, and insurance canvassers exhibit substantially higher earnings growth with age than steel-mill workers and railway operators. For these occupations, the contribution of firm-specific tenure to earnings is likely to be much lower than the contribution of occupation-specific tenure. As the tables suggest, occupations with low values of $\phi_{22.5}$, that we associate with OLM markets, exhibit either relatively large or relatively low earnings differentials. This result could depend on our fairly restrictive definition of the SLM sector. If we use a more restrictive criterion and assign to the SLM sector all the occupations where relative earnings are less than 1.5, the slope coefficient in the regression of relative pay on a constant and on $\phi_{22.5}$ attracts a negative sign but is not significantly different from zero.[14] This piece of evidence is only apparently in contrast with one implication of the model developed in chapter 2, suggesting that wage differentials are wider in OLM than in ILM firms. That implication refers to wage differentials conditional on age and seniority, while the current evidence compares groups of individuals with different age and seniority.

[14] A similar result holds if we use the adjusted measure $\hat{\phi}_{22.5}$.

Table 3.5 *Average age, seniority, occupational tenure, share of large firms, and relative earnings, bottom 20 occupations, ranked by value of $\phi_{22.5}$*

Occupation	$\phi_{22.5}$	Age	Seniority	Occ.tenure	percent L. firms	Rel. ear.
System engineer	0.19	30.1	6.7	7.2	31.5	2.39
Computer programmer	0.02	26.2	4.0	4.1	19.2	2.09
Truck driver	0.12	39.9	9.1	11.2	10	1.37
Miner (digger)	0.22	43.2	9.9	11.8	14.7	1.45
Knitter	0.17	43.2	13.2	14.8	7.7	1.36
Tailor	0.11	41.3	11.4	13.4	7.2	1.64
Sewing machine worker	0.13	39.6	9.3	10.9	1.3	1.52
Wood pattern-maker	0.16	40.9	12.2	14.1	3.9	1.56
Furniture-maker	0.12	41.1	12.3	12.3	2.4	1.44
Woodwork-painter	0.23	40.9	11.3	14.0	2.6	1.46
Sheet metal worker	0.21	37.8	10.9	12.3	15.5	1.62
Iron worker	0.09	41.3	11.9	13.9	18.4	1.47
Mechanical draftsman	0.05	32.6	8.9	9.5	25.4	1.85
Insurance canvasser	0.00	41.5	7.3	9.8	86.1	2.61
Cook	0.00	34.7	7.3	11.8	13.4	1.73
Pilot	0.22	37.9	13.9	15.3	77.7	1.76
Medical doctor	0.00	37.6	4.6	10.3	32.8	2.88
Pharmacist	0.00	35.2	7.1	10.2	24.0	2.04
Clinical X-ray technician	0.15	35.2	8.4	11.3	26.6	1.85
Clinical exam. technician	0.00	34.8	8.8	10.9	31.6	2.24

Note: For explanation of *L* and Rel. ear., see table 3.4.

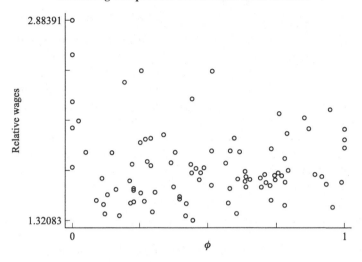

Figure 3.3 Relative pay and ϕ

The usefulness of our measure depends on whether its variation among occupations can be accurately predicted by the variation in average firm size and average seniority. If this prediction is accurate, our suggested measure is clearly redundant. We check this by regressing ϕ_j on a constant, average seniority and firm size, and obtain the following result[15]

$$\phi_j = \underset{(0.085)}{0.022} + \underset{(0.008)}{0.029 T_j} + \underset{(0.141)}{0.323 L_j}$$

$$R^2 = 0.31, \ N = 92$$

where L is firm size (measured as the employment share of large firms in each occupation). It turns out that the combined effect of average seniority and average firm size explains only about 30 percent of the variation among occupations. We conclude from this that our measure provides useful additional information on the degree of internalization of occupations.

Earnings profiles in internal and in occupational labor markets

Standard human capital theory predicts that individual productivity increases with firm-specific tenure, as workers accumulate over time

[15] Standard errors within parentheses. We have experimented with powers and interactions of the explanatory variables, with little change in the results.

non-portable human capital. Since earnings are linked to productivity, earnings also increase with tenure. If the accumulation of human capital occurs at a decreasing rate, as in the classical Mincerian earnings function, individual productivity and earnings are a concave function of firm-specific tenure. When human capital is portable and its accumulation occurs mainly in the market, however, occupation-specific tenure is likely to matter more than firm-specific tenure in the determination of individual earnings. Internal labor markets are often designed to foster the accumulation of firm-specific human capital, because employment security and long-term employment contracts help overcome the "hostage problem," thus allowing both firms and workers to recoup their investment costs.[16] On the other hand, occupational labor markets are typical of occupations and skills that are fairly general and portable from firm to firm.

This discussion suggests that firm-specific tenure should matter more for earnings growth in occupations that fit into the ILM type (high value of ϕ), while occupation-specific tenure should be more important for occupations belonging to the OLM type (low value of ϕ). To be more precise, define W_{ij}, A_{ij}, and T_{ij}, respectively, as hourly earnings, age net of seniority, and seniority of individual i working in occupation j. A slightly modified version of the standard earnings equation is

$$\ln W_{ij} = \alpha_j + \gamma_1 T_{ij} + \gamma_2 T_{ij}^2 + \gamma_3 A_{ij} + \gamma_4 A_{ij}^2 + \gamma_5 T_{ij} A_{ij} + \gamma_6 L_{ij} + \varepsilon_{ij}$$
$$(3.4)$$

where ln is for logarithm, α_j is an occupation-specific effect, γ_i are parameters, L is a firm-size dummy taking the value of one if the individual is employed by a firm with more than 1,000 employees and of zero otherwise, and ε is the error term, that we assume to have zero mean and constant variance. Notice that we are restricting the impact of education and labor market experience before joining the current firm to be the same. Even though this restriction is likely to be rejected by the data, we are forced to impose it because of the lack of information on education.[17]

Equation (3.4) can be adequately modified as follows to account for possible differences in earnings profiles between ILM-type and OLM-type occupations

---

[16] See Lynch (1993) for a discussion of the "hostage problem."
[17] Lack of information on education makes it impossible to evaluate the returns to labor market experience, in both the same and in other occupations.

$$\ln W_{ij} = \gamma_0 \phi_j + \gamma_1 T_{ij} + \gamma_2 T_{ij}^2 + \gamma_3 A_{ij} + \gamma_4 A_{ij}^2 + \gamma_5 T_{ij} A_{ij} + \gamma_6 L_{ij}$$
$$+ \beta_1 \phi_j T_{ij} + \beta_2 \phi_j T_{ij}^2 + \beta_3 \phi_j A_{ij} + \beta_4 \phi_j A_{ij}^2 + \beta_5 \phi_j T_{ij} A_{ij} + \varepsilon_{ij}$$
$$(3.5)$$

where β_i are parameters. First, the random occupation-specific effect, α_j, has been replaced by an occupation-specific variable, ϕ_j, measuring the degree of internalization of each occupation. Second, the RHS variables in (3.4) have been interacted with ϕ_j. Since ϕ_j measures the degree of internalization of an occupation, the impact of a marginally higher degree of internalization on the relationship between earnings and firm-specific tenure can be captured by evaluating the following partial derivative

$$\lambda = \frac{\partial \ln W}{\partial T \partial \phi} = \beta_1 + 2\beta_2 T + \beta_3 A \qquad (3.6)$$

for different values of seniority and net age.[18] Since more internalization is likely to yield steeper wage–seniority profiles, we expect the sign of this derivative to be positive.

Equation (3.5) allows for explicit effects of the degree of internalization on the wage–seniority profile, but restricts the impact of firm size on the intercept alone. As discussed in the previous section, the measure ϕ is positively correlated with firm size so that interacting it with average net age and tenure may simply capture firm-size effects on earnings profiles. To see whether our suggested measure adds something to the standard firm-size effect, we interact all the explanatory variables on the RHS of (3.5) with the firm-size dummy, L. Conditional on these additional interactions, significant interactions between ϕ and seniority suggest that ILM effects spread beyond large firms and are linked to occupations as well as to firm size.

The empirical implementation is based on a dataset of 92 occupations, ten age groups and three firm sizes. Excluding missing values, we have 2,585 valid observations. Table 3.6 presents the summary statistics of the main variables used in the regressions, both for the whole sample and for the subsamples of large, small, and medium-sized firms. The empirical models in (3.4) and (3.5) refer to individuals. Since our data are based on grouped observations, however, we need to introduce a few adjustments. First, the firm-size dummy is defined as equal to one when employees in a

---

[18] For instance, given the estimated values of the parameters, λ can be evaluated by setting net age equal to 20 and seniority equal to 5. Alternatively, it can be evaluated at the sample means of net age and seniority for each firm size. In what follows, we shall use the expression "wage–seniority profile" to describe the relationship between earnings and seniority.

Table 3.6 *Summary statistics*

Variable	Mean	St. dev.	Min.	Max.
All firms				
ln hourly wage	3.16	0.39	1.88	4.95
Age net of seniority	25.74	7.34	15	59.5
Firm-specific seniority	11.52	8.06	0.5	41
Large firms				
ln hourly wage	3.35	0.37	2.06	4.95
Age net of seniority	23.02	5.59	15	54.7
Firm-specific seniority	14.63	10.02	0.5	41
Small and medium-sized firms				
ln hourly wage	3.07	0.36	1.88	4.63
Age net of seniority	27.02	8.04	15	56
Firm-specific seniority	10.07	7.25	0.5	35.3

cell are employed by a firm with more than 1,000 employees, and to zero otherwise. Second, the error term with grouped data is assumed to have an heteroskedastic variance, varying with the number of observations in each cell, and each equation is estimated by weighted least squares, using as weights the number of individuals in a cell.[19]

The results are reported in table 3.7. In column (1) we show the estimates of (3.5) and in column (2) we present the estimates of the more general specification, including the interactions with the firm-size dummy, L. Since the former specification is nested into the latter, we can test whether the restrictions in the more parsimonious model are supported by our data. It turns out that a likelihood ratio test cannot reject the more general specification, including interactions between the firm-size dummy and all the other variables.[20] An additional and relevant hypothesis that can be tested is whether the interactions of our measure ϕ with net age and seniority are jointly significant in the regressions presented in table 3.7. For each column, we compute the likelihood ratio test when the null hypothesis is the joint exclusion of these interactions. As reported at the bottom of each column, the test is equal to 86.89 in the parsimonious model and to 122.99 in the more general model. Both values imply that

---

[19] In this chapter we ignore the important issue of the endogeneity of tenure; that is discussed in detail in chapter 4.

[20] The likelihood ratio test is equal to 132.92. With 11 degrees of freedom, the alternative hypothesis cannot be rejected at the 5 percent level of confidence.

Table 3.7 *Earnings profiles interacted with $\phi = \phi_{22.5}$, weighted least squares; dependent variable: log of hourly earnings, each regression includes a constant term*

Variables	Coefficients (1)	Coefficients (2)
ϕ	0.869 (0.211)[a]	1.475 (0.266)
Age net of seniority	0.113 (0.007)	0.122 (0.008)
Age net of seniority squared	−0.001 (0.0001)	−0.001 (0.0001)
Seniority	0.074 (0.006)	0.061 (0.008)
Seniority squared	0.0001 (0.0001)	0.001 (0.0002)
Age net of seniority × seniority	−0.0025 (0.0002)	−0.003 (0.0002)
ϕ × seniority	0.012 (0.010)	0.058 (0.015)
ϕ × seniority squared	−0.0015 (0.0002)	−0.003 (0.0004)
ϕ × age net of seniority	−0.063 (0.014)	−0.113 (0.018)
ϕ × age net of seniority squared	0.0006 (0.0002)	0.0013 (0.0003)
ϕ × net age × seniority	0.0016 (0.0003)	0.0015 (0.0004)
L^b	0.200 (0.009)	0.334 (0.248)
$\phi \times L$		−1.284 (0.524)
Age net of seniority × L	–	−0.030 (0.017)
Age net of seniority squared × L	–	−0.0007 (0.0004)
Seniority × L	–	0.050 (0.012)
Seniority squared × L	–	−0.0017 (0.0003)
Age net of seniority × seniority × L	–	−0.0007 (0.0004)
ϕ × seniority × L	–	−0.098 (0.022)
ϕ × seniority squared × L	–	0.0027 (0.0005)
ϕ × age net of seniority × L	–	0.127 (0.037)
ϕ × age net of seniority squared × L	–	−0.002 (0.0006)
ϕ × net age × seniority × L	–	0.001 (0.0008)
R^2	0.639	0.656
Nobs[c]	2.585	2.585
Joint significance of interactions with ϕ	$\chi^2(5) = 86.89^*$	
Joint significance of interactions with ϕ		$\chi^2(10) = 122.99^*$
Joint significance of interactions with L		$\chi^2(11) = 132.92^*$

Notes:
[a]Standard errors within parentheses.
[b]The dummy variable L is equal to one when employees in a cell are employed by a firm with more than 1,000 employees, and to zero otherwise.
[c]In all tables in this chapter: number of observations.
*The test cannot reject the hypothesis of joint significance at the 5 percent level.

the alternative hypothesis of jointly significant interaction terms cannot be rejected by the data. We conclude from this that the interaction of our measure ϕ with net age and seniority significantly improves our ability to explain the cross-section relationship between earnings and human capital variables.

Rather than discussing each estimated coefficient in detail, we prefer to summarize the contribution of the indicator ϕ by computing its estimated marginal impact on the slope of the wage–seniority profile. This is done in two ways. First, we evaluate λ for large and small–medium-sized firms, using the sample means of net age and seniority. Second, we set a common value for net age, 20, and allow seniority to take the values of 5, 10, 15, and 20. The results of this exercise are presented in the first part of table 3.10. When evaluated at the sample means, a marginal increase in the degree of internalization positively affects the slope of the wage–seniority profile in both types of firm, but especially in large firms.

When seniority is allowed to vary and net age is set at 20 years, the estimated value of λ is positive for seniority spells lower than 10 years and negative for longer spells. This finding suggests that occupations with high ϕ, that fit into the ILM type, yield steeper wage–seniority profiles early on in a worker career, while occupations with low ϕ, that fit into the OLM type, have steeper earnings profiles when seniority is fairly high. A possible explanation of this result is the presence of a selection bias in ILM-type occupations. Some of these occupations – for example, ticket sellers, motormen, and train conductors – are clearly linked by promotion patterns, and the best-performing employees are expected to move up the career ladder as their tenure increases. If stayers are less able than leavers, the negative effect of seniority on λ when seniority is high can simply reflect this selection process.

The relationship between earnings profiles and degree of internalization is illustrated in figure 3.4, based on the regression results in column (1) (for all firms) and in column (2) (for small, medium-sized and large firms) of table 3.7. These figures are computed by using the estimated coefficients, by setting net age at 20, and by letting seniority vary between 1 and 20. Starting from all firms, simulated earnings in occupations with a high value of ϕ ($\phi_{22.5} = 0.8$) start from a lower value but grow faster than earnings in occupations with a low value of ϕ ($\phi_{22.5} = 0.1$). Earnings growth in the former group of occupations slows down after 10 years of tenure but earnings remain higher through the entire simulated period. Turning to small, medium-sized, and large firms, we can see that the behavior of simulated earnings does not change qualitatively with firm size. The main difference is quantitative, as earnings differentials in the two types of occupation are smaller in firms with more than 1,000 employees.

The findings in table 3.7 are open to two main potential drawbacks. First, we are using the unadjusted measure of ϕ, $\phi_{22.5}$. Since this measure is correlated with seniority by construction, and seniority in Japan is positively correlated with both earnings and firm size, it is not surprising that ϕ shows these same correlations in the data. Second, our regressions ignore education. Without a measure of schooling it is difficult to know the extent to which the estimated coefficients for variable ϕ in table 3.7 are biased by a specification error.

Table 3.8 deals with the first objection by presenting regression estimates where the measure $\phi_{22.5}$ has been replaced by the adjusted measure $\hat{\phi}_{22.5}$. As the second part of table 3.10 shows, the use of the adjusted measure does not bring any qualitative change to the results discussed above: the estimated value of λ when sample means are used is positive in both types of firm and the marginal impact of internalization is positive for low seniority spells and negative for high spells.

We deal with the second objection as follows. First, we estimate model (3.5), in both the parsimonious and in the more general specification that includes interactions with the dummy L, on the subset of 57 blue-collar occupations. By focusing on blue-collar jobs, we are minimizing the impact of education, because it is unlikely that educational requirements vary substantially among these occupations. On the one hand, very few university graduates are employed in blue-collar jobs. On the other, more than 70 percent of blue-collar workers aged less than 60 are high school graduates.[21] The estimated earnings profiles are presented in table 3.9. Columns (1) and (2) in the final part of table 3.10 display the estimated values of λ when only blue-collar occupations are considered. Compared to the estimates based on the whole set of occupations, the marginal contribution of a higher ϕ on the slope of the wage–seniority profile is positive for both short and for long seniority spells. Evaluated at sample means, this contribution is also positive. Once again, the qualitative results are very similar to the results discussed above: earnings profiles are steeper in occupations with a high value of ϕ, especially when individuals are employed in small and medium-sized firms.

Second, we use an alternative data source, the 1992 Survey on the Employment Structure (*Shugyou Kouzou Chousa*), to look at the relationship between the degree of internalization and the average level of education. This survey provides information on individual educational attainment, but does not have data on occupational tenure. Without

---

[21] See Ohkusa (1995).

Table 3.8 *Earnings profiles interacted with $\phi = \hat{\phi}_{22.5}$, weighted least squares; dependent variable: log of hourly earnings, each regression includes a constant term*

Variables	Coefficients (1)	Coefficients (2)
ϕ	−0.586 (0.269)[a]	−0.408 (0.326)
Age net of seniority	0.093 (0.007)	0.096 (0.008)
Age net of seniority squared	−0.001 (0.0001)	−0.001 (0.0001)
Seniority	0.063 (0.005)	0.056 (0.008)
Seniority squared	0.0002 (0.0001)	0.001 (0.0002)
Age net of seniority × seniority	−0.0019 (0.0002)	−0.002 (0.0002)
ϕ × seniority	0.054 (0.012)	0.075 (0.018)
ϕ × seniority squared	−0.0013 (0.0003)	−0.002 (0.0005)
ϕ × age net of seniority	0.023 (0.018)	0.007 (0.023)
ϕ × age net of seniority squared	−0.0003 (0.0003)	−0.000003 (0.0003)
ϕ × net age × seniority	−0.0006 (0.0004)	−0.0008 (0.0005)
L^b	0.209 (0.009)	0.195 (0.260)
ϕ × L		−0.489 (0.721)
Age net of seniority × L	–	−0.018 (0.018)
Age net of seniority squared × L	–	0.0007 (0.0003)
Seniority × L	–	0.040 (0.012)
Seniority squared × L	–	−0.0011 (0.0003)
Age net of seniority × seniority × L	–	−0.0008 (0.0004)
ϕ × seniority × L	–	−0.077 (0.027)
ϕ × seniority squared × L	–	0.0011 (0.0007)
ϕ × age net of seniority × L	–	0.069 (0.052)
ϕ × age net of seniority squared × L	–	−0.002 (0.0009)
ϕ × net age × seniority × L	–	0.002 (0.001)
R^2	0.633	0.640
Nobs	2.585	2.585
Joint significance of interactions with ϕ	$\chi^2(5) = 45.49^*$	
Joint significance of interactions with ϕ		$\chi^2(10) = 58.29^*$
Joint significance of interactions with L		$\chi^2(11) = 106.42^*$

Notes:
[a] Standard errors within parentheses.
[b] The dummy variable L is equal to one when employees in a cell are employed by a firm with more than 1,000 employees, and to zero otherwise.
*The test cannot reject the hypothesis of joint significance at the 5 percent level.

Table 3.9 *Earnings profiles interacted with $\phi = \phi_{22.5}$, weighted least squares; dependent variable: log of hourly earnings, each regression includes a constant, blue-collar occupations only*

Variables	Coefficients (1)	Coefficients (2)
ϕ	0.387 (0.244)[a]	1.264 (0.305)
Age net of seniority	0.069 (0.010)	0.092 (0.013)
Age net of seniority squared	−0.0007 (0.0001)	−0.0009 (0.0002)
Seniority	0.083 (0.006)	0.075 (0.010)
Seniority squared	−0.0005 (0.0002)	−0.0002 (0.0003)
Age net of seniority × seniority	−0.002 (0.0002)	−0.0022 (0.0003)
ϕ × seniority	−0.014 (0.010)	0.032 (0.017)
ϕ × seniority squared	−0.0005 (0.0003)	−0.001 (0.0004)
ϕ × age net of seniority	−0.017 (0.017)	−0.090 (0.023)
ϕ × age net of seniority squared	−0.0001 (0.0003)	0.0011 (0.0003)
ϕ × net age × seniority	0.0015 (0.0004)	0.0007 (0.0005)
L^b	0.186 (0.009)	0.543 (0.563)
ϕ × L		−1.960 (0.930)
Age net of seniority × L	–	−0.009 (0.045)
Age net of seniority squared × L	–	−0.0004 (0.0008)
Seniority × L	–	−0.011 (0.016)
Seniority squared × L	–	−0.0008 (0.0004)
Age net of seniority × seniority × L	–	0.0016 (0.0008)
ϕ × seniority × L	–	−0.035 (0.028)
ϕ × seniority squared × L	–	0.0011 (0.0006)
ϕ × age net of seniority × L	–	0.151 (0.077)
ϕ × age net of seniority squared × L	–	−0.002 (0.0016)
ϕ × net age × seniority × L	–	−0.0006 (0.001)
R^2	0.789	0.798
Nobs	1.607	1.607
Joint significance of interactions with ϕ	$\chi^2(5) = 19.35^*$	
Joint significance of interactions with ϕ		$\chi^2(10) = 35.18^*$
Joint significance of interactions with L		$\chi^2(11) = 86.87^*$

Notes:
[a]Standard errors within parentheses.
[b]The dummy variable L is equal to one when employees in a cell are employed by a firm with more than 1,000 employees, and to zero otherwise.
*The test cannot reject the hypothesis of joint significance at the 5 percent level.

Table 3.10 *Estimated values of the marginal impact of a higher ϕ on the slope of the wage–seniority profile (λ)*

All Occupations	Small and medium-sized firms (1)	Large firms (2)
λ (sample means)	0.032	0.043
λ ($T = 5\ A = 20$)	0.055	0.011
λ ($T = 10\ A = 20$)	0.022	0.004
λ ($T = 15\ A = 20$)	−0.011	−0.002
λ ($T = 20\ A = 20$)	−0.045	−0.009
All occupations, adjusted ϕ	**Small and medium-sized firms**	**Large firms**
λ (sample means)	0.009	0.021
λ ($T = 5\ A = 20$)	0.037	0.021
λ ($T = 10\ A = 20$)	0.015	0.009
λ ($T = 15\ A = 20$)	−0.007	−0.002
λ ($T = 20\ A = 20$)	−0.030	−0.013
Blue-collars only	**Small and medium-sized firms**	**Large firms**
λ (sample means)	0.033	0.023
λ ($T = 5\ A = 20$)	0.036	0.0007
λ ($T = 10\ A = 20$)	0.025	0.0009
λ ($T = 15\ A = 20$)	0.014	0.001
λ ($T = 20\ A = 20$)	0.002	0.001

Note: T = seniority; A = age net of seniority.

occupational tenure, we can still compute a measure of the degree of internalization by exploiting available information on the current and on the previous job. In particular, we assign to the function $\Lambda[\cdot]$ in (3.1) zero if the worker has had a previous job in the same occupation and one if the worker has had no previous job or had a job in a different occupation. The underlying idea here is that if job changes occur mainly within the same occupation, that occupation is likely to be of the OLM type. We then compute the average value of ϕ and average educational attainment, where educational attainment is a dummy variable equal to one if the individual is a university graduate and zero otherwise, for each available occupation. Compared to the Survey on the Wage Structure, the Survey on the Employment Structure has a different and less detailed occupational classification. In particular, the occupational classification in the latter survey closely tracks the industrial classification and is organized into 12 occupational groups, including professionals, managers,

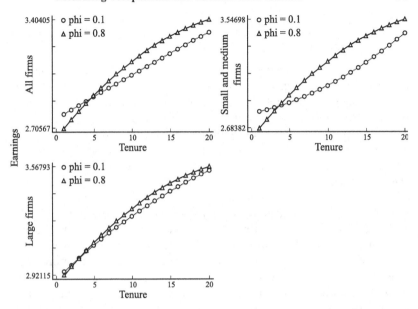

Figure 3.4 Earnings, tenure, and ϕ

clerical workers, sales personnel, workers in the services sector, security personnel, workers in agriculture and fishery, workers in the transportation and telecommunications sector, and blue-collar workers in industry. While this classification is clearly less adequate than the more detailed classification provided by the former survey, it provides a useful handle to evaluate the relationship between schooling and the degree of internalization of an occupation. Focusing on the occupations with a relatively large number of employees, it turns out that managers and clerical workers have a higher value of ϕ than sales personnel and professionals. Moreover, the value of the estimated degree of internalization for blue-collar workers in industry is lower than the value estimated for managers and clerical workers but higher than the value estimated for sales personnel.[22] A weighted regression of the estimated ϕ on a constant and on the average level of education for the set of available occupations yields the following result[23]

---

[22] Our computations are based on Ohkusa (1995). The estimated value of ϕ turns out to be equal to 0.913 for managers, 0.878 for clerical workers, 0.853 for blue-collar workers in industry, 0.851 for professionals, and 0.805 for sales personnel.

[23] Standard errors within parentheses.

$$\phi_j = \underset{(0.022)}{0.833} + \underset{(0.082)}{0.054} \,(\% \; college \; degree)_j + \text{residuals}$$

$$R^2 = 0.04, \; N = 12$$

Thus we do not find evidence in these data of a significant correlation between measured degree of internalization and educational level. The lack of a significant correlation between estimated ϕ and average educational level is not very surprising. For instance, when compared to clerical workers, professionals are both more highly educated (% college = 0.499) and exhibit a relatively lower degree of internalization. At the same time, when compared with sales personnel (% college = 0.301), they are more highly educated but have a higher degree of internalization. Similar considerations can be drawn from a comparison of blue-collar workers in industry (% college < 0.10), clerical workers (% college = 0.352) and managers (% college = 0.327). On the one hand, managers are less educated than clerical workers but have a higher degree of internalization. On the other hand, they are both more educated than blue-collar workers and experience a higher degree of internalization. With due caution, the lack of a significant correlation between average educational attainment and degree of internalization suggests that the specification error arising from omission of education in (3.4) and (3.5) is unlikely to affect in a substantial way the estimates of the coefficients associated with our measure of the degree of internalization ϕ.[24]

Summary

The distinction between internal and occupational labor markets requires the development of informative indicators, that go beyond standard measures such as firm size and average seniority, which are too vague. In this chapter we have developed an alternative measure, ϕ, based on the comparison between firm-specific and occupation-specific tenure, and have applied it to Japanese occupational data. While the suggested measure is positively correlated both with average seniority and with average firm size, these variables explain only about one-third of its total variation. Moreover, a classification of the top and of the bottom 20 occupations based on the value of ϕ is in line with common economic sense.

To test whether this measure has an autonomous information content, we have used it in the estimate of Japanese wage–seniority profiles. It turns out that the slope of these profiles is positively correlated with our

[24] We hasten to stress that omission of education could still bias our estimates if education is correlated with tenure and net age.

measure ϕ. In particular, occupations with a higher degree of internalization (a higher ϕ) tend to have steeper earnings profiles, independently of firm size. Interestingly, we find that the impact of a high value of ϕ on the slope of wage–seniority profiles is larger among small and medium-sized firms. We find this suggestive of the fact that ILM employment systems extend beyond large firms. Apparently, it is not firm size alone that identifies the presence of these systems, but also the type of occupation. When an occupation is organized in internal labor markets, pay and HRM practices are affected, in both large and small and medium-sized firms.

Appendix   List of the 92 occupations

System engineer
Computer programmer
Electronic computer operator
Car driver, private
Truck driver, private
Boiler man
Watchman
Odd jobber
Miner–digger
Miner–pillar setup worker
Baker
Spinning-loom adjusting worker
Silk weaving machine adjusting worker
Knitter
Tailor
Sewing machine worker
Timber worker
Wood pattern worker
Furniture-maker
Joiner
Woodwork-painter
Paper-making worker
Paper container maker
Type-picker and type-setter
Photo-relief engraver
Process plate engraver
Relief printer
Offset printer
Chemical analyst

General chemical operative
Chemical fiber spinning
Glass former
Pottery worker
Steel-making worker
Metal-fusing worker
Furnace manipulation worker
Metal molder
Non-pattern forging worker
Pattern forging worker
Iron and steel tempering worker
Steel rolling and drawing worker
Metallic materials testing worker
Metallic materials inspecting worker
Non-ferrous metal smelter
Metal press machine operator
Welder
Sheet-metal worker
Electroplating worker
Metal painter
Slinger
Lathes operator
Milling machine operator
Boring machine operator
Iron worker
Finisher
Polisher
Machine assembler
Machine inspecting worker
Mechanical draftsman
Assembler of communication equipment
Radio, television assembler
Heavy electric equipment assembler
Light electric equipment inspecting worker
Car assembler
Equipment to propel ship installer
Ship plumber
Plastic mold worker
Sales clerk, department store
Salesman (except sales clerk, department store)
Salesman of motor vehicles
Salesman of household utensils

Insurance canvasser
Cook
Probationer cook
Waiter
Motorman, private railways
Train conductor, private railways
Ticket seller and ticket examiner, private railways
Bus driver
Pilot
Radio operator
Generation or transformation of electricity worker
Barber
Laundryman
Automobile repairman
Machine mender
Medical doctor
Pharmacist
Clinical X-ray technician
Clinical examination technician
School teacher
Journalist

4 Earnings and seniority in internal labor markets

Overview[1]

In chapter 3, we developed an empirical measure to classify occupations between internal and occupational labor markets by contrasting tenure with an employer with tenure within an occupation. The measure was then applied to a subset of the 141 occupations available in the dataset.

In this chapter we focus on *ranks* or *job levels* rather than occupations, and study from an empirical viewpoint the relationship between seniority and earnings. Jobs that do not have a well defined occupational content but fit into a ranking hierarchy – such as department head, section head, subsection head, and foreman – are usually organized in Japan into ILM employment systems. A key feature of internal labor markets is the frequency of long-term employment relationships, that help to foster the accumulation of human capital.

Seniority affects earnings not only directly, by influencing productivity, as predicted by human capital theory, but also indirectly, by sorting individuals into different tasks, that are often ordered by degree of responsibility, skills, and authority. When earnings are partly attached to jobs,[2] the allocation of workers to jobs has important implications for earnings growth, because individuals can earn more not only by staying longer on a job but also by moving to a more important job, either within the firm (internal promotion) or between firms (inter-firm mobility). In internal labor markets, internal promotion is important and the relationship between seniority and earnings is partly accounted for by the fact that seniority can affect promotion prospects.[3]

---

[1] This chapter is a substantial update of Brunello and Ariga (1997).
[2] See the discussion in Lazear (1995).
[3] See chapter 5.

Review of the literature

In the literature, empirical earnings functions stress the relationship between earnings, seniority, labor market experience, and education. In an influential paper, Hashimoto and Raisian (1985) use cross-sectional data to compare earnings profiles in Japan and the United States, and conclude that "growth rates in earnings attributable to tenure are far greater in Japan than in the United States" (p. 732).[4]

In another paper, Collier and Knight (1985) compare earnings profiles in Japan and the United Kingdom. They choose Japan "as the country most commonly identified with institutionalized seniority pay and life-time employment, and Britain as the country which has not attracted particular attention in this respect" (p. 19). Their main finding is that the seniority premium, defined as the percentage difference between pay of those who have completed ten years of tenure with the same employer and pay of those with less than one year of service, is about twice as large in Japan than in Britain.[5] The rather limited importance of seniority in British earnings profiles is confirmed by a study by Booth and Frank (1996), who use data from the 1991 wave of the British Household Panel Survey (BHPS) and find that tenure is never significant in the earnings functions they estimate.

These differences in earnings profiles are often given a human capital interpretation. According to the human capital view, steeper wage trajectories are caused by the growth of skills in firms that put greater emphasis on training and retraining of employees. Since differences in the accumulation of human capital are widely regarded as a critical factor in explaining international differences in productivity growth,[6] evidence of steeper earnings profiles in Japan can be used to explain, at least in part, Japan's remarkable economic performance after the Second World War.[7]

Clearly, the human capital view is not the only possible explanation of upward-sloping earnings profiles. Two well known alternatives are the

---

[4] See also Mincer and Higuchi (1987); Clark and Ogawa (1992).

[5] Additional evidence for Britain is provided by Marsden (1990), who compares the four major European countries and finds that the seniority premium is lowest in the United Kingdom and highest in France. Marsden's definition is slightly different from Collier and Knight's (1985) definition of seniority premium. Marsden uses this evidence to corroborate his view of the British labor market as an occupational market, that differs from the internal labor markets prevailing in France and in Japan.

[6] See Barro and Lee (1992); Crafts (1992); Mankiw, Romer and Weill (1992).

[7] The relationship between human capital accumulation and economic growth need not be one-sided. According to Mincer and Higuchi (1988): "the question remains why the emphasis on human capital formation on the job is so much greater in Japan than in the US. Our answer is that such emphasis is conditioned by rapid economic growth."

agency and the matching explanation. According to the agency explanation, earnings increase with tenure even if productivity does not, because firms need to provide adequate incentives to their employees. In the matching explanation, earnings increase with tenure simply because good matches last longer. We view these explanations as complementary rather than as mutually exclusive, because the design of earnings profiles is likely to respond to both incentive and sorting problems (moral hazard and adverse selection problems) and human capital accumulation. On the one hand, the solution of incentive problems can foster the accumulation of skills. On the other, an adequate assignment of workers to positions can be used to preserve these skills within the firm.[8]

The job matching explanation challenges conventional estimates of earnings profiles, based on cross-section data. When worker, job, and/ or match quality are unmeasured, they represent omitted variables and the cross-section evidence need not reflect the "true" relationship between earnings and tenure. A growing number of studies, mainly in the United States, has explicitly addressed this problem and suggested alternative ways of dealing with omitted variables. Devine and Kiefer (1991) survey part of this literature and conclude that "some part of wage growth in a match can be attributed to a pure tenure effect, but there is no consensus on what proportion it represents" (p. 271).[9] If the size of the bias induced by omitted variables varies substantially among different countries, an implication of this literature is that comparative evidence on the relative contribution of tenure to earnings growth, such as that presented by Hashimoto and Raisian (1985), could be misleading.

In this chapter, we address this issue by focusing on two specific questions. First, we ask whether the substantial tenure effects found in most estimates of Japanese earnings functions reflect the "true" relationship between tenure and earnings. Second, we compare British and Japanese earnings profiles and verify whether there are substantial differences in seniority premia in the two countries. Britain is often perceived as a typical OLM labor market and Japan as a typical ILM labor market. An implication of the model developed in chapter 2 is that within-rank wage differentials, driven by seniority, should be more important in ILM than in OLM firms, where between-rank wage differentials matter relatively more.

We build on a simple idea. Worker-, job-, and/or match-specific quality are unobserved by the econometrician but are revealed in the market

---

[8] See Carmichael (1983); Aoki (1988).
[9] Contributions also include Topel (1991); Altonji and Williams (1996).

place as labor market experience increases. In particular, if firms learn about quality, they should use this information to allocate workers to jobs and to provide the right skill to the right person. This allocation does not necessarily take place within firms, but can involve labor turnover in the market place. Given that "better" workers should be assigned to jobs involving more sophisticated skills and a higher degree of responsibility, the observation of the position filled by the employee in the firm, that we call rank (or job level), is likely to be informative, to some extent, of her quality and of the quality of her match.[10] Under some assumptions, this information can be used to construct an unbiased estimator of the effects of tenure on earnings growth.

The chapter has three main results. First, tenure effects are less important than the effects estimated with the traditional approach, used by Hashimoto and Raisian (1985). The difference, however, is small. Second, we distinguish conditional from unconditional tenure effects, with rank, or the position filled by the employee in the firm, as the conditioning variable. It turns out that within-rank earnings growth is important earlier on in a career, and between-ranks earnings growth becomes more important as tenure increases, especially among medium-sized firms.

Third, and last, both conditional and unconditional seniority premia are smaller in the United Kingdom than in Japan. The difference is particularly sharp in the manufacturing sector. While the ratio between unconditional and conditional premia in the finance industry[11] is about the same in the two countries, this ratio is much higher in British than in Japanese manufacturing. This suggests two things. First, earnings profiles do not differ across industries in Japan as sharply as they do in the United Kingdom. Second, between-rank earnings growth, associated with the allocation of the right person to the right job, is relatively more important in the British than in Japanese manufacturing. Our evidence thus confirms that ranks matter relatively more for earnings in OLM labor markets, while seniority matters relatively more in ILM labor markets.

---

[10] Rosen (1982) shows that firms should assign workers of superior talent to top positions. See also Kremer (1993). Malcomson and McLeod (1988) show that a firm hierarchy can solve both moral hazard and adverse selection problems, with abler workers self-sorting into their appropriate rank in the hierarchy.

[11] The industry includes banking, security, insurance, and non-bank financial intermediary (NBFI) sectors.

The empirical relationship between earnings and seniority: Japanese data

We start from the following specification of the earnings function, used by Hashimoto and Raisian (1985) (hereafter, HR) in their estimate of earnings profiles in Japan and the United States

$$\ln W_{it} = \alpha_0 + \alpha_1 T_{it} + \alpha_2 T_{it}^2 + \alpha_3 X_{it} + \alpha_4 X_{it}^2 + \alpha_5 X_{it} T_{it}$$
$$+ \sum_j \alpha_{6j} E_{ij} + \sum_t \alpha_t YD_t + \mu_i + \varepsilon_{it} \qquad (4.1)$$

where W is hourly earnings, inclusive of bonuses, T is tenure or seniority, X is pre-job experience,[12] measured as age *minus* tenure *minus* 6 *minus* years of schooling, E is a set of educational dummies, YD is a vector of time dummies, ε is an error term and t is for time. Compared to HR, we use hourly rather than monthly earnings, as is customary in most of the literature on earnings functions, and experience net rather than gross of tenure. Since our sample observations are cell means of male earnings stratified by firm size, educational attainment, age group, and industry, as in the HR estimates, the index i corresponds to a cell.

Clearly, standard estimates of (4.1) yield unbiased estimators of the effects of tenure, experience, and education if the RHS variables are uncorrelated with the error term. Following Abraham and Farber (1987), however, suppose that the error term can be decomposed as follows

$$\varepsilon_{it} = \tau_{it} + \eta_{it} \qquad (4.2)$$

where η is a disturbance uncorrelated with the regressors in (4.1) and τ is a disturbance that captures the unobserved (to the econometrician) quality of the group of employees, their jobs, and their matches. Since workers with more education and experience typically end up in better matches, unobserved quality, τ, can be expressed as follows

$$\tau_{it} = \rho X_{it} + \sum_j \xi_j E_{ij} + \mu_i \qquad (4.3)$$

where μ captures the time-invariant component of unobserved quality that is not correlated, by construction, to education and pre-job experience.[13] Substituting (4.2) and (4.3) into (4.1) yields

---

[12] Since tenure and gross experience are strongly correlated in Japan, we prefer to use net experience.
[13] The job matching model explains the cross-sectional correlation between wages and tenure by arguing that individuals differ in their suitability to different firms. In the model, there are both individual and match-specific effects (see Garen, 1988). In the pure learning model, ability is time-invariant. See Farber and Gibbons (1996).

$$\ln W_{it} = \alpha_0 + \alpha_1 T_{it} + \alpha_2 T_{it}^2 + [\alpha_3 + \rho]X_{it} + \alpha_4 X_{it}^2 + \alpha_5 X_{it}T_{it} \quad (4.4)$$
$$+ \sum_j [\alpha_{6j} + \xi_j]E_{ij} + \sum_t \alpha_t YD_t + \mu_i + \eta_{it}$$

If workers in a particular cell are, on average, better than workers in other cells – or, alternatively, if they fill better jobs or enjoy better matches – they will stay longer with their match and enjoy, at the same time, higher earnings. In this case, observed tenure and unobserved quality, μ, are positively correlated and standard estimates of the effect of tenure on earnings growth are upward-biased.[14]

Abraham and Farber (1987) suggest correcting the bias by including in the earnings function (4.4) the completed length of a job match, either observed or estimated from a Weibull proportional hazard model.[15] Unfortunately, we do not have any information on the completed length of a match, so we must use a different approach. As anticipated in the introduction, our idea is simple and straightforward. If workers and matches are of different quality, and this quality is observed by firms over time, revealed information should be used in the allocation of workers to jobs and to skills. Thus, better workers in better matches should climb the job ladder faster and be allocated to job slots requiring more sophisticated skills and paying higher salaries.[16] While the econometrician cannot observe quality directly, she can infer it by looking at the allocation of workers within firms and among jobs requiring different skills.

Denote R as the rank filled by an employee in the firm. Here, "rank" means both the position filled in the job hierarchy and the skill content of a job, and we assume that there is a positive correlation between position held and skill. With G ($G > 1$) ranks, the variable R assumes the value one in the bottom rank and the value G in the top rank. The allocation of workers to ranks is likely to depend on both observable quality, measured by tenure, experience, and education, and unobservable quality, given by μ. Rank, however, is not correlated with the disturbance η. In

[14] Since the covariance between cell μ and cell T is equal to

$$\frac{1}{N^2}\sum_i \sum_j E(\mu_i T_j)$$

where N is the number of individuals in the cell, our assumption that cell μ and cell T are positively correlated is equivalent to requiring that individual μ and T are positively correlated for each individual and across individuals in the cell.
[15] Alternative methods are used by Altonji and Shakotko (1987); Marshall and Zarkin (1987); Topel (1991).
[16] Waldman (1984) shows that high-ability workers are always allocated to positions with a high marginal product of ability.

general, the relationship between measured variables and the allocation to ranks can involve non-linearities and interaction terms. In what follows, we posit only that unobservable quality affects R both linearly and independently of other variables such as tenure, education, and job experience.

Let Z be a vector of additional variables that affect allocation to rank. Moreover, assume that the error term in the rank equation can be decomposed in a time-variant and a time-invariant component, as the error term τ_{it} in (4.3). Then the rank equation is given by

$$R_{it} = \beta_0 + \beta_1 T_{it} + \beta_2 X_{it} + \sum_j \beta_{3j} E_{ij} + \beta_4 Z_{it} + \beta_5 \mu_i \qquad (4.5)$$

Equation (4.5) can be used to substitute μ out of (4.1) and obtain

$$\ln W_{it} = \delta_0 + \delta_1 T_{it} + \alpha_2 T_{it}^2 + \delta_2 X_{it} + \alpha_4 X_{it}^2 + \alpha_5 X_{it} T_{it}$$
$$+ \sum_j \delta_{3j} E_{ij} + \delta_4 R_{it} + \delta_5 Z_{it} + \sum_t \alpha_t YD_t + \eta_{it} \qquad (4.6)$$

where the following restrictions hold

$$\delta_0 = \alpha_0 - \frac{\beta_0}{\beta_5}, \; \delta_1 = \alpha_1 - \frac{\beta_1}{\beta_5}$$

$$\delta_2 = \rho + \alpha_3 - \frac{\beta_2}{\beta_5}, \; \delta_{3j} = \xi + \alpha_{6j} - \frac{\beta_{3j}}{\beta_5}$$

$$\delta_4 = \frac{1}{\beta_5}, \; \delta_5 = -\frac{\beta_4}{\beta_5} \qquad (4.7)$$

Conditional on rank, R, the impact of tenure on earnings is given by δ_1, which is lower than α_1 in (4.1) if β_1/β_5 is positive – that is, if both higher unobserved time-invariant ability, μ, and observed tenure affect rank allocation in the same direction. The unconditional impact of tenure on log wages is given by

$$\frac{\partial \ln W}{\partial T} = \delta_1 + 2\alpha_2 T + \alpha_5 X + \delta_4 \frac{\partial R}{\partial T}$$

Using (4.5), we obtain that

$$\frac{\partial \ln W}{\partial T} = \alpha_1 + 2\alpha_2 T + \alpha_5 X$$

Since the RHS variables are uncorrelated with the error η by construction, standard estimates of (4.6) yield unbiased estimates of the effects of tenure, experience, and education on earnings, conditional on rank. By conditioning on rank, these estimates measure only within-rank earnings differentials. Tenure, experience, and education, however, contribute to earnings growth both directly and indirectly, by affecting allocation to rank. Estimates of unconditional tenure effects, composed of both within-rank and between-rank earnings differentials, can be obtained by estimating parameters α_1, α_2 and α_5.

This strategy requires a consistent estimate of parameters β_i in (4.5). Since tenure in this equation is correlated with the error term, ordinary least squares cannot be used. To deal with this problem, we use instrumental variables. Because tenure depends both on wages and on rank, we use as instruments educational dummies, job experience, and the variables included in Z. As additional instruments, we use a polynomial of the third order in the variable AGE, the average age net of tenure of workers in the cell, and year dummies.

The underlying assumption is that rank allocation, conditional on tenure, experience, and education, does not depend either on age or on year dummies.[17] We test this assumption with both the Sargan Criterion and the test of the over-identifying restrictions suggested by Main and Reilly (1993) and Card and Vella (1997). In the maintained assumption that the error term in the equation allocating workers to rank contains only unobserved ability, μ, we can use the results of the estimates of (4.5) and (4.6) to derive from (4.7) consistent estimates of the vector of parameters α.

The empirical strategy described so far assumes that ranks have cardinal as well as ordinal meaning. Such a strong assumption is useful to illustrate the key points of the strategy and can be partially relaxed by replacing the variable R in (4.5) with the latent variable, P, interpreted as the competence level reached by an individual. In this case, substitution of unobserved quality, μ, out of (4.1) yields a new version of (4.6), with P in place of R. Estimation of (4.5) can then be implemented by using an ordered-response model, that associates the observable ranking R with competence levels P as follows

$$R_i = 1 \text{ if } P_i < \mu_0;$$

$$R_i = j \text{ if } \mu_0 \leqslant P_i < \mu_j \text{ if } \mu_j \leqslant \mu_{j\max};$$

$$R_i = j_{\max} \text{ if } P_i \geq \mu_{j_{\max}} \tag{4.8}$$

Since P is not observable, the empirical analysis of (4.6) requires that we proxy it either with a set of rank-specific dummies or with the observed variable R.

---

[17] Age is also used as an instrument by Hersch and Reagan (1990); Sloane and Theodossiou (1993).

Both procedures are applied to the data extracted from the third volume of the Survey on the Wage Structure (*Chingin Kouzou Kihon Chousa*). The source is the same used by HR, with the major difference that we select data stratified by rank. This choice has two consequences. First, we cannot use the occupational data used in chapter 3, because of the lack of information on rank. Second, we have no information on firms with fewer than 100 employees.

In this chapter, we focus on male workers in large firms (that have more than 1,000 employees), and in medium-sized firms (that have 100 to 499 employees), and pool together the data for two periods, 1980–4 and 1990–4. The first period covers the years after the second oil shock and the second the years after the burst of the economic bubble. Since the selected years cover a 15-year period, the data can also be used to study changes in earnings profiles over time. This is done in chapter 9.

As mentioned above, the data are cell means of hourly earnings (gross of bonuses), tenure and age, cross-classified by firm size, age group, and rank. In these data, a rank corresponds rather closely to the position occupied by the employee in the organizational hierarchy. The top rank is department director (*bucho*) and the other ranks are, respectively, division director (*kacho*), subdivision director (*kakaricho*), and unranked (*hishokkai*).[18]

This classification by rank has the merit of tracking closely the hierarchical structure within Japanese firms and the demerit of being rather gross, since it ignores all the grades within each rank (including the unranked). As discussed in Aoki (1988) and in chapter 5, Japanese firms typically have both a vertical and a horizontal hierarchical structure. The former is associated with the function assigned to the job and the latter defines the relative status of the individual within the firm. While a given status does not necessarily imply assignment to a particular function, such a function cannot be performed unless a given status has been achieved. Our data refer to functional positions in the vertical hierarchy and ignore movements in the horizontal hierarchy that could occur within each functional rank.

Table 4.1 presents the weighted means and standard deviations of monthly earnings, average age, experience, and tenure in the rank in 1994, the last year in the sample.[19] In general, average tenure, age, and earnings increase with rank. Workers in large firms, independently of their rank, are older, better paid, and better educated, and have been with the same firm longer than their colleagues in medium-sized firms.

[18] We exclude foremen because this rank is typical of the industrial sector and is virtually absent in the rest of the economy.
[19] The weight is the number of individuals in the cell.

Table 4.1 *Weighted means and standard deviations, Japan, 1994*

Means and St. dev.	Large firms	Medium-sized firms
Tenure unranked	15.86 (8.7)[a]	11.15 (5.44)
Tenure rank 1[d]	19.59 (10.0)	15.96 (7.5)
Tenure rank 2[d]	21.65 (8.81)	17.68 (7.2)
Tenure rank 3[d]	21.88 (9.7)	17.51 (8.4)
Age unranked	40.00 (11.5)	40.00 (11.5)
Age rank 1	41.19 (10.7)	40.69 (10.9)
Age rank 2	43.72 (9.4)	43.21 (9.5)
Age rank 3	45.56 (8.6)	43.20 (9.6)
Monthly wage unranked[e]	634.3 (194.8)	523.9 (147.3)
Monthly wage rank 1	722.4 (163.2)	572.1 (104.6)
Monthly wage rank 2	869.4 (196.8)	674.5 (101.7)
Monthly wage rank 3	1025.9 (253.9)	804.9 (145.3)
Education unranked (years)[c]	10.75 (2.6)	10.75 (2.6)
Education rank 1	11.06 (2.5)	10.71 (2.6)
Education rank 2	11.01 (2.5)	10.92 (2.6)
Education rank 3	11.39 (2.5)	10.92 (2.5)
Experience unranked[b]	7.38 (3.6)	12.09 (6.7)
Experience rank 1	4.52 (2.1)	8.01 (4.1)
Experience rank 2	4.96 (1.9)	8.60 (3.5)
Experience rank 3	6.31 (2.9)	8.82 (3.7)

Notes:
[a]Standard deviations in parentheses.
[b]Experience is net of tenure.
[c]Education is measured by expected years of schooling, as in HR.
[d]Rank 1 is for subdivision directors, rank 2 for division directors, and rank 3 for department directors.
[e]Monthly wage is in 000 yen.

To assess the direction and the size of the bias that characterize standard estimates of (4.1) in the presence of unobserved differences in worker, match, and job quality, we fit both (4.1) and (4.6) by ordinary least squares and use the White procedure to correct standard errors for the heteroskedasticity induced both by aggregation and by unknown sources.

The estimate of (4.6) requires that we specify Z. As discussed at length in chapter 5, a natural candidate is time spent in the rank before promotion. With fast tracks, the longer the time spent in the rank, the lower the probability of being allocated to a higher rank. Unfortunately, we do not

Table 4.2 *Estimated earnings equations, Japanese men*[a]

	Large firms		Medium-sized firms	
	(4.6)	HR[b]	(4.6)	HR
T	0.065**	0.067**	0.059**	0.068**
T^2	−0.0009**	−0.0007**	−0.001**	−0.0009**
X	0.009	0.005**	0.028**	0.011**
X^2	−0.0004	−0.0006**	−0.0009**	−0.0005**
E_1	0.125**	0.143**	0.142**	0.166**
E_2	0.206**	0.234**	0.257**	0.279**
E_3	0.414**	0.464**	0.438**	0.469**
$SHARE$	0.179**	–	0.184**	
R	0.201**	–	0.182**	–
R^2	0.91	0.78	0.92	0.80
Nobs[c]	1105	1105	1175	1175

Notes:
[a]Pooled data 1980–4 and 1990–4; dependent variable: ln W; method: ordinary least squares.
[b]HR refers to the specification used by Hashimoto and Raisian (1985).
**The estimated coefficient is significant at the 5 percent level of confidence. Heteroskedasticity-consistent standard errors.
Each regression includes a constant and nine year dummies.
[c]In all tables in this chapter: number of observations.

have the data to construct such a variable. Instead, we define the variable *SHARE*, the number of employees in the rank relative to total employment. This variable captures the availability of positions in each rank, that we assume to be determined by both technological requirements and the rate of growth of the firm.[20] Given ability, tenure, experience, and education, allocation to a higher rank is less likely when the relative number of positions is smaller.

Results of the estimates are presented in table 4.2, for both large and medium-sized firms. For both types of firm, the inclusion of rank R and *SHARE* increase substantially the adjusted R^2.[21] Next, we estimate (4.5).

[20] See chapter 10 for a detailed discussion.
[21] We have also experimented with a more flexible specification that uses rank dummies in place of R. Since the estimated coefficients of tenure, experience, and education change very little, we retain the original specification in the text.

Table 4.3 *Estimates of the rank function, by instrumental variables*[a]

	Large firms	Medium-sized firms
T	0.005	0.019**
X	0.021**	−0.007**
E_1	0.088	0.072
E_2	0.067	0.073
E_3	0.121**	0.108**
$SHARE$	−2.700**	−2.597**
R^2	0.67	0.65
SC^b	0.58 (11)	0.18 (11)
$TEST^c$	0.43 (12)	0.22 (12)
Nobs	1105	1175

Notes:
[a] Additional instruments are year dummies and a third-order polynomial in age net of tenure.
[b] SC is the Sargan Criterion for instrument validity
[c] $TEST$ is a Lagrange Multiplier test (LM) for the over-identifying restrictions (see Main and Reilly, 1993).
Probability values of the tests in the table; degrees of freedom in parentheses.
**The estimated coefficient is significant at the 5 percent level of confidence.

First, we retain the linear specification with rank R as the dependent variable and use instrumental variables. The results in table 4.3 show that the allocation of workers to higher ranks is positively affected by tenure and negatively affected by the relative number of employees in the rank with respect to total employment.[22] The instrumental variables strategy is tested using the Sargan Criterion, a misspecification test of whether any variable from the instrument set can be omitted from (4.5).[23] It turns out that the null hypothesis of no misspecification cannot be rejected by the data. A similar result is obtained when testing for the validity of the over-identifying restrictions. This test is a Lagrange Multiplier test (LM) and is computed by running an auxiliary regression involving the ordinary least squares residuals from the original specification, the set of explanatory variables and the full set of additional instruments.

[22] Interactions and quadratic terms are excluded after a sequential specification search that eliminates estimated coefficients that are not significantly different from zero.
[23] See Sargan (1984).

Table 4.4 *Estimates of the rank function, using the ordered probit model*

	Large firms	Medium-sized firms
FT^a	0.018**	0.053**
X	0.003	−0.030**
E_1	0.108	0.178
E_2	0.117	0.224**
E_3	0.190	0.298**
SHARE	−70.233**	−64.671**
$\mu_1{}^c$	1.474**	2.630**
μ_2	2.459	2.420
$\ln L^b$	−643.2	−597.5
Nobs	1175	1105

Notes:
$^a FT$ is the fitted value from a regression of tenure on the full set of instruments, including those specified in table 4.3.
$^b \ln L$ is the value of the log-likelihood.
$^c \mu_i$ are the threshold values of the ordered probit.
**The estimated coefficient is significant at the 5 percent level of confidence.

Second, we use a discrete choice framework and estimate (4.5) with an ordered probit model. This model estimates both the parameters of (4.5) and the endogenous range thresholds, under the assumption that errors are normally distributed.[24] The results are presented in table 4.4, where we retain the same specification used in table 4.3. They confirm the finding that tenure effects have a significantly positive impact on rank allocation in both types of firm.

The relative contribution of tenure to earnings growth can be more easily evaluated by considering a hypothetical distribution of workers, who differ only in their tenure and experience.[25] Assuming that both tenure and pre-job experience start from zero, with a new entry in the labor market, we construct the distribution of hourly earnings at regular intervals of five years of additional tenure, maintaining pre-job experience equal to zero. Results are shown in table 4.5.[26]

[24] Since tenure is endogenous, we replace it with the fitted value from a regression of tenure on the full set of instruments.
[25] Our results from a number of cross-sections can be considered as relevant information on the wage–tenure relationship for any particular cohort only if stability in the relationship among cohorts is assumed to hold. See Jonsson and Klevmarken (1978) for details.
[26] This exercise is equivalent to that performed by HR and by Clark and Ogawa (1992).

Table 4.5 *Estimated earnings growth caused by tenure, Japanese men[a]*

Tenure	Conditional (1)	Unconditional (2)	Unconditional (3)	HR (4)
		Large firms		
0	100	100	100	100
5	135.4	136.0	137.8	137.5
10	175.3	176.9	181.6	181.8
15	216.8	219.9	228.7	231.2
20	256.2	261.1	275.2	282.7
		Medium-sized firms		
0	100	100	100	100
5	130.3	132.6	136.9	137.2
10	160.7	166.3	177.4	179.3
15	187.4	197.2	217.4	222.9
20	206.6	221.2	251.8	263.8

Notes:
[a]Entries are hourly earnings at various years of tenure. Hourly wages at zero tenure and experience are normalized to 100.
Column (2) refers to the instrumental variables method and column (3) to the ordered probit method.

According to our estimates, ten years of tenure, conditional on rank, increase earnings over earnings at zero tenure and zero pre-job experience, respectively, by about 75 percent and 60 percent in large and medium-sized firms. On the other hand, 20 years of tenure increase earnings over the initial value by about 156 percent in large firms and by about 107 percent in medium-sized firms. As column (4) in table 4.5 suggests, HR estimates of tenure effects imply a seniority premium in large firms equal to about 82 percent and 183 percent, respectively, after 10 and 20 years of tenure. In medium-sized firms, the premium is equal to 79 percent and 164 percent.

We thus conclude that tenure effects conditional on rank are sizeable but smaller than the effects predicted by HR estimates. As illustrated by figures 4.1 and 4.2, the gap is relatively small for large firms but significant for medium-sized and small firms.

Columns (2) and (3) in table 4.5 show the unconditional tenure effects, obtained by estimating (4.5) either by instrumental variables or by ordered probit and using the results to infer the value of the vector of

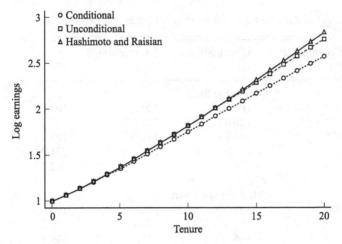

Figure 4.1 Wage–tenure profiles, Japanese large firms

parameters α in (4.1). It turns out that, when we use the ordered probit, unconditional seniority premia in large firms are equal to about 82 percent after 10 years and to about 175 percent after 20 years. In medium-sized firms, these premia are equal to about 77 percent after 10 years and to about 152 percent after 20 years.

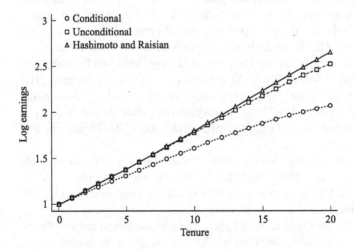

Figure 4.2 Wage–tenure profiles, Japanese medium-sized firms

When we use instrumental variables, unconditional seniority premia in large firms are equal to about 77 percent after 10 years and to about 161 percent after 20 years. In medium-sized firms, these premia are equal to about 66 percent after 10 years and to about 121 percent after 20 years. Unconditional premia are thus lower when we use instrumental variables to estimate the rank allocation equation than when we use the ordered probit model. In either case, the estimated unconditional premia are lower than the HR premia. The difference, however, is small.

We draw from these results a number of observations. First, standard estimates of Japanese earnings profiles are biased because they fail to take into proper account the fact that tenure is endogenous. The size of the bias, however, is small. Second, tenure "pays" more in large than in medium-sized firms. Third, the difference between unconditional and conditional earnings growth is larger among medium-sized firms, suggesting that the contribution of between-rank earnings growth declines as firm size increases.

Fourth, the gap between within-rank and between-rank earnings growth, measured by the ratio between unconditional and conditional earnings growth, increases monotonously with tenure. In particular, when we use the ordered probit specification, this ratio after 20 years of tenure is equal to 1.074 and to 1.220, respectively, in large and medium-sized firms. Independently of tenure, the ratio is rather low. As mentioned above, this could depend on the fact that we are focusing on relatively few ranks and on the vertical hierarchy, thus ignoring promotion from grade to grade within each rank.

Earnings and seniority in Japan and the United Kingdom

As mentioned earlier in the chapter, Collier and Knight (1985) tabulate average earnings of male employees in the United Kingdom and in Japan by age group and years of service, and find that the seniority premia paid to Japanese workers are much higher than the premia received by British workers. They use these findings to suggest that internal labor markets are more widespread in Japan than in the United Kingdom but, quite correctly, refrain from attributing differences in these premia to differences in either human capital accumulation or incentive mechanisms.

In this section, we estimate conditional tenure effects on earnings profiles in Japan and the United Kingdom, using datasets that are as similar as possible. Japanese data were described above. UK data are collected from the New Earnings Survey (NES). The appealing feature of these data is that they contain, albeit only for the years 1975, 1976, and 1979, explicit information on tenure. Unfortunately, no information on education is provided. The data that we can use are cell means of hourly earnings (gross of incentive pay), tenure, and age of workers, cross-classified by age group, industry, and socioeconomic group. Socioeconomic groups in the ESRC Data Archive dataset are obtained by reclassifying the original data by occupation "to capture the socio-economic identity which attaches to individual occupations or the elements of social and economic hierarchy often relevant to the analysis of pay" (Gregory and Thomson, 1990, p. 485).

These groups are managers, professionals, intermediate non-manuals, junior non-manuals, foremen, skilled manuals, semi-skilled manuals, and unskilled manuals. For our purpose, we associate socioeconomic groups with ranks. We hasten to stress, however, that the mapping from these groups to hierarchical levels is looser in British than in Japanese data. Compared to the Japanese definition of rank, occupational and skill content prevails in the British definition. Clearly, the difference is not only in the definition of the data. Comparative work on Japan and the United Kingdom suggests that the design of careers and job ladders differs rather sharply between the two countries. In Japan, the hierarchical structure is finely graded and without a major gap between ranks. In the United Kingdom, job ladders are limited by clearer demarcation lines between manual and non-manual workers, and between managerial staff and production workers (see Dore, 1987, for a very instructive comparison).

Differences in the design of the internal organization of firms are accompanied by differences in the selection process and in the allocation of workers to jobs. According to Dore "Japan . . . has developed what is probably the most . . . meritocratic system of schooling and occupational selection in the world . . . [on the other hand] . . . meritocracy never really has triumphed in Britain over back-door family influence" (Dore, 1987, pp. 99, 103).

As already mentioned, the British data do not contain information on educational levels.[27] Moreover, cell means are stratified by industry. In what follows, we select manufacturing and finance. The manufacturing sector is at the core of Japanese economic success, and the financial sector is comparatively important in the British economy.[28] For the sake of comparison, we also select a similar sample of observations from the

---

[27] An alternative source is the BHPS, containing information on both education and tenure. A preliminary investigation of the 1991 wave shows, however, that the number of available individual observations with the required characteristics is slightly less than 600. This number is too low to compute cell means by rank, age group, and educational level, the format required for a meaningful comparison with available Japanese data.

[28] In 1988, banking and finance covered 11% of total employment in the United Kingdom, more than in Germany or France.

Japanese data. Unfortunately, a major break in the data occurs in 1975, and we can use Japanese data only from 1976 onwards. Hence, we select the period 1976–9, the closest we can get to the period imposed by restrictions on the British data.

Next, we focus on male workers in the age range 20–59 for Japan and 21–59 for Britain, to avoid plaguing the estimates with differences in the degree of labor market attachment exhibited by different segments of the labor force. Since the UK data do not allow us to separate large from small firms, we will consider, for both countries, the aggregate data.[29]

Lack of information on education implies that we cannot compute labor market experience, X, used in the previous section. We replace this variable with AGE, average age in the cell, which adds together average schooling, experience, and tenure. For both countries, we estimate the following earnings and rank functions

$$\ln W_{it} = \gamma_0 + \gamma_1 T_{it} + \gamma_2 T_{it}^2 + \gamma_3 AGE_{it} + \gamma_4 AGE_{it}^2$$
$$+ \gamma_5 AGE_{it} T_{it} + \gamma_6 R_{it} + \gamma_7 SHARE_t + \eta_{it} \qquad (4.9)$$

$$R_{it} = h_0 + h_1 T_{it} + h_2 AGE_{it} + h_3 SHARE_t + h_4 \mu_i \qquad (4.10)$$

To avoid the collinearity induced by the strong correlation between age and tenure, we use age net of tenure. For comparison, we also map UK socio-economic groups into the variable R. In particular, we assign to unskilled and semi-skilled manuals and to junior non-manuals rank 1, to skilled manuals, foremen, and intermediate non-manuals rank 2, to professionals rank 3, and to managers rank 4.[30]

A summary of the main variables used in this section is given in table 4.6, where we present, for the two selected industries, the weighted means and standard deviations of tenure, age, and the nominal hourly wage in 1979, when information is available for both countries. The summary statistics show that average tenure in the United Kingdom is much shorter than in Japan. In addition, the average age of workers in upper ranks is lower in the United Kingdom than in Japan.

The estimates of (4.9) and (4.10) are shown in tables 4.7 and 4.8. To save space, we present only the results based upon the instrumental variables technique applied to (4.10), where endogenous tenure has been instrumented by year dummies and by AGE^2. With the sole exception of Japanese manufacturing, both the Sargan Criterion and the LM test

---

[29] Japanese data are limited to regular workers who are employed in firms with more than 100 employees.

[30] Compared to the previous section, Japanese manufacturing data include foremen, who are treated as subsection directors.

Table 4.6 *Means and standard deviations, Japan and the United Kingdom, 1979, manufacturing and finance*

Rank	Manufacturing			Finance		
	Tenure	Age	Wage[b]	Tenure	Age	Wage
Japan						
Unranked†	11.4 (5.0)[a]	34.6 (10.1)	30.9 (5.7)	8.8 (5.3)	32.7 (10.4)	43.6 (13.7)
Rank 1[c]	18.0 (5.6)	39.8 (7.4)	40.6 (4.7)	15.7 (6.2)	36.4 (6.7)	62.7 (11.8)
Rank 2[d]	18.9 (4.2)	42.7 (6.3)	51.0 (4.9)	21.3 (4.5)	42.6 (5.8)	84.7 (7.2)
Rank 3[e]	21.4 (3.7)	47.6 (6.2)	65.7 (7.4)	23.9 (3.9)	47.3 (5.7)	100.9 (12.4)
Britain						
Unranked†	8.3 (3.8)	40.3 (11.7)	9.1 (0.5)	6.9 (3.6)	34.7 (11.9)	8.4 (1.1)
Rank 1[c]	10.2 (5.0)	40.1 (11.3)	10.3 (0.2)	9.4 (5.5)	38.2 (10.7)	10.9 (1.3)
Rank 2[d]	10.6 (6.6)	38.5 (11.5)	12.5 (1.4)	8.2 (6.5)	34.6 (10.8)	12.9 (3.2)
Rank 3[e]	12.7 (6.2)	42.2 (10.3)	13.8 (1.4)	13.7 (7.4)	40.6 (10.5)	15.8 (2.7)

Notes:
[a] Standard deviations in parentheses.
[b] Japanese wages are in 0000 yen per month; UK data are in 00 per week.
[c] Rank 1 is for subdivision directors and foremen in Japan, skilled manuals, foremen and intermediate non-manuals in Britain.
[d] Rank 2 is for division directors in Japan and professionals in the UK.
[e] Rank 3 is for department directors in Japan and managers in Britain.
† Unranked is for workers without rank in Japan, for unskilled, semi-skilled manuals and junior non-manuals, in the United Kingdom.

Table 4.7 *Estimated earnings equations, Japanese and British men[a]*

	Japan		Britain	
	Manufacturing	Finance	Manufacturing	Finance
T	0.079**	0.106**	0.061**	0.096**
T^2	−0.002**	−0.0015**	−0.002**	−0.001
AGE	−0.017	0.067	0.058**	0.064**
AGE^2	0.0004	−0.0008	−0.002**	−0.001**
AT	0.0016**	−0.0009	−0.001**	−0.001
$SHARE$	0.501**	−0.039	−0.200**	−0.855
R	0.277**	0.117**	0.134**	0.113**
R^2	0.94	0.93	0.90	0.77
Nobs	158	122	120	116

Notes:
[a]For definitions, see table 4.2.
Pooled data 1976–9 for Japan and 1975, 1976, and 1979 for Britain, dependent variable: ln W.
Each regression includes a constant and year dummies.
Standard errors are heteroskedasticity-consistent.
**The estimated coefficient is significant at the 5 percent level of confidence.

Table 4.8 *Estimates of the rank function, by instrumental variables[a]*

	Japan		Britain	
	Manufacturing	Finance	Manufacturing	Finance
T	0.029**	0.049**	0.123**	0.035
AGE	0.003	−0.008	−0.090**	−0.026**
$SHARE$	−2.750**	−2.508**	−3.049**	−15.295**
SC	0.98 (2)	0.95 (2)	0.94 (2)	0.23 (2)
$TEST$	0.00 (3)	0.17 (2)	0.98 (3)	0.32 (2)
R^2	0.92	0.59	0.49	0.64
Nobs	158	122	120	116

Notes:
[a]For definitions, see table 4.3.
Additional instruments are year dummies and a second-order polynomial in age net of tenure.
**The estimated coefficient is significant at the 5 percent level of confidence.

Table 4.9 *Estimated earnings growth caused by tenure, Japanese and British men[a]*

Tenure	Manufacturing		Finance	
	Conditional	Unconditional	Conditional	Unconditional
Japan				
0	100	100	100	100
5	161.4	168.0	151.1	155.1
10	231.1	250.4	211.7	224.2
15	293.5	331.0	275.0	299.6
20	330.6	388.0	331.1	371.2
Britain				
0	100	100	100	100
5	129.8	140.9	141.6	144.5
10	153.4	180.7	191.1	198.8
15	169.4	210.6	245.5	260.5
20	161.1	223.3	300.3	325.0

Note: [a]Entries are hourly earnings at various years of tenure; hourly wages at zero tenure and experience are normalized to 100.

cannot reject the null hypothesis of no misspecification. Results are mixed for Japanese manufacturing: while the Sargan Criterion cannot reject the null, the LM test rejects it.

As before, we find it convenient to illustrate both conditional and unconditional tenure effects by generating from the estimates a distribution of hourly earnings for different tenure spells, starting from zero tenure and 18 years of average age net of tenure. The results are presented in table 4.9 and illustrated in figures 4.3–4.6.

First, returns to tenure in manufacturing are significantly higher in Japanese than in British manufacturing, thus confirming the evidence discussed above. In the finance industry, however, the difference is not as sharp and conditional returns to tenure are about the same in the two countries. Notice that most stylized facts about Japanese labor have been drawn from the manufacturing sector. This piece of evidence warns against easy generalizations to other sectors of the Japanese economy.

Next, earnings growth in Japan, both conditional and unconditional, is about as high in manufacturing as in finance, and the difference between unconditional and conditional tenure effects is fairly small in

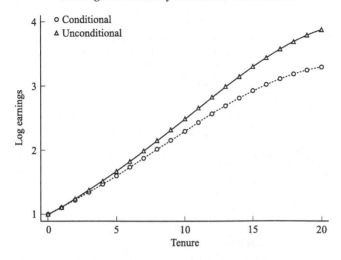

Figure 4.3 Wage–tenure profiles, Japanese manufacturing

both industries. In sharp contrast, earnings growth in the United Kingdom is much higher in finance than in manufacturing. In more detail, and conditional on rank, earnings in the manufacturing sector are only about 61 percent higher after 20 years of tenure than earnings at zero tenure. This percentage increases to 200 percent after the same spell in the finance sector.

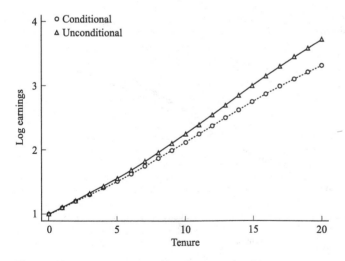

Figure 4.4 Wage–tenure profiles, Japanese banking

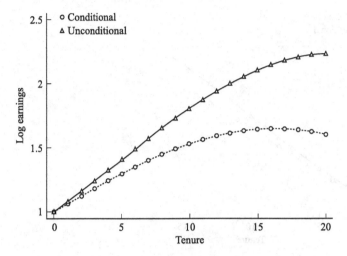

Figure 4.5 Wage–tenure profiles, UK manufacturing

The estimated ratio of unconditional to conditional earnings growth in British manufacturing is 1.39 (223.3/161.1) after 20 years of tenure. This compares to a ratio of 1.17 (388.0/330.6) in Japanese manufacturing. In contrast, the ratio of unconditional to conditional earnings after 20 years of tenure is quite similar in British and Japanese banks (1.08 in Britain and 1.12 in Japan). These numbers suggest that the contribution of

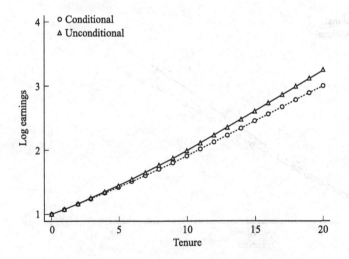

Figure 4.6 Wage–tenure profiles, UK banking

between-rank earnings growth to total earnings growth is more important in Britain than in Japan for manufacturing, but not for finance.

Strictly speaking, differences in the definition of variables and data warn against making too much of the above comparison between the two countries. The common view on the organization of pay in Japanese and British manufacturing is summarized by Dore (1987) as follows. Pay in Britain is tied to the job, and reflects the going rate in the market. On the other hand, pay in Japan is organized in incremental scales, and progression from one scale to the other is regulated by both merit and seniority. These differences are often viewed as depending on the stronger emphasis given by Japanese firms to long-term (implicit) employment contracts, substantial investment in firm-specific skills, cooperative industrial relations and slow promotion patterns. As a result, the Japanese labor market has a distinctive "ILM" flavor, with limited inter-firm mobility, especially among large and medium-sized firms (see Aoki, 1988). The evidence discussed above partially supports this view, both because earnings growth caused by pure, within-rank, tenure effects are larger in Japan than in the United Kingdom, and partly because pay differentials caused by rank allocation are larger in British manufacturing. Notice, however, that our measure of the position filled by the employee in the corporate hierarchy, rank, is too broad to capture the variety of job grades in the promotion ladder. As stressed above, conditional seniority effects estimated in this chapter are likely to include some promotion effects, involving mobility between grades within the same rank.[31]

Tenure effects on earnings growth in Japan and the United Kingdom do not differ in the finance sector as much as they do in the manufacturing sector.[32] An obvious question is why international differences in earnings growth caused by tenure vary between the two industries. A key factor in this story, we believe, is the distinction between manual and non-manual workers. Koike (1988) tabulates earnings by age and tenure in Japan and the United Kingdom, and finds that earnings profiles of non-manual workers do not differ much in the two countries. On the other hand, he also finds that the earnings profiles of British manual workers are remarkably flat in comparison to their Japanese counterparts.

---

[31] Abraham and Medoff (1980) use job grade-level dummies in earnings regressions and find that between-job-level earnings differentials are more important than within-job-level differentials.

[32] In the Japanese banking sector, the branch manager is an important rank that we cannot use because of the lack of data. This may have some effect on our findings, especially on the estimated rank effect on earnings.

Koike explains this difference by arguing that Japanese blue-collars accumulate through frequent job rotation a much wider range of skills than their British colleagues, making them much more similar to white-collar employees.[33] Since blue-collar workers are concentrated in manufacturing and are rare in finance, our findings are partly caused by composition effects and partly by Japanese human resource development (HRM) on the shop floor.

Summary

Standard estimates of earnings profiles ignore the fact that, with unobserved heterogeneity, cross-section evidence need not reflect the "true" relationship between earnings and tenure. In this chapter, we have argued that the observation of the position filled by an employee in the firm hierarchy is informative of both her quality and the quality of her match. Under some additional assumptions, this information can be used to construct an unbiased estimator of the effects of tenure on earnings growth.

We have applied this simple idea to Japanese and British data. We found that tenure effects are less important than the effects estimated with the traditional approach, used by Hashimoto and Raisian (1985). The difference, however, is small. Conditional effects make up a substantial part of the overall impact of tenure on earnings, especially for short–medium tenure spells and for large firms. Within-rank earnings growth is important earlier on in a career, and between-rank earnings growth becomes more important as tenure increases, especially among small firms. Finally, both conditional and unconditional seniority premia are smaller in the United Kingdom than in Japan, and the ratio of unconditional to conditional premia, measuring the importance of between-rank earnings growth, is higher in the former. This difference is particularly significant in the manufacturing sector.

An important question not addressed in this chapter is whether the expected returns to seniority change over time. With the pronounced slow-down of the Japanese economy after the burst of the bubble in the early 1990s, both the feasibility of long-term employment commitments and the role of seniority in promotion and earnings growth have been questioned.[34] We shall come back to this question in chapter 9.

---

[33] This view on the "white-collarization" of Japanese blue-collars is described in detail by Koike (1995).

[34] See Clark and Ogawa (1992).

5   Recruitment and promotion in Japanese firms

Overview[1]

In this chapter, we study *recruitment and promotion patterns* in Japanese internal labor markets. We do this in two ways. First, we use personnel data to look at entry, exit, and promotion in large Japanese companies. In spite of the revival in the interest on internal labor markets, empirical research in these areas has been relatively scarce, both in Japan and elsewhere. The reason is that personnel data, the main source of information, are not usually available to the applied researcher. Second, we review in detail other empirical studies, both in Japan and elsewhere, and place our own research in a wider perspective.

The common view on recruitment and promotion in large Japanese firms can be summarized as follows: (1) promotion is seniority-based and a late selection approach prevails;[2] (2) the allocation of workers to jobs is centralized; (3) there is extensive job rotation, with internal transfers; (4) there are well defined ports of entry, and a strong preference for recruitment of school graduates.

Relevant evidence in support of the common view comes from the pioneering work by Ronald Dore (1973) on *Hitachi Corporation*, a company also studied by Aoki (1988) in his economic treatise on the Japanese firm. Important additional Japanese evidence is provided by the well known fieldwork carried out by Kazuo Koike (1981). In the United States, relevant empirical research is reviewed by Baker, Gibbs and Holmstrom (1994a) in their influential work based on the personnel data file of a large American firm.

---

[1] This chapter is based upon Ariga, Ohkusa and Brunello (1999).
[2] "Late selection" is a short cut for "cumulative, small, cohort–peer differentiating selection," a characterization suggested by Ronald Dore in private correspondence.

A distinguishing feature of the evidence from Japan is that it is based mainly on established, old, and large *keiretsu* firms operating in mature manufacturing sectors or in the finance industry. Hitachi Corporation is a typical example. Because of this, an important research question is whether the common view holds beyond the "Hitachi experiment." In this chapter we address this question by using two types of data. The first dataset is drawn from the personnel files of a large Japanese manufacturing company (hereafter, firm ABO) and contains information on the career history of more than 5,000 employees for the period 1971–94. Compared to the Hitachi benchmark, firm ABO is relatively young, profitable, high-tech, and has grown rapidly during the late 1970s and 1980s to become known world-wide as one of the leaders in its line of products. Moreover, it does not belong to any *keiretsu* and is without any specific "main bank" relationship. Hence, it provides an interesting contrast with the benchmark case.

The second dataset is based on the information published by a specialized magazine, *Bekkan Chuo Roudou Jihou*, containing the records of trials held in Japanese local labor courts because of alleged unfair labor practices. The standard allegation is unfair promotion, and the firm involved in the trial usually produces substantial evidence on past promotion decisions to argue its case. Because the design of the data is not motivated by econometric research, however, it is fairly hard to find ideal information in the records. The four firms considered in the final part of this chapter are a branch of a local bank (firm B), an establishment of a firm involved in the installation and maintenance of elevators (firm C) and two local broadcasting firms (firm D and E). Needless to say, the selection of these firms is driven only by data availability and we do not claim here to provide evidence that can be extended to the whole Japanese economy. The former two firms have already been investigated by Tomita (1992) and Ohtake (1994), while the remaining two firms have not yet (to our knowledge) received academic attention.

We start with a brief review of the existing theoretical and empirical literature and move on to a detailed analysis of firm ABO. First, we present the data and give an overview of human resource management (HRM). Next, we turn to an econometric investigation of the dataset and to the discussion of the relevant results. In the second part of the chapter, we present the evidence based on data drawn from firms B–E and then compare in detail the results drawn from our five case studies with other relevant findings in the related empirical literature. A brief summary concludes the chapter.

A brief review of the literature

The study of internal labor markets has for long been the province of institutional economists and sociologists. New developments in the economic theory of incentives and contracts in the presence of incomplete information, however, have attracted the attention of economists, who have produced important empirical research in the area.

One strand of this research focuses on specific institutional settings. In his pioneering work, Rosenbaum (1984) studies career mobility in American corporate hierarchies. A similar focus is taken by Abraham and Medoff (1980), Baker, Gibbs and Holmstrom (1994a) and McCue (1996).[3] These empirical contributions try to clarify and test propositions derived from theoretical models of internal labor markets that operate in an environment characterized by imperfect information. Similar work has been carried out in other institutional settings – for example, by Bourguignon and Chiappori (1995), who look at a French company, and by Imada and Hirata (1995), who study a large Japanese company.

Another strand of empirical research takes a more comparative perspective, with the purpose of illustrating and eventually explaining why promotion policies adopted by large firms in various institutional contexts differ. Important examples here are Dore (1973) and Koike (1988, 1991), who focus on the comparison between perceived Western and Japanese practices. Itoh (1991) summarizes the common view on the promotion policies of Japanese large corporations as follows:[4]

Workers in the Japanese firm tend to experience a wider range of closely related jobs than those in the Western firm . . . the promotion pattern in Japan is a late selection approach; *the majority are not differentiated from their cohort for 10 to 15 years* and then only a minority is selected to go on to upper management positions. (Itoh, 1991, p. 350, emphasis ours)

In more detail, promotion policies in Japan are perceived as having the following key characteristics:

(a) Promotion is based mainly upon internal upgrading (*internal promotion*)

---

[3] See also Itoh, Kumagai and Ohtake (1998). This is not an exhaustive list of all the relevant contributions. We refer the reader to Baker, Gibbs and Holmstrom (1994a); Gibbons (1996); Prendergast (1998) for detailed reviews of the American literature.

[4] Aoki (1988) argues in a similar fashion that
new entrants to the firm are placed in the bottom rank. However, they are promoted over certain periods on a rank-by-rank basis as their performances meet certain standards. In each period, they move up one rank, at most, but a differential arises among employees in the long run because of discriminating treatment with respect to the speed of promotion, which results in substantial variation in one's lifetime earnings and separation payments. (1988, p. 95)

(b) Individuals belonging to the same entry cohort, who share similar educational background and have been hired in the same year by the firm, are not differentiated in their career for a considerable period of time (about 10 years[5]); competition is ongoing with constant evaluation but differentiation within each cohort is delayed (*late selection*)

(c) Competition for promotion does not generally involve individuals belonging to different entry cohorts.[6]

The contrast between early selection of stars in the United States and late selection in Japan is taken to be a stylized fact in the comparison of HRM policies in the two countries.[7] The empirical evidence supporting this fact, however, is not abundant. In the United States, Rosenbaum (1984) finds evidence of early selection in the personnel data of a large firm. In particular, he shows that an early promotion significantly affects the probability of a further promotion in the job ladder. Baker, Gibbs and Holmstrom (1994a) show that fast tracks are typical of the promotion policy of a large American firm operating in the service sector.

The evidence for Japan is also based on case studies. Spilerman and Ishida (1994), for instance, use Japanese data and show that there is little career differentiation among workers during the first 10 years of tenure in the firm. Moreover, most workers move up the corporate hierarchy at roughly the same rate. After 10–15 years, differentiation becomes noticeable. Similarly, Matsushige (1995a) uses the results of a survey of 164 large Japanese firms carried out by the Japanese Institute of Labor and confirms the late selection approach in the race for promotion to both lower and higher management levels.[8]

Economic theory has tried to explain promotion patterns by considering vertical movements in a career ladder, as a learning device, or as an incentive mechanism, or finally as a tool to foster the accumulation of human capital. The separation between these three perspectives is partially artificial, and most authors recognize that they closely interact.[9] Here, we briefly consider each approach separately.

Let individual productivity be determined by a time-invariant characteristic, ability, that is gradually revealed over time. The *learning hypothesis* suggests that promotion to higher ranks, that yield better pay, could

---

[5] See Koike (1991); Spilerman and Ishida (1994).
[6] See Yashiro (1995). In the ensuing discussion, we shall focus mainly upon point (a).
[7] A good example is Prendergast (1992).
[8] Additional evidence is discussed in Inoue (1982); Hanada (1987); Tachibanaki (1992); Tomita (1992); Ohtake (1995); Takeuchi (1995); Yashiro (1995).
[9] According to Baker, Gibbs and Holmstrom (1994a), "the distinction between ability and human capital may be artificial." See also the discussion in Prendergast (1998).

result from repeated observations of worker performance by the employer. With learning, firms can improve the allocation of workers to jobs and at the same time retain good employees by upgrading them to higher-paying jobs.[10] The speed of promotion depends on whether the current employer is better informed than the market on worker productivity. In this case, promotion reveals valuable information and leads to higher labor costs because of offer matching. Because of this, the rate of promotion is slower than in the situation where the employer and the market share the same information.[11]

The *incentive hypothesis* is based on the rank-order tournament model developed by Lazear and Rosen (1981). Individual workers do not differ in their ability but control an action that is not directly observable by the employer, who must design appropriate incentives to elicit the desired level of effort. Under some conditions, firms prefer to induce individual effort by focusing on relative rather than on absolute performance. This can be done by setting up promotion tournaments, with prizes for the winner(s) of the competition. Compared to pay for performance, these schemes have the advantage of being verifiable.[12] Tournaments have also disadvantages. One is that a worker can win both by outperforming competitors and by damaging their performance. Another is collusion.[13]

According to the *human capital hypothesis*, promotion to jobs requiring more complex skills and higher responsibility depends on the accumulation of firm-specific human capital.[14] If skills are developed mainly by learning-by-doing (or by on-the-job training), company seniority has a positive influence on observed promotion patterns. Moreover, when job ladders consist of jobs with closely related skills, the degree of proximity of these skills in lower- and upper-rank jobs leads naturally to promotion as a mechanism that fosters skill formation.[15] Easy jobs in lower ranks and hard jobs in higher ranks, that are correlated because of either technical or information-related reasons,[16] imply that job and company experience lead to promotion from lower to upper ranks.

These hypotheses have implications for the patterns of promotion in large private corporations, and in particular for the contrast between early selection and late promotion. As remarked by Itoh (1991), late

[10] See Baker, Jensen and Murphy (1988); Harris and Holmstrom (1982).
[11] See Waldman (1984).
[12] See Malcomson (1984).
[13] See Lazear (1995) for a detailed discussion.
[14] See, for instance, Abraham and Medoff (1985); Demougin and Siow (1994).
[15] See chapter 2 for a model that emphasizes the technical proximity of skills.
[16] See Jovanovic and Nyarko (1996) for a model that emphasizes the learning effects of mobility from easier to harder jobs.

promotions can occur in the learning approach when they convey to the market relevant information on individual ability. The incentive to delay promotions is higher the lower is accumulated firm-specific human capital, because of the higher transferability of skills. Since Japanese firms are widely perceived to invest more in firm-specific human capital, this explanation is apparently at variance with the stylized evidence on relative promotion speed.

Late selection in promotion tournaments is unlikely to be the optimal strategy of firms that sort workers of different abilities. In particular, Meyer (1991) shows that it is always optimal for an organization to bias the final promotion contest in favor of the current leader, the worker with the best cumulative performance. Thus, winning the first contest increases the probability of winning future contests. While Meyer's model explains the early selection approach taken by American companies, it does not fit with the late selection policy allegedly used by Japanese firms.

Late selection can be explained by a model that emphasizes human capital accumulation rather than learning or incentives. When skills in lower and upper ranks are significantly correlated, late selection can be the optimal promotion policy. In chapter 2, we have shown that firms where jobs are designed to require closely related skills focus on internal training and adopt internal labor market (ILM) practices. Since these firms recruit workers with average ability, few workers are candidates for an early selection treatment and late selection prevails. On the other hand, firms that focus on jobs that require skills developed in the market place are less likely to organize internal labor markets and to reduce the heterogeneity of new entrants with respect to ability. In these firms, early selection prevails.

The incentive approach suggests that late selection has both costs and benefits. The costs derived from a less efficient allocation of training resources and from the failure to retain abler employees trade off with the benefits implied by better incentives for the losers of early promotion tournaments. If the contribution of potential losers is important, firms could find it optimal to reduce the speed of promotion. According to Itoh

the argument here predicts slower promotion in the Japanese firm because mid-career separation of able workers seems more costly in Japan, and because the incentives of the losers seem particularly important for Japanese-type work organization in which responsibility is delegated to lower levels of hierarchy. (1991, p. 368)

Finally, the choice of promotion speed can depend on institutional differences. Prendergast (1992) focuses on differences in the degree of labor market competition in the United States and Japan. Late selection is a viable option in Japan because of the poor labor market opportunities for workers in mid-career who quit their jobs in large firms. While American firms cannot retain high-quality employees with a late selection policy because of substantial market competition and labor turnover, limited offer matching from the labor market makes this option possible in Japanese companies.

Recruitment and promotion: evidence from individual firm ABO

The firm

The firm was established in the late 1950s and grew rapidly during the 1960s and the 1970s. In 1971, it employed more than 1,000 employees. By 1980, this number had increased to roughly 4,000; by 1984, it reached 10,000. Employment peaked in the mid-1980s to stabilize at about 13,000 in the last 10 years. Although the firm grew quite rapidly, its main lines of business have changed little since its inception.[17] It is listed on all the major stock exchanges in Japan.

The firm is organized into eight major product divisions. Together with the headquarters, these divisions make up the core of the hierarchical structure. There are 15 major factories located in Japan and an extensive network of branch offices in Japan, Europe, and the United States. The organization is framed according to major product groups. Because of the nature of its products, this firm classifies and controls human resources and positions not only according to the functional classification of jobs and to employee capabilities, but also in terms of product lines. A broad group of product lines makes up a division and each of the major eight divisions is headed by an executive, typically a senior vice president. Since several divisions have sizeable internal "sales" and "purchases," each division functions as a profit center and the firm extensively uses internal accounting prices to assess the productivity and profitability of each division.

Divisions have considerable discretion and are to a certain extent autonomous entities. Each division has its own sales section and a considerable degree of freedom in developing new product lines, reshuffling its internal organization, etc.; its sales staff works in each regional branch office and is under the direct control of the division headquarters, not of the head of the regional office. The relative independence of each division

---

[17] In the late 1980s, the firm acquired a medium-size firm to extend the scope of its business and participated in a major joint venture in a related field.

also applies to HRM. Transfers of employees across divisions are rare and exceptional and recruitment decisions are decentralized. For example, divisions with their own establishments (factories) independently hire production employees. Moreover, even in the recruitment of engineers and managerial workers, the interviews of candidates with division staff largely determine the outcome of the recruitment decision.

The data

The personnel data of firm ABO include the promotion history of incumbent employees since their entry into the firm to our observation point, June 1994. The data are limited to stayers – that is, to employees who are currently employed after joining the firm from 1971 onwards. There are 5,502 valid records, one for each employee recruited by the personnel division at the company's headquarters. The data cover virtually all white-collar workers and engineers, but exclude most blue-collar workers, who are hired by the plants located both all over Japan and overseas. Part-time workers are also excluded. For each employee, the available data contain the following information: education, year of entry in the firm, year of graduation from school, type of recruitment, promotion history, and position held in 1994. Recruitment can be on a regular basis (*teiki saiyou*) or on an irregular basis (*chuto saiyou*). Regular recruitment is done during the annual recruitment period and focuses mainly on new school graduates. Irregular recruitment, on the other hand, is done on a case-by-case basis and involves mainly individuals who have separated from their previous firm. Promotion history is fully available since 1971, when the firm introduced a formal ranking system.

The rank system

Each employee is given a specific rank and the rank is the basis both for personnel management and for the compensation system. It is important to clarify what is meant here by "rank." Japanese firms are often characterized by a dual hierarchical structure, one focusing on vertical and the other on horizontal ranks. Vertical ranks are associated with specific job positions and entail different levels of authority and responsibility in the hierarchy. Examples are department director (*bucho*) and division director (*kacho*). Horizontal ranks are grades used to differentiate individuals in terms of status and pay. Promotion to a higher horizontal rank does not imply *per se* a change in authority, responsibility, and even type of job. Quite importantly, however, vertical and horizontal ranks are closely inter-related, since promotion to a vertical rank often requires a

Table 5.1 *Ranks and positions in the Japanese firm*

Positions a	Function/responsibility	Shikaku b		Rank in our chapter
	Management	Riji		–
		Sanji	1	16
			2	15
			3	14
	Administration/Professional	Huku-Sanji	1	13
			2	12
			3	11
	Supervision/monitoring/Semi-professional	Syuji	1	10
			2	9
		Syuji-ho	1	8
			2	7
	General/senior tasks	Syumu	1	6
			2	5
		Syumu-ho	1	4
			2	3
	General tasks	Shain I	1	2
			2	1
		Shain II	1	0
			2	

Positions column (vertical ranks): Team leader; Head of *Kakari* (squad); Head of section; Head of department; Head of divisions; Head of major department factories.

Right-side annotations:
- ① Interviews
- ② Essay
- ③ Special off-the-job training
- → Written examination (at rank 7)
- → Master (at rank 3)
- → 4-year college (at rank 2)
- → 2-year college / Senmon Gakko (vocational school) (at rank 1)
- → Senior high (at rank 0)
- → Junior high

Notes: a Vertical ranks.
b Horizontal ranks.

specific horizontal rank as a prerequisite. In particular, promotion to a higher vertical rank is usually not possible unless the required horizontal rank has been reached.[18] In this chapter, we focus on horizontal ranks, both because of data limitations and because the concept of "ranking hierarchy" developed by Aoki (1988) as a key feature of large Japanese firms focuses on the horizontal hierarchy. Table 5.1 shows the details of the ranking system. Excluding executives who are members of the board (*Riji*),[19] there are eight major groups (*shikaku*), that are further divided into 17 ranks,[20] ranging from rank 0 to rank 16. Together with *Riji*, the top *shikaku*, *Sanji*, makes up the governing body of the corporation. In 1994, less than 1 percent of the employees in our sample was in this

[18] See Aoki (1988).
[19] Since *Riji* are not employees, they are not included in the data.
[20] The distinction between *shikaku* and rank has no substantial content and is only a descriptive device. In particular, we define somewhat improperly each *shikaku* as a group of ranks. Following the company guidelines, we treat the two ranks at the bottom of the hierarchy as equivalent to a single rank (rank 0).

group. Next, *Huku-Sanji* is for upper–middle management (that is, the heads of smaller departments and of important sections.[21]

In 1994, 7 percent of the employees in our sample was in this group. The third and the fourth *shikaku*, *Syuji* and *Syuji-ho*, are mainly for lower management (that is, heads of smaller sections (*Ka*) and squads (*Kakari*)). This group includes about 38 percent of employees in our sample. Employees ranked below *Syuji-ho* (about 54 percent of the employees in our sample) are generally non-managerial workers, with the exception perhaps of those ranked as top *Syumu*, who are often team leaders.

Roughly speaking, *Shain I, II, Syumu-ho*, and *Syumu* are for jobs in non-managerial ranks, such as clerks and senior clerks, and *Syuji-ho* and *Syuji* are for jobs in low–medium management. As we show below, differentiation in promotion among employees belonging to the same recruitment cohort starts in this firm significantly earlier than suggested by the common view on late selection in large Japanese firms. In particular, differentiation is already visible as early as in the *Syumu-ho shikaku*.

Table 5.1 also shows that there are two key promotions in the career ladder: the first to *Syuji-ho* (rank 7) and the second to *Huku-Sanji* (rank 11). Candidates for promotion to these ranks are screened not only by regular performance evaluation but also by written exams and interviews. Promotion to these ranks is important because it provides an entry ticket for careers in middle and upper management.

Since its introduction in 1971, the rank system has not changed. This stability is sharply in contrast with the frequent changes in the organization of the corporate hierarchy. Over time, the firm has built, changed, and eliminated entire sections, departments, and even divisions at a fairly rapid pace. This contrast highlights the unique function of the horizontal ranking system in the allocation and evaluation of employees.

Recruitment

Since our data are limited to the stock of employees in June 1994, we lack full information on the annual flow of recruited employees and observe only the time and the type of recruitment of each incumbent. Information on separation patterns is clearly important, but failure to control for turnover is presumably less of a problem in Japan than elsewhere, because of the relatively low separation rates registered by large Japanese manufacturing firms. While "lifetime employment" is likely to

---

[21] Currently, employees with ranks higher than *Huku-Sanji* are not paid for overtime work.

exaggerate the length of job spells in Japanese large firms, the empirical evidence suggests that Japanese workers hold fewer jobs and stay longer on their jobs than their American counterparts.

The firm studied in this chapter hires both regular and irregular recruits. As mentioned above, regular recruits are hired during the annual recruitment period and are almost entirely new school graduates. Irregular recruits are hired at need and usually have previous labor market experience. Both types are hired on a permanent basis, and are eligible for permanent employment in the firm. The share of irregulars on the total number of incumbents is 38.5 percent.[22] If we divide the current stock of employees by year of entry in the firm, irregular recruits are 64 percent, 46 percent and 11 percent of all the incumbents hired, respectively, from 1971–5, from 1981–5, and from 1991–4. These numbers suggest that the relative importance of irregulars has declined with the stabilization of employment levels after the mid-eighties.[23]

Average previous labor market experience in our sample is equal to 4.88 years for the cohort hired between 1971 and 1975, to 4.26 years for the cohort hired 10 years later, and to only 1.49 years for the latest cohort, which was recruited from 1991 to 1994. Since regular recruits are hired after graduation from school and tend to have zero previous experience, the observed decline in average experience reflects the decline in the relative share of irregulars on total employment.

As the firm grew, it gradually built its reputation as one of the world's leading companies in the field. Partially because of this, the relative importance of *chuto saiyou* declined over time. Nevertheless, even nowadays sizeable hirings occur among employees with previous job experience.[24] Figure 5.1 shows that, while there is a clear positive trend in the number of regular recruits, the number of irregular recruits exhibits substantial fluctuations on a year-to-year basis without any significant trend.

Since these data focus mainly on white-collars, it is difficult to draw a comparison with the national average. It is fair to say, however, that this company does not fit well in this respect with the perceived view on

[22] In another case study of a large Japanese steel-maker, Imada and Hirata (1995) find that the share of irregular recruits in the total stock of employees is 15.5 percent, much less than in our firm. Imada and Hirata also find that there are very few irregular recruits in the medium–high ranks, another important difference with the firm studied in this chapter.

[23] Later in the chapter, we argue that it is difficult to explain the observed trend exclusively in terms of differences in turnover behavior.

[24] In 1990, 37 percent of recruits were irregular recruits and in 1995 the firm hired more irregulars than regulars. Furthermore, about 25 percent of the board members in this firm are irregular recruits, and some of them have fairly short tenure. Compare this with Hitachi Corporation, which has a board of about the same size. In Hitachi, only 10 percent are irregular recruits and only one of them has less than 20 years' tenure.

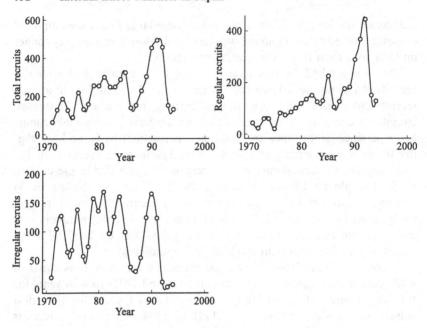

Figure 5.1 Hirings data

recruitment in large Japanese firms, summarized by Dore (1973) as follows:

the orthodox way to get into Hitachi has been to be recruited immediately on leaving school or university. A proportion of those recruited decide, usually within a year or two, that a lifetime with Hitachi is not for them. Ideally the company replaces them with new school-leavers the following April. (1973, p. 32)

Another important feature of this firm is the composition of employment by education. This is clearly an education-intensive company. Among the employees who entered the firm during the early 1970s and stayed on, about 31 percent were university graduates or postgraduates. This proportion was close to 73 percent for the employees recruited 10 years later. Regular recruits are more likely to be at least college graduates than irregular recruits: among those recruited from 1991 to 1994, about 88 percent of the former had at least a college degree, compared to 75 percent of the latter.[25]

---

[25] Over time, the level of education has risen quite sharply for both types of recruits. In the early 1970s, 53 percent of regular recruits had at least a college degree, compared to about 90 percent 20 years later. Similarly, 19 percent of irregular recruits hired in the early 1970s had at least a college degree, compared to 75 percent 20 years later.

Mainly because of their previous job experience, irregular recruits are older than regular recruits at the time of entry into the firm. In particular, while no regular recruit is older than 30 at recruitment, this percentage is close to 29 percent among irregular recruits. Initial rank allocation also varies substantially with the type of recruitment. Table 5.2 presents the initial distribution of employees in the ranking hierarchy according to type of recruitment and education level, for both the whole sample and three cohorts of recruits, the 1971–5, the 1981–5, and the 1991–4 cohort. Consider the whole sample. Regular recruits with less than college education are almost entirely allocated to rank 0 upon recruitment. On the other hand, regular recruits with at least college education are allocated to the first two ranks, with very few exceptions to this rule.[26]

Compared to regulars, irregular recruits are more spread out in their initial allocation in the ranking hierarchy. While the majority of employees with less than college education is in rank 0, about 20 percent are allocated to rank 3 or higher. The presence of multiple ports of entry is even clearer among irregular recruits with at least college education. Here, about one-third of the total is in rank 2 or below, about one-quarter is in ranks 3 and 4 and the rest (38 percent) is allocated to ranks higher than or equal to 5. Quite remarkably, about 1.7 irregular recruits out of 10 are initially placed at rank 7 or higher, corresponding to *Syuji-ho* or higher in table 5.1.[27] These findings are broadly confirmed by the tables based upon cohort-specific data. Notice that multiple ports of entry for irregular recruits apply not only to the 1971–5 high-growth period, but also later on, when firm growth was remarkably slower.

In summary, the hiring policy of this firm is somewhat in contrast with the common view on typical recruitment patterns in large Japanese firms, as described, for instance, by Dore. First, the firm recruits from outside to fill vacancies in higher ranks. Second, it recruits employees with diverse job experience, education, and age.[28] Third, irregular recruits are placed initially in a rather wide range of ranks, which strongly suggests that the firm uses multiple ports of entry for this type of recruitment.

---

[26] Initial allocation by educational attainment for regular recruits is called *syonin kakuzuke*.
[27] This result is in line with those by Baker, Holmstrom and Gibbs (1994a), who find evidence of considerable hiring from outside at all levels of the firm.
[28] Apparently, this is also not in line with Aoki's view that Japanese (large) firms prefer to have a homogeneous labor force. See Aoki (1988).

Table 5.2 *Allocation to initial rank*
  (a) Whole sample, by years of education and type of recruitment

	Regulars	Regulars	Irregulars	Irregulars
	< 16	≥ 16	< 16	≤ 16
0	86.6	–	65.7	0.2
1	5.0	52.8	8.7	3.0
2	7.0	45.8	6.4	30.5
3	0.9	0.9	5.0	16.7
4	0.5	0.2	4.0	11.6
5	–	0.2	3.0	12.3
6	–	0.05	1.9	9.0
7	–	–	2.7	5.6
≥ 8	–	0.05	2.6	11.1
Total	100	100	100	100

(b) Cohort 1971–5, by education and type of recruitment

	Regulars	Regulars	Irregulars	Irregulars
	< 16	≥ 16	< 16	≥ 16
0	73.2	–	68.9	1.5
1	3.1	–	11.3	1.5
2	17.5	83.2	3.2	33.8
3	3.1	5.3	2.9	8.8
4	3.1	5.3	1.9	2.9
5	–	4.4	2.5	2.9
6	–	0.9	1.6	13.2
7	–	0.9	3.2	8.8
≥8	–	–	4.5	26.6
Total	100	100	100	100

Promotion policy

A key feature of internal labor markets is that vacant positions in higher ranks are filled mainly by upgrading incumbents from lower ranks (*internal promotion*). Table 5.3 shows the percentage of individuals promoted to ranks 5, 7, 9, and 11 who started from a rank lower than 3, classified

Table 5.2 (continued)

(c) Cohort *1981–5, by education and type of recruitment*

	Regulars	Regulars	Irregulars	Irregulars
	< 16	≥ 16	< 16	≥ 16
0	69.4	–	76.8	0.3
1	13.9	–	4.5	0.3
2	16.7	99.4	6.1	47.2
3	–	0.6	3.5	21.3
4	–	–	3.8	8.7
5	–	–	1.3	8.7
6	–	–	0.6	2.7
7	–	–	1.3	4.2
≥ 8	–	–	2.1	6.6
Total	100	100	100	100

(d) Cohort 1991–4, by education and type of recruitment

	Regulars	Regulars	Irregulars	Irregulars
	< 16	≥ 16	< 16	≥ 16
0	100.0	–	23.5	–
1	–	93.7	17.6	9.4
2	–	6.2	11.7	5.6
3	–	–	14.8	11.3
4	–	–	11.8	18.8
5	–	–	14.8	25.5
6	–	–	2.9	14.2
7	–	–	2.9	3.8
≥ 8	–	–	–	11.4
Total	100	100	100	100

Notes: Ranks in rows, type of recruitment and years of education in columns.
Workers with a college degree or more have at least 16 years of schooling.

Table 5.3 *Percentage promoted to a given rank who started from a rank lower than 3*

	Regulars	Regulars	Irregulars	Irregulars
Rank	All employees	College only	All employees	College only
5	98.0	98.0	76.3	53.4
7	96.5	96.7	56.9	41.2
9	94.0	94.7	69.7	37.5
11	89.7	89.6	31.4	27.9

by type of recruitment and by educational attainment. While the vast majority of regular employees promoted to each of these ranks has been internally upgraded from lower ranks, quite independently of educational attainment, this percentage falls to less than 50 percent among irregular employees with at least a college degree. This evidence suggests that internal upgrading is common practice in this firm, especially for regular hires but also for irregular hires.

Additional evidence on internal promotion is given by the ratio of the individuals initially allocated to a given rank over the total number of individuals promoted to that rank. The higher this percentage, the less important internal promotion. Focusing on individuals with at least a college degree and on ranks 5, 7, 9, and 11, we find that only six regular employees out of 1,545 promoted to rank 5, have been originally allocated to that rank and that no regular employee has been initially allocated to the higher ranks. Turning to irregular employees, this percentage is higher but still low and equal to 22.3, 8.9, 4.8, and 4.5 percent, respectively, for ranks 5, 7, 9, and 11. Overall, this evidence suggests that internal promotion is important in this firm.

Next, we outline the broad features of promotion outcomes in this firm by computing for each individual in the sample the duration elapsed from entry in the firm to promotion to at least a selected rank. The higher this duration, the slower the promotion process. Completed spells end up in a promotion. Censored spells refer to individuals who did not get promoted to at least a given rank by 1994, our observation point, provided that they started from a lower rank.

Since we wish to compare the careers of regular and irregular workers, we line them up by initial rank in the firm. As shown in table 5.2, the vast majority of regular workers is initially allocated by the firm to ranks 1 and 2 if they have at least a college degree, and to rank 0 if they have

Table 5.4 *Log rank tests of the null hypothesis that survivor functions do not vary with type of recruitment, probability values, selected ranks*

Promoted at least to rank	Initial rank 1 or 2	Initial rank 0
3	0.000	0.029
5	0.015	0.000
7	0.073	0.001
9	0.625	0.015

lower education. Because of this, it makes sense to focus on these ranks and to consider the two groups separately in figures 5.2–5.9. These figures show for selected ranks the Kaplan–Meier survivor functions both for regular (*type 1*) and for irregular (*type 2*) recruits. Table 5.4 presents the log rank tests of the null hypothesis that these survivor functions do not vary with the type of recruitment. With the exception of promotion to at least rank 9 of workers initially allocated in ranks 1 and 2, the test always rejects the null hypothesis at the 10 percent level of confidence.

Consider first figures 5.2–5.5, that focus on workers initially allocated to ranks 1 and 2. Starting from promotion to at least rank 3 (figure 5.2), 95.7 percent of regular recruits are promoted at least to this rank after

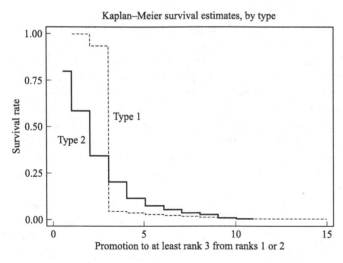

Figure 5.2 Kaplan–Meier survivor estimate: promotion to at least rank 3 from initial rank 1 or 2

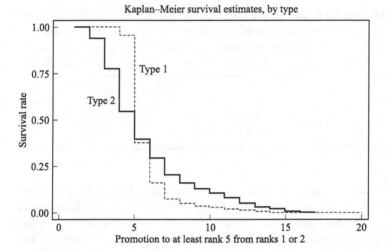

Figure 5.3 Kaplan–Meier survivor estimate: promotion to at least rank 5 from initial rank 1 or 2

three years in the company, with a clear peak in the hazard rate in the third year since entry. After three more years, only 2 percent of the initial stock still survives in the ranks below rank 3. For irregular recruits, the hazard rate does not exhibit any significant peak: after three years, 80 percent have been promoted to at least rank 3; after three more years, the survivor rate in lower ranks is 5.4 percent.

Next consider promotion to at least rank 5 (figure 5.3). During the first four years in the firm, regular workers have a lower hazard than irregulars and, in the fourth year after entry, the survivor rate is about 96 percent for the former and about 55 percent for the latter. This rate falls rapidly in the next two years to 16 percent among regulars, and much less rapidly to 30 percent among irregulars. Hence, there is a significant peak in the hazard experienced by regulars in their fifth and sixth year in the firm. Importantly, about one-sixth of the regulars initially allocated to ranks 1 and 2 are left behind in the promotion race at the end of their sixth year. This proportion increases to about one-third among irregulars.

A similar pattern can be observed for higher ranks. In the case of promotion to at least rank 7 (figure 5.4), for instance, no regular employee makes it within five years from entry, 43 percent make it within eight years and 10 percent do not make it even after 11 years. On the other hand, 14 percent of the irregulars are promoted within five years, 59 percent within eight years and 24 percent do not make it after 11 years.

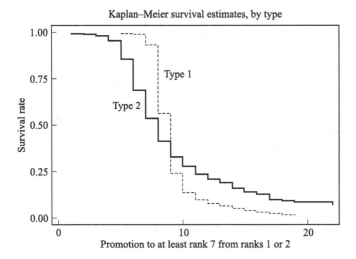

Figure 5.4 Kaplan–Meier survivor estimate: promotion to at least rank 7 from initial rank 1 or 2

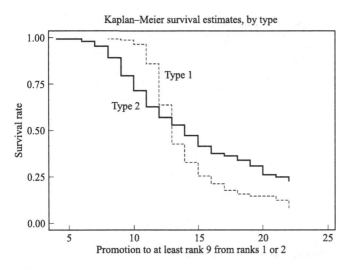

Figure 5.5 Kaplan–Meier survivor estimate: promotion to at least rank 9 from initial rank 1 or 2

To summarize, the timing of promotion is much more dispersed among irregular recruits in all ranks. Moreover, the survival rate at long durations is generally higher among irregulars than among regulars. These findings suggest two things. First of all, the firm applies to irregular and regular recruits, who are initially allocated to ranks 1 and 2 and have in most cases at least a college degree, different promotion policies. In particular, there seems to be no benchmarking in the timing of promotion for irregular workers, contrary to what happens for regular recruits. Secondly, irregular recruits seem to be more heterogeneous than their regular counterparts.

Figures 5.6–5.9 show the promotion patterns of regular and irregular workers that are initially allocated to rank 0. Compared to workers with higher education, promotion at least to ranks 3, 5, 7, and 9 is slower, and the difference between regulars and irregulars less sharp. In particular, we notice that the hazard from lower ranks experienced by regular workers does not exhibit significant peaks. Thus heterogeneity and lack of benchmarks for promotion appear to be features shared by both types of employees when education and initial allocation in the ladder are relatively low. This makes sense because the vast majority of employees with less than a college degree was originally hired at individual establishments, rather than at the firm headquarters. Those who appear in our data were able to advance enough from their initial rank allocation to be included in the data.

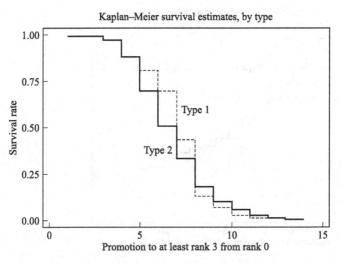

Figure 5.6 Kaplan–Meier survivor estimate: promotion to at least rank 2 from initial rank 0

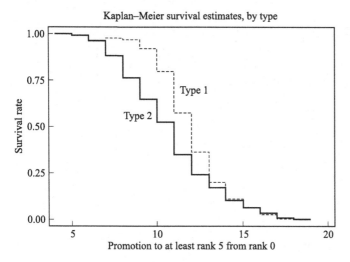

Figure 5.7 Kaplan–Meier survivor estimate: promotion to at least rank 5 from initial rank 0

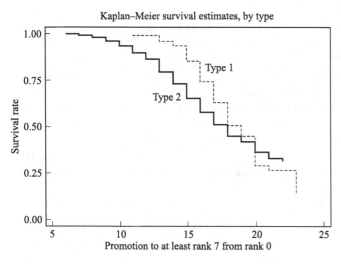

Figure 5.8 Kaplan–Meier survivor estimate: promotion to at least rank 7 from initial rank 0

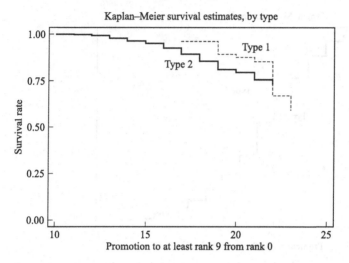

Figure 5.9 Kaplan–Meier survivor estimate: promotion to at least rank 9 from initial rank 0

A closer look at the promotion policy of this firm requires that we control for the underlying heterogeneity of the population of employees. Important dimensions of this heterogeneity are the year of entry in the firm, the level of education, and the type of recruitment. In what follows, we choose one entry cohort, 1979 (15 years before the observation point), focus on individuals with at least a college degree and with initial rank equal to 2, and tabulate the timing of repeated promotion from entry to 1994, after distinguishing between regular and irregular recruits.[29] Consider first regular recruits. As shown in the last column of table 5.5, all of them have been through five promotions. Only 46 percent of all incumbents, however, have managed eight promotions or more during the past 15 years.[30] Right from the start of the promotion tournament, a small percentage of individuals is persistently allocated to a higher rank. The modal year of promotion has a high density in the first promotion round, with 94.3 percent of incumbents being promoted in that year. In the second round, however, the modal year (five years after entry) has a density of 62.8 percent, and about 37 percent of the employees in this

---

[29] We choose 1979 for two reasons: first, recruits have had a 15-year career in the firm before our observation point; second, the size of this cohort is sufficiently large. Recall that our information is limited to stayers.

[30] Needless to say, this does not exclude the fact that they can be promoted after 1994, our observation point.

Table 5.5 *Promotion patterns for the cohort hired in 1979, college graduates or more, initial rank = 2*

(a) Regular recruits, Nobs = 70[d]

P[a]	Min R[a]	Max R	MPY[a]	EPY[b]	LPY[b]	CV[c]	LP[c]
1st P	3	3	82 (94.3)	(1.4)	(4.3)	0.005	(−)
2nd P	4	5	84 (62.8)	(21.4)	(15.7)	0.009	(−)
3rd P	5	6	86 (42.8)	(50.1)	(7.1)	0.009	(−)
4th P	6	7	87 (35.7)	(5.7)	(58.6)	0.011	(−)
5th P	7	8	88 (40.0)	(31.4)	(28.6)	0.012	(9)
6th P	8	9	89 (31.8)	(9.1)	(59.1)	0.015	(26)
7th P	9	10	90 (28.8)	(5.8)	(65.4)	0.017	(54)
8th P	10	10	91 (28.1)	(37.4)	(34.5)	0.015	(89)
9th P	11	11	94 (50.0)	(50)	(−)	0.010	(100)

(b) Irregular recruits, Nobs = 28

P	Min R	Max R	MPY	EPY	LPY	CV	LP
1st P	3	3	79 (60.7)	(−)	(39.3)	0.026	(−)
2nd P	4	5	84 (25.0)	(57.1)	(17.7)	0.023	(−)
3rd P	5	6	84 (25.0)	(64.4)	(10.6)	0.022	(−)
4th P	6	9	87 (32.1)	(57.2)	(10.7)	0.022	(4)
5th P	7	10	88 (25.9)	(55.4)	(18.5)	0.021	(15)
6th P	8	11	89 (25.0)	(46.0)	(29.0)	0.023	(26)
7th P	9	12	90 (23.8)	(33.2)	(43.0)	0.021	(59)
8th P	10	13	91 (25.0)	(58.3)	(16.7)	0.014	(85)
9th P	11	11	94 (60.0)	(40.0)	(−)	0.015	(100)

Notes:
[a]P is promotion, R is rank, MPY is modal year of promotion.
[b]EPY and LPY are, respectively, the percentages of workers promoted earlier and later than the modal year.
[c]CV is the coefficient of variation and LP is the percentage of workers having their last promotion.
[d]In all tables in this chapter: number of observations.
Percentages in parentheses.

cohort have been promoted either before (21.4 percent) or after (15.7 percent) the modal year. The spread between the modal year and the actual year of promotion increases with the number of promotions, as shown by the increase in the coefficient of variation.

The situation is different for irregular recruits. Here, the modal year of promotion is closer to the recruitment year in the earliest part of the career and has in general a lower density than in the case of regular recruits. For instance, the modal year of the first promotion is the first year in the firm, and 60.7 percent of irregulars make it in that year. The modal years of the second and third promotion are the same for regulars and irregulars, but with a density of 25 percent, compared, respectively, to about 63 and 43 percent. Moreover, the coefficient of variation is about three times as large for irregulars than for regulars (0.023 versus 0.009), which points to the higher dispersion in the timing of promotion.

Focusing on the same entry cohort and on individuals with at least a college degree, table 5.6 shows promotion outcomes after three, five, eight, 10, and 15 years in the firm for incumbents who are initially allocated to rank 2, by type of recruitment. Consider first regular recruits. As illustrated by the first part of table 5.6, almost all the incumbents who were allocated to rank 2 in 1979 are in rank 3 by 1982. Hence, there is virtually no differentiation after three years. Differentiation in promotion starts in the next two years: by 1984, about 76 percent of workers starting in 1979 from rank 2 have been promoted to rank 4, 16 percent are in rank 3, and the rest have been promoted to a rank higher than 4. Eight years after entry, differentiation is sharper: about 50 percent of those who started in 1979 from rank 2 are in rank 6 by 1987, 33 percent are in rank 7 and 16 percent lag behind in rank 5. While differentiation continues later on, it starts during the fourth and the fifth year after entry, about six years earlier than predicted by the common view.

Compared to regular recruits, irregular recruits start the promotion race from a broader range of ranks (see table 5.2, p. 134). The basic pattern, however, is unchanged: diversification in promotion patterns starts early on for both types of recruitment, during the first five years for regular recruits and in the initial allocation for irregular recruits.

These data suggest that the speed of promotion is already significantly different among recruits five years after recruitment. Hence, the promotion policy of this firm deviates in a significant way from the stylized view, that emphasizes late selection in promotion patterns. If any evidence exists of automatic and simultaneous promotion outcomes, this is limited to regular recruits during their first three or four years with the firm.

It is interesting to compare our findings with those from other studies. In another case study of a Japanese firm, Takeuchi (1995) has informa-

Table 5.6 *Percentage of employees promoted to rank i, 1979–1994, regular and irregular recruits with at least a college degree, initial rank = 2, cohort hired in 1979*

(a) 1979–82

Rank	3	4	5	6	Total
Regulars	98.5	1.5	–	–	100
Irregulars	56.5	26.1	13.0	4.3	100

(b) 1979–84

Rank	3	4	5	6	7	≥8	Total
Regulars	15.7	75.7	7.1	1.4	–	–	100
Irregulars	14.8	37.0	22.2	11.1	11.1	3.7	100

(c) 1979–87

Rank	3	5	6	7	8	≥9	Total
Regulars	–	15.7	50.0	32.9	1.4	–	100
Irregulars	3.6	3.6	32.1	32.1	17.9	10.7	100

(d) 1979–89

Rank	4	6	7	8	≥9	Total
Regulars	–	5.7	51.4	38.6	4.3	100
Irregulars	3.6	3.6	32.1	25	35.6	100

(e) 1979–94

Rank	6	7	8	9	10	≥11	Total
Regulars	–	5.7	20	24.3	38.6	11.4	100
Irregulars	3.6	7.1	10.7	28.6	25	25	100

tion on 66 employees of a large financial company, who were recruited by the firm in 1966. These individuals were all *simultaneously* promoted to senior clerk (*shunin*)[31] after three years. After two more years, all with the exception of a single case were promoted to team leader rank (*kakari-chou-shoku*). After eight years, more than 80 percent were promoted to deputy section chief rank (*kacho-dairi-shoku*), and the rest were promoted by the 10th year in the firm. A substantive difference in promotion patterns appears in the promotion to section chief rank (*kacho-shoku*), to which only 82 percent of the initial stock of entrants was promoted between the 12th and the 22nd year of tenure.

Compare these numbers with those in tables 5.5 and 5.6, which refer to the 1979 cohort and focus on regular recruits, who are the most likely to experience late selection in promotion. After three years, all incumbents have been promoted to rank 3. After five years, about 76 percent of incumbents have been promoted to rank 4, 16 percent remained in rank 3, and 8.5 percent have been promoted to ranks 5 or higher. The timing of the second promotion (mainly to rank 4) also differs: 21.4 percent of incumbents were promoted by their fourth year after entry, 62.8 percent in their fifth year and the rest have been promoted later. Eight years after entry, about 16 percent of all incumbents have been promoted to rank 5, 50 percent to rank 6, 33 percent to rank 7, and 1.4 percent to rank 8 or 9.

The contrast is even sharper when we consider irregular recruits. Five years after entry, only 51.8 percent of them were at least in rank 4 and more than 14 percent were in ranks higher than 7. Eight years after entry, about 40 percent were in ranks lower than 7, 32 percent were in rank 7 and the rest in ranks higher than 7. Relative to the common view on late selection, that suggests little or no differentiation during the first 10 years in the company, our firm is clearly differentiating earlier on.

Exits

As already mentioned, our data do not contain direct information on turnover. To produce a rough estimate of turnover behavior, we have obtained from the firm an update of the personnel data in the summer of 1996. By matching the 1994 and 1996 datasets, we are able to identify those workers who were employed in 1994 but left any time between 1994

---

[31] These are titles of specific (horizontal) ranks (*shikaku*), not of functional positions (vertical ranks). For example, having a *kacho-shoku* rank indicates that the employee is a potential candidate for section chief (*kacho*), just as an employee with a *fuku-sanji* rank in our data is a candidate for section chief, or for head of a small department.

and 1996. It turns out that 234 employees out of 5,502 (4.25 percent) left the firm during the period. This is equivalent to a quit rate of about 2 percent per year, much less than 6 percent, the average quit rate in the 1980s reported by Aoki (1988, p. 65) for firms with more than 1000 employees. The estimated distribution of leavers is not much affected by the type of recruitment. In particular, the percentage of leavers among regular recruits (*teiki saiyou*) is 3.90 percent over the two years, compared to 4.76 percent among irregular recruits (*chuto saiyou*).

To check these figures, we have also obtained detailed data on the total number of hirings in each year, classified by education, sex, and recruitment type. Since our data do not cover the majority of production workers, table 5.7 focuses only on college graduates and shows the proportion of hired employees still in the company either in 1994 or in 1996, by year of recruitment. It turns out that, on average, 78.6 percent of the regular hirings and 65.8 percent of the irregular hirings between 1972 and 1994 are still with the firm in 1994. If we use a constant annual attrition rate, these figures indicate that the average annual exit rate is 2.89 percent for regulars and 3.96 percent for irregulars, somewhat higher than the rate found by matching the 1994 and 1996 datasets.[32]

Table 5.7 also shows that exit rates exhibit a strong pro-cyclical pattern. In particular, the cohort hired during the period 1983–7 (boom years) shows a higher propensity to quit, independently of recruitment type. Perhaps more importantly, once we exclude the rather exceptional turnover during the boom years 1983–7, the table indicates that our estimate of exit rates based upon matching the 1994 and the 1996 datasets is not too inaccurate a description of actual turnover. In this case, the average annual exit rate is 2.15 percent for regulars, and 2.98 percent for irregulars.

Comparing overall survival rates in 1994 and 1996, we find that the exit rate is modest and equal to about 3.2 percent during this two-year period, even including the cohorts hired in the boom years (1983–7). If we focus instead only on the cohorts hired between 1991 and 1994, the two-year attrition rate increases to 6.1 percent among regular hirings, and to 10.2 percent among irregular hirings. We also find that about one-third of leavers have been recruited between 1991 and 1994, compared to only about one-fifth of stayers. These findings confirm that exits are concentrated heavily among cohorts with shallow tenures.

---

[32] Since quits are concentrated among workers with short tenures, the observed difference could be explained by the fact that, by matching the 1994 and the 1996 datasets, we ignore quits by individuals hired in 1995 who left within a year.

Table 5.7 *Hirings and survivors among college graduates, by year of recruitment, 1972–1994*

	Percentage survived in 1994		Percentage survived in 1996	
Year	Regulars	Irregulars	Regulars	Irregulars
1972	87.5	57.1	87.5	52.4
1973	88.9	72.4	85.2	55.2
1974	100.0	70.0	100.0	60.0
1975	87.5	75.0	81.3	66.7
1976	100.0	68.6	96.0	57.1
1977	90.9	71.5	82.4	71.5
1978	87.9	65.5	87.9	62.1
1979	90.8	66.2	89.2	62.0
1980	73.9	67.1	72.8	59.5
1981	67.9	64.5	67.1	63.4
1982	77.4	67.5	76.1	65.0
1983	61.6	53.5	59.7	53.5
1984	55.9	48.9	55.3	47.8
1985	63.9	59.4	61.1	58.4
1986	72.1	48.1	70.4	40.7
1987	74.4	52.8	71.3	50.0
1988	83.9	77.1	81.4	62.5
1989	76.7	76.8	75.0	72.0
1990	78.7	77.3	72.6	73.3
1991	90.2	82.4	84.5	74.5
1992	93.7	75.0	88.9	25.0
1993	92.1	100.0	85.1	100.0
1994	100.0	100.0	95.9	45.5

When we compare stayers and leavers and identify the latter by comparing data for 1994 and for 1996, we find that the leavers in our sample have on average lower education, higher previous job experience, and marginally higher age. Moreover, they are more frequently found in the bottom and in the top ranks, and in particular in *Shain I* and *II*, *Huku-Sanji*, and *Sanji*.

To sum up, we find that irregular recruits are more likely to quit the firm than regular recruits, although the difference is rather small (roughly 1 percent per year). We also find that exit rates vary pro-cyclically, suggesting that cohort effects are important to explain exit behavior, especially in the first years with the firm.

Econometric analysis

In this section, we use a simple econometric model to study the main factor influencing promotion probabilities in firm ABO. The empirical specification is based on the following model

$$I_{it} = \beta_0 + \beta_1 T_{it} + \beta_2 T_{it}^2 + \beta_3 TR_{it} + \beta_4 TR_{it}^2 + \beta_5 D_{it} \qquad (5.1)$$
$$+ \sum_j \beta_{6j} R_{ijt} + \sum_i \delta_i S_i + \sum_t \gamma_t X_t + \varepsilon_{it}$$

where I is a latent variable, T is tenure in the firm, TR is tenure in the rank, D is the number of years required for promotion from the previous to the current rank,[33] R is a dummy indicating the current rank, S is an individual dummy, X is a time dummy, β, γ, and δ are parameters, ε is a normally distributed error term, i is the subscript for individuals, j for ranks, and t is the subscript for time. The data are longitudinal in the following sense: for each individual, we pool together all her promotion history, summarized by the string of promotions from entry to the current observation point, 1994.[34]

Next, define a discrete variable, P_{it}, such that

$$P_{it} = 1 \text{ iff } I_{it} \geq 0 \qquad (5.2)$$
$$P_{it} = 0 \text{ iff } I_{it} < 0$$

where $P_{it} = 1$ means that individual i was promoted to a given rank at time t, and $P_{it} = 0$ means that promotion has not occurred. Given the assumption that the error term is normally distributed, the model (5.1)–(5.2) can be estimated using a probit specification.

Notice that there are two potentially important selection problems in our data. First and foremost, we observe only stayers from entry to 1994. If stayers are likely to be more successful in promotion tournaments, our sample is likely to over-emphasize promotion probabilities in any rank. Second, we observe only employees hired at the headquarters of the firm. To see the implications of this, divide our sample into two subsamples, one for employees with college education or more, and the other for employees with less than college education. The personnel division at the headquarters is responsible for monitoring, evaluating, and promot-

[33] When the current rank is the second available rank, we use years from joining the firm to promotion to the first rank.
[34] We include in the sample only individuals who have experienced at least one promotion event.

ing employees belonging to the first group from their recruitment onwards.

With the sole exception of those who have been assigned to a job at the headquarters from the start, employees belonging to the second group are managed almost exclusively by the personnel section in the local plant where they are employed. Unless these employees are promoted to a position that makes them candidates for managerial jobs, their personnel records remain in the plant where they are assigned and are not in our data. Thus, we can observe only those employees who do not have college education *and* have survived a substantial selection process. This additional selection problem suggests that we treat these two groups separately in the regression analysis. Needless to say, the results for the group of employees with less than college education must be interpreted with additional caution.

The empirical model specified in (5.1) and (5.2) is designed to flexibly encompass the predictions derived from different theoretical setups. Suppose that the observed pattern of promotion in the firm is generated by a pure learning model. In this model, individuals differ only because they are endowed with idiosyncratic ability, both unknown and time-invariant, and the firm learns about this ability by repeated observation and evaluation of individual performance. An implication of the pure learning model is that observed differences in promotion patterns are simply the consequence of differences in time-invariant ability, captured in the model above by the set of individual dummies, S_i.

An important departure from the pure learning model occurs when employees differ not only because of their innate ability, but also in other dimensions – such as, for instance, outside labor market opportunities. If this additional heterogeneity is correlated with innate ability and affects the turnover decision of individuals, focusing on a sample of stayers could lead to a spurious correlation between promotion outcomes and tenure variables.[35]

Individual ability need not be time-invariant, however, especially when individuals invest heavily in firm-specific human capital. In this case, ability could be conceived of as "purely the varying rate at which individuals accumulate human capital" (Baker, Gibbs and Holmstrom, 1994a, p. 903). When firm-specific human capital is important, tenure in the firm and in the current rank have a positive impact, on both promotion probabilities and earnings profiles.

---

[35] See Mincer and Jovanovic (1981).

Table 5.8 *Summary statistics, full sample, means and standard deviations (in parenthesis)*

Variable	All workers	Less than college	College or more
Promotion rate	0.43 (0.49)	0.40 (0.49)	0.46 (0.50)
Tenure	10.94 (4.21)	12.29 (4.17)	9.79 (3.89)
Tenure in the rank	1.79 (1.14)	1.88 (1.14)	1.70 (1.13)
Duration	2.05 (1.09)	2.29 (1.17)	1.84 (0.98)
Experience	4.05 (5.11)	5.73 (5.59)	2.63 (4.15)
Education	14.19 (2.40)	11.77 (1.04)	16.24 (0.73)
Age	35.46 (5.80)	35.81 (6.33)	35.17 (5.29)
% irregular hirings	0.54 (0.50)	0.73 (0.44)	0.37 (0.48)
Nobs	27407	12590	14817

In this section, we are especially interested in the estimate of coefficient β_5, associating the probability of promotion to a given rank with the time spent in earning promotion to the current (and lower) rank. According to the pure learning approach, the estimate of coefficient β_5 should be zero, and fast-track effects should be fully captured by differences in innate ability. To put it differently, fast tracks are in the genes. If individual characteristics are time-varying, however, and individuals with higher ability receive more intensive training and/or are allocated to "elite" tasks and career ladders, the estimate of β_5 should be negative, even after explicitly controlling for time-invariant individual effects. In this case, fast tracks are *not only* in the genes.

Independently of whether ability is innate or time-varying, fast tracks in promotion imply that individuals with a consistently higher promotion probability (i.e. with a high estimated value of δ_i) should be promoted faster to any rank and consequently should experience relatively low values of D, the time to promotion to the current rank. Hence, with fast tracks, a regression of estimated individual fixed effects on D should attract a significantly negative sign.

The relationship between promotion outcomes, tenure, and duration in the previous rank is likely to vary when different generations of employees are considered. Because of this, we divide the sample further by year of birth and by the educational level of each employee and estimate model (5.1)–(5.2) for the cohort born between 1948 and 1958.[36] Table 5.8 shows the summary statistics of the main variables for the full sample

---

[36] We exclude younger cohorts because of their relatively short careers in the firm.

and tables 5.9 and 5.10 present our results, separately for workers with less than college education and workers with at least college education, respectively. We focus on marginal effects.[37]

It turns out that, with the exception of a few cases, the effect of D on the probability of promotion is negative and significant. On the other hand, the effect of tenure in the firm is positive but decreasing, a pattern often observed in the Mincerian earnings functions. Next, the effect of tenure in the current rank is also positive and with a concave pattern, with a peak between the third and the fifth year since access to the rank. Finally, the last row in each of the regression results presented in tables 5.8–5.10 shows the estimated coefficient from the regression of fitted individual fixed effects, $\hat{\delta}_i$, on D, duration in the previous rank. The evidence for most cohorts is that there is a statistically significant and negative correlation.

We conclude from this evidence that fast-track effects persist even after taking account of individual fixed effects. Hence, they cannot be explained only by the impact of innate ability on promotion: if fast tracks are simply the consequence of the fact that employees endowed with higher innate ability are promoted faster, the number of years in the previous rank should not affect promotion probabilities in a regression that includes individual effects.

To assess the relative importance of tenure, tenure in the current rank, and time to promotion to the current rank, we compute the weighted average of each estimated coefficient in tables 5.9 and 5.10, using as weights the size of each age cohort. These average values are shown in the last column of each table. By evaluating tenure and tenure in the rank at their sample means,[38] we estimate that a one-year increase in tenure, conditional on tenure in the current rank, current rank, and time to promotion to the current rank, increases the probability of promotion to a higher rank by 0.47 among college graduates and by 0.24 among

---

[37] In general, the probit model is defined as

$$\text{Prob}(y_i \neq 0 \mid x_j) = \Phi(x_j b)$$

The marginal effect of x_j is given by

$$\frac{\partial \Phi}{\partial x_j} = \phi(\bar{x}b)b_j$$

where $\bar{x}$ is the sample mean of x.

[38] The marginal effect of tenure T is given by

$$\frac{\partial \Phi}{\partial T} = \phi(\bar{x}b)\left[b_1 + b_2\frac{\partial T^2}{\partial T}\right]$$

where b_1 and b_2 are the coefficients associated with T and T^2.

Table 5.9 *Estimates of model (5.1)–(5.2), by age cohorts, employees with less than college education, marginal effects*[a]

Regressors	1948	1949	1950	1951
T	0.31 (0.00)[b]	0.25 (0.00)	0.32 (0.00)	0.33 (0.00)
T^2	−0.006 (0.00)	−0.04 (0.02)	−0.005 (0.00)	−0.004 (0.00)
TR	0.36 (0.00)	0.30 (0.00)	0.30 (0.00)	0.58 (0.00)
TR^2	−0.05 (0.00)	−0.04 (0.00)	−0.04 (0.00)	−0.09 (0.00)
D	−0.04 (0.16)	0.007 (0.82)	−0.06 (0.04)	−0.12 (0.00)
Pseudo R^2	0.32	0.30	0.29	0.37
Nobs	458	657	808	543
Corr $[\delta_i, D]$[c]	−0.746 [−6.33]	−0.281 [−3.12]	−0.439 [−4.15]	−0.911 [−4.17]

Regressors	1952	1953	1954	1955
T	0.34 (0.00)	0.27 (0.00)	0.47 (0.00)	0.45 (0.00)
T^2	−0.005 (0.02)	−0.003 (0.06)	−0.007 (0.00)	−0.006 (0.00)
TR	0.41 (0.00)	0.22 (0.00)	0.38 (0.00)	0.43 (0.00)
TR^2	−0.06 (0.00)	−0.02 (0.02)	−0.06 (0.00)	−0.06 (0.00)
D	−0.07 (0.11)	−0.04 (0.12)	−0.03 (0.42)	−0.06 (0.05)
Pseudo R^2	0.28	0.28	0.34	0.37
Nobs	796	860	734	1058
Corr $[\delta_i, D]$	−0.715 [−4.87]	−0.793 [−7.96]	−0.675 [−4.41]	0.187 [0.75]

Regressors	1956	1957	1958	Average
T	0.61 (0.00)	0.78 (0.00)	0.97 (0.00)	0.459
T^2	−0.008 (0.00)	−0.009 (0.03)	−0.02 (0.00)	−0.009
TR	0.40 (0.00)	0.24 (0.26)	0.18 (0.14)	0.344
TR^2	−0.08 (0.00)	−0.032 (0.58)	−0.04 (0.10)	−0.051
D	−0.11 (0.00)	−0.08 (0.18)	−0.15 (0.00)	−0.067
Pseudo R^2	0.37	0.46	0.43	
Nobs	723	471	765	
Corr $[\delta_i, D]$	−0.543 [−1.91]	−0.735 [−3.37]	−0.344 [−1.12]	

Notes:
[a]Each regression includes rank, time, and individual dummies.
[b]Probability values in parentheses and *t*-ratios in brackets.
[c]Corr $[\delta_i, D]$ is the estimated coefficient in the regression of the estimated individual effects on a constant term and on D.

Table 5.10 *Estimates of model (5.1)–(5.2), by age cohorts, employees with at least college education, marginal effects*

Regressors	1948	1949	1950	1951
T	0.24 (0.00)	0.25 (0.00)	0.39 (0.00)	0.43 (0.00)
T^2	−0.0002 (0.82)	−0.003 (0.01)	−0.003 (0.07)	−0.003 (0.09)
TR	0.32 (0.00)	0.32 (0.00)	0.23 (0.06)	0.57 (0.00)
TR^2	−0.06 (0.01)	−0.05 (0.00)	−0.06 (0.00)	−0.14 (0.00)
D	−0.07 (0.01)	−0.01 (0.64)	−0.09 (0.03)	−0.09 (0.07)
Pseudo R^2	0.31	0.28	0.30	0.36
Nobs	588	884	711	815
Corr $[\delta_i, D]$	−0.528 [−6.50]	−0.984 [−9.59]	−0.473 [−8.49]	−0.463 [−5.51]

Regressors	1952	1953	1954	1955
T	0.36 (0.00)	0.46 (0.00)	0.50 (0.00)	0.61 (0.00)
T^2	−0.002 (0.47)	−0.004 (0.16)	−0.005 (0.10)	−0.004 (0.27)
TR	0.71 (0.00)	0.66 (0.00)	0.31 (0.00)	0.24 (0.03)
TR^2	−0.17 (0.00)	−0.16 (0.00)	−0.09 (0.00)	−0.08 (0.00)
D	−0.13 (0.03)	−0.09 (0.06)	−0.13 (0.01)	−0.16 (0.04)
Pseudo R^2	0.35	0.36	0.35	0.41
Nobs	727	846	739	768
Corr $[\delta_i, D]$	−0.539 [−8.46]	−0.629 [−9.69]	−0.861 [−6.39]	−0.755 [−10.25]

Regressors	1956	1957	1958	Average
T	0.83 (0.00)	0.82 (0.00)	1.31 (0.00)	0.594
T^2	−0.006 (0.13)	−0.009 (0.04)	−0.020 (0.00)	−0.006
TR	0.52 (0.00)	0.35 (0.01)	0.51 (0.00)	0.435
TR^2	−0.19 (0.00)	−0.13 (0.00)	−0.20 (0.00)	−0.124
D	−0.39 (0.00)	−0.15 (0.01)	−0.14 (0.11)	−0.133
Pseudo R^2	0.43	0.43	0.49	–
Nobs	817	975	1007	–
Corr $[\delta_i, D]$	−1.103 [−11.14]	−1.187 [−7.38]	−1.595 [−8.59]	–

Note: For definitions, see table 5.9.

employees with less than college education. We also estimate that a conditional one-year increase of tenure in the rank increases the probability of promotion by 0.013 in the former group and by 0.152 in the latter group. Finally, a conditional one-year increase in the time to promotion to the current rank reduces the probability of promotion by 0.133 among college graduates and by 0.067 among employees with lower educational attainment. We draw from this that, even in the presence of significant fast-track effects, tenure in the firm remains the key factor for promotion to higher ranks.

Next, we investigate whether fast-track effects apply not only to higher but also to low–medium ranks. In previous sections of this chapter, we have presented evidence against the common view about late selection in promotion and showed that workers of this firm, who were recruited in a given year, start being differentiated in the speed of promotion from the early stages of their career. In particular, selection appears to begin within five years after regular recruitment. A related, but distinct, question is whether fast-track effects appear from the early stages of a career.[39] To answer this question, we estimate model (5.1)–(5.2) only for individuals whose current rank is low–medium – that is, between rank 5 and rank 8. It turns out that our results are qualitatively similar to those in table 5.9 and 5.10. In particular, the estimate of coefficient β_5 is consistently negative and significantly different from zero. This is additional evidence that fast-track effects characterize promotion outcomes, even for workers in low to medium ranks.

Firm growth and promotion policy

As mentioned above, the firm grew rapidly during the 1970s and the early 1980s, and at a much slower pace afterwards. The average annual rate of growth of real sales and employment during the period 1975–84 was, respectively, 19 and 14 percent. In the next 10 years, growth fell, respectively, to 3 and 2 percent. Because of this, total employment stabilized after years of rapid expansion.

An interesting question is whether these remarkable changes in the rate of growth of the firm had any significant impact on its HRM policies, and in particular on the patterns of promotion. To answer this question, we have run regressions similar to those presented in tables 5.9 and 5.10 after augmenting the set of explanatory variables with the annual rate of growth of real sales in the firm, but failed to detect a systematic relationship between this variable and the probability of promotion.

---

[39] This effect is also known as *star treatment*.

This result is apparently at variance with the view that higher growth fosters promotion of incumbent employees by creating vacancies in upper-rank positions.[40] A tentative explanation of our finding is that this firm, during its high-growth period, relied to a large extent on external hirings to fill vacancies in medium–high ranks, thus limiting the opportunities for the internal promotion of incumbents. Reliance on external hirings was perhaps unavoidable during that period, because the skills necessary to sustain growth could not be developed fast enough within the firm.[41]

Exits and promotion

As discussed above, the estimated effect of tenure on promotion could be biased by endogenous selection if leavers and stayers differ in their promotion outcomes. For instance, if leavers are less able and have a lower promotion probability than stayers, the sample of stayers turns out to be composed of individuals with long tenure, higher ability, and better promotion records. When unknown ability influences both promotion and the decision to stay or leave, tenure and the error term are correlated, and the estimated coefficient of tenure is biased.

In more detail, suppose that the observed pattern of promotion is generated by a variant of Jovanovic's learning model (Jovanovic, 1979), and assume that each rank represents the conditional expectation of unknown productivity which, in turn, is a time-invariant random variable drawn from a common distribution. In this case, the presence of unknown heterogeneity generates the well known upward bias in cross-section regressions of wages (or promotion) on tenure, because less productive employees quit. Whether or not such a bias contaminates our panel regressions depends crucially upon the extent to which the fixed individual effect captures variations in unknown productivity. If, as in Jovanovic's original formulation, heterogeneity is fully represented by an additive and time-invariant random variable, the estimated coefficient of tenure in our regressions is unbiased, with the only major departure from the standard set of assumptions being the non-normality of the error term.[42]

---

[40] See Aoki (1982) and chapter 10.
[41] The trade off between internal promotion and external recruitment is discussed by Lazear (1995) and Chan (1996). In particular, Lazear argues that "the more heterogeneity there is in the population, the more likely is outside hiring" (1995, p. 136). The reason is that the difference between outsider and insider ability must be large for the firm to be willing to hire outsiders.
[42] See Jovanovic (1979); Lancaster (1990).

To check whether leavers and stayers differ in their promotion outcomes, we can use the information on only about 200 individuals who quit the firm between 1994 and 1996. Using this information, we have augmented (5.1) with the interactions between each explanatory variable and a dummy equal to one if the individual left in the last two years and to zero otherwise, and tested for the joint significance of these additional terms. It turns out that we can never reject the null hypothesis that stayers and leavers exhibit a similar behavior. Additional evidence is provided by the Kaplan–Meier survivor functions, similar to those described in figures 5.2–5.9. The log rank tests on the absence of significant differences in the survival rates of stayers and leavers cannot reject the null in most cases.[43]

The lack of a significant difference in the promotion outcomes of leavers and stayers could be driven by the fact that our information on leavers is far from complete. For instance, leavers are likely to be concentrated among young employees. Since many leavers in our sample have been with this firm for more than 10 years, we could be simply missing the core of turnover behavior. Needless to say, a more satisfactory treatment of turnover must await better data.[44]

Recruitment methods and promotion policy

The evidence presented so far indicates that there are systematic differences in the way the firm treats regular and irregular recruits. That regulars and irregulars are treated differently in promotion tournaments, not only in the firm studied in this chapter, is without dispute, at least in Japan.

We have shown that this firm manages promotions of regular recruits to each rank by using benchmark years. When ranks are relatively low, the majority of employees belonging to the same cohort are promoted to a specific rank in the benchmark year. We find no evidence of benchmarking for irregular recruits. In a sense, this is to be expected: conditional upon education and the year of entry, regular recruits of a particular cohort have more or less the same age, have entered the labor market and have been screened at the same time, and have similar job assignments, in terms of both skill requirements and responsibility. Benchmarking does not work nearly as well for irregulars: recruits of a

---

[43] The p-value of the test is 0.023 for rank 3, 0.123 for rank 5, 0.558 for rank 7, and 0.134 for rank 9.
[44] In future work, we plan to obtain better information on turnover behavior by using the same methodology employed in this chapter and extending it to additional annual updates on the promotion history of this firm.

given cohort have different experience and age, and are initially allocated to a wider range of ranks. Accordingly, their work assignment, responsibility, and positions differ from the start.

Our findings also suggest that benchmarking applies only to relatively homogeneous cohorts, and is more likely for regular recruits with limited experience in the firm, who have been hired at the headquarters. Although benchmarking in promotion earmarks an important distinction between regular and irregular recruits, it is not clear whether overall promotion prospects differ between the two groups.

To investigate this issue, we have run regressions that replace individual fixed effects with time-invariant characteristics such as years of education and previous labor market experience outside the firm. It turns out that the latter variable attracts a negative and significant coefficient among college graduates (p-value = 4.7 percent). Its marginal effect on promotion, however, is very small. We have also run regressions with fixed effects separately for regulars and irregulars, but found no substantial differences between the two groups.

These findings suggest that differences in the promotion outcomes between the two groups reflect primarily differences in the underlying heterogeneity of candidates, rather than a different promotion policy.

Discussion

We have found that, in firm ABO, promotion outcomes are positively influenced by both tenure in the firm and tenure in the rank; fast-tracks effects are significant; fast tracks persist even after controlling for innate ability; and early differentiation in promotion is sharper among irregular recruits.

As we have argued above, it is difficult to explain most of these results by a pure learning model, where individuals differ only because of their innate and time-invariant ability. Although our results are consistent with different models of promotion, our preferred story is a human capital model that incorporates heterogeneity of jobs and skills, such as in the model presented in chapter 2. Such a model can explain all our major findings in a coherent manner.[45]

Assuming that the positive correlation between tenure and promotion remains even after controlling for endogenous selection, this correlation can easily be explained if skills are firm-specific. Fast-track effects that survive even after controlling for individual fixed effects naturally arise if

---

[45] See also the discussion in Gibbons and Waldman (1999).

the employees who are best in the accumulation of the required skills in lower-ranked jobs receive more intensive training, which makes them more likely to perform better in upper-rank jobs as well. The difference in the intensity of training received by employees early on can account for the persistent negative effect of time spent in the promotion to the current rank on promotion outcomes.

Overall, our findings suggest that the promotion policy of this firm deviates in important ways from the stylized view of promotion in large Japanese firms. At the same time, we find concrete signs that some of the features considered typical of Japanese firms are present also in this firm. First, tenure in the firm has a large and positive impact on the probability of promotion. Second, regular recruits are allocated initially to ranks on the basis of their education and have a similar career history for the first three or four years after recruitment. In this limited sense, this firm appears to intentionally ignore individual differences very early on in the first promotion rounds.

Evidence from other firms

In this subsection, we consider additional evidence on promotion patterns drawn from the *Bekkan Chuo Roudou Jihou*, a specialized magazine that contains the records of trials held in Japanese local labor courts because of alleged unfair labor practices. The personnel data extracted from this magazine refer to a branch of a local bank, to an elevator maintenance company, and to two local TV network companies.

The data from the local bank and from the elevator maintenance company include information on the evaluation of individual performance, and can be used to investigate the relationship between this evaluation and promotion. On the other hand, the data from the two TV network companies do not include information on performance evaluation, but contain the promotion history of employees.

The local bank has more than 1,000 employees and is organized in a ranking hierarchy of 9 ranks. Promotion to higher ranks depends on both the evaluation of performance and oral and written exams. The available data refer to the subset of 336 employees in ranks 4–6. The elevator maintenance company has close to 4,000 employees and a ranking hierarchy composed of eight ranks below division director (*kacho*). Finally, with about 250 employees each, the two TV network companies are smaller in size and have a less sophisticated career ladder than firms B and C.

Starting from the two broadcasting companies (firms D and E), available information includes firm-specific tenure, education, age, year of entry in the firm, and year of promotion to a hierarchical rank. This information allows us to compute both complete and interrupted spells in a hierarchical rank and to relate these spells to individual character- istics and time spent in the firm. In particular, let us define the survival time in a rank as the time interval from entry to exit from the rank. This interval is a random variable with distribution function $F(\tau) = \text{Prob}(\tau \leqslant t)$. The survivor function is defined as the probability that a spell is still alive at time t and is denoted as $R(t) = 1 - F(t)$. Given that the spell is alive at time t, the probability that it will end with promotion to a higher rank between t and $t + dt$ is given by $f(\tau \mid \tau > t)$. At time $\tau = t$ the conditional density is a function of t alone and is known as the hazard rate

$$h(t) = f(\tau \mid \tau \geq t) = -\frac{r(t)}{R(t)}$$

where $r(t) = R'(t)$.

Assuming a proportional hazard model and a Weibull distribution for the baseline hazard and simplifying the hierarchical structure of each firm into three ranks (low, medium, high), we estimate the following empirical model[46]

$$h(t) = t^{\alpha} \exp(\beta_0 + \beta_1 T + \beta_2 E + \beta_3 A + \beta_4 D + v) \tag{5.3}$$

where T is individual tenure in the firm, E is a dummy for educational attainment, equal to one for upper secondary and tertiary education and to zero otherwise, A is age at entry in the firm, and D is the time to promotion to the current rank. If the firm under study organizes labor in an internal labor market, we expect seniority to affect the hazard positively. Conditional on seniority, age of entry and education are also expected to have a positive impact on the hazard, because they signal either the accumulation of previous labor market experience or ability to learn. Finally, time to promotion to the current rank should affect the probability of promotion to the next rank negatively if there are fast tracks in promotion. The results of the estimate of (5.3) are presented in table 5.11 for firm D and in table 5.12 for firm E.[47]

Overall, the empirical evidence suggests that firm-specific tenure, edu- cation, and age of entry affect the hazard positively. Furthermore, con- ditional on seniority, age, and education, the hazard to a higher rank is

[46] We obtain qualitatively similar results with a Cox proportional hazard model.
[47] Owing to the nature of the data, we do not have information on attrition, and in particular on those workers who have quit the firm.

Table 5.11 *Weibull hazard model, firm D; dependent variable: hazard to ranks 1, 2, and 3, the regressions include a constant and a duration dependence parameter*

	Coefficients		
Variables	Rank 1	Rank 2	Rank3
Higher than sec. edu.	1.819 (0.177)[a]	1.518 (0.367)	−0.109 (0.230)
Tenure	0.141 (0.034)	0.306 (0.058)	−0.025 (0.042)
Age at entry	0.083 (0.031)	0.027 (0.047)	0.030 (0.036)
Time to promotion to current rank	–	−0.138 (0.061)	−0.013 (0.034)
Pseudo R^2	0.250	0.265	0.150
Nobs	166	166	166

Note: [a]Standard errors in parentheses.

generally lower the higher the number of years spent in the previous rank. Thus, fast flyers in the bottom rank are likely to fly faster to the medium and the high rank, and there is evidence of the presence of fast tracks. The positive and significant impact of seniority on the hazard suggests that the two local broadcasting firms considered in this study tend to favor incumbents in the promotion decision, much in line with ILM-type firms. At the same time, available information on both recruiting and the treatment of employees with special skills indicates that a significant share of the employees in these firms are trained outside the firm. Special skills include broadcasting and program production jobs, such as cameraman, news editor, program director, and designer.

When seniority matters, perhaps because firm-specific human capital is accumulated with time spent in the firm, promotion decisions do not rely exclusively on performance.[48] Other things being equal, senior employees have an advantage over junior staff. Many popular descriptions of the Japanese employment system have over-played the importance of promotion by seniority, raising questions on the specific incentive design adopted by (mainly large) Japanese firms. These popular views have been corrected by the influential work of Aoki (1988) and Koike (1988), who stress that strong competition among peers is at least as important as seniority in the promotion decision.[49]

[48] See Abraham and Medoff (1985).
[49] Work in this area includes Tachibanaki (1995).

Table 5.12 *Weibull hazard model, firm E; dependent variable: hazard from ranks 1, 2, and 3, the regressions include a constant and a duration dependence parameter*

	Coefficients		
Variables	Rank 1	Rank 2	Rank 3
Higher than sec. edu.	0.994 (0.269)[a]	1.709 (0.430)	0.934 (0.557)
Tenure	−0.123 (0.036)	0.304 (0.072)	0.248 (0.057)
Age at entry	0.041 (0.036)	0.074 (0.050)	0.093 (0.053)
Time to promotion to current rank	–	0.027 (0.115)	−0.087 (0.061)
Pseudo R^2	0.146	0.113	0.12
Nobs	88	88	88

Note: [a]Standard errors in parentheses.

The personnel data of firms B and C, containing information on the evaluation of performance, allow us to ascertain the relative importance of tenure and performance in the promotion decision. Information on employees of firm B includes age, education, performance evaluation, tenure in the rank, and eventual promotion to a higher rank.[50] Information on employees of firm C is more limited and includes only age adjusted for years of education, performance evaluation, union membership, and eventual promotion to a higher rank.[51]

Table 5.13 presents the results of probit models of the probability of promotion to a higher rank for both firms. Starting from firm B, the estimates suggest that both seniority (overall and in the rank) and performance matter for promotion. Turning to firm C, our results indicate that age net of education, a close proxy to seniority, does not affect significantly the promotion decision, that relies only on performance evaluation. This evidence suggests that firm B fits well into the ILM-type firm, where internal promotion is important, while firm C is closer to the OLM-type firm, where incumbents and outsiders compete on merit, with little influence of seniority.

[50] See Tomita (1992) for more details.
[51] See Ohtake (1994).

Table 5.13 *Probit estimates of the probability of promotion to a higher rank, firm B and firm C; the dependent variable is a dummy variable equal to one in the event of promotion, and to zero otherwise*

	Coefficients	
Variables	Firm B	Firm C
Tenure	1.062 (0.285)[a]	–
Tenure squared	−0.023 (0.007)	–
Age	−0.042 (0.018)	−1.204 (1.04)
Age squared	–	0.017 (0.01)
Tenure in the rank	0.223 (0.042)	–
Job evaluation	0.619 (0.110)	1.334 (0.267)
Log likelihood	−146.3	−39.92
Nobs	334	172

Note: [a]Standard errors in parentheses.

A review of the evidence

In this section, we compare four case studies of internal labor markets, including a middle-sized firm in the US service industry, studied by Baker, Gibbs and Holmstrom (1994a, hereafter firm BGH), a large Japanese steel firm studied by Imada and Hirata (1995, hereafter firm IH), our own study of a large hi-tech firm, discussed in the first part of this chapter (firm ABO), and a Japanese subsidiary of a large US bank, studied by Itoh, Kumagai and Ohtake (1998, hereafter firm IKO). The primary reason for choosing these four firms is the relative richness of available information. Not only do these studies offer a detailed econometric analysis of internal labor markets, they also provide a wide range of information on institutional design, hierarchical structure, and major recent changes. Table 5.14 summarizes the key features of these firms.

Firm BGH

We use this firm as the benchmark for the three Japanese cases. It is clear that this firm represents reasonably well the main features of internal labor markets in American firms. First of all, this firm experiences sizeable turnover and the average annual exit rate for employees in the bottom levels of the hierarchy is 12 percent. Promotion flows and exit flows are comparable in size in the lower rungs of the career ladder.

Table 5.14 *Key features of the four firms*

	IH	ABO	IKO	BGH
Country	Japan	Japan	Japan	United States
Industry	Manufacturing	Manufacturing	Banking	Services
Size (000)	35	4–13	0.5–1.5	3–10
Firm growth	Slow	Fast/Slow	Fast	Fast
Number of divisions	Small	Large	Large	–
Centralized recruiting	Yes	Limited	Limited	–
% Irregular recruits	Small	Large	Majority	Large
Job rotation	Yes	Yes	–	–
SSS	Yes	Yes	No	No
Multiple ports of entry	No	Yes	Yes	Yes
Annual exit rate (%)	1	2–4	Large	12–15
Late selection	Yes	Partially yes	No	No
Fast tracks	Partially Yes	Yes	Yes	Yes
Tenure effects	Yes	Yes	Partially yes	Negative

Recruitment occurs in multiple ports of entry, and the selection of incumbents for upper-level ranks starts at the very early stage of a career. Controlling for other variables, tenure in the firm has a relevant negative effect on promotion, a feature shared by many similar studies of American firms. While institutional details are scarce, we notice that this firm decentralizes recruitment, promotion, and pay decisions. BGH also rejects the hypothesis that individual pay follows a rigid administrative rule and is governed primarily by position and performance.

Firm IH

This firm is diametrically different from BGH, and in almost every aspect it confirms the conventional wisdom on Japanese internal labor markets. Key features include: (a) relatively rigid administrative rules controlling the speed of promotion; (b) benchmarking based upon the year of entry; (c) a strong preference in recruitment for new school graduates; (d) regular rotation and frequent horizontal transfer of employees. The institutional setup is also highly typical and includes a highly centralized personnel policy, the SSS skill-based pay system (*Shokuno Shikaku Seido*), with its emphasis on horizontal ranks, and an enterprise union. The exit rate is extremely low, at less than 1 percent per year.

Firm ABO

As we saw above, the firm studied in this chapter is something of a mixed breed but, we believe, well within the spectrum of the prototype Japanese large firm. The firm shares with other major Japanese firms important institutional features. For instance, the building block of ILM policy is the SSS ranking and pay system. Although limited in scope, the promotion policy shows clear signs of benchmarking, at least among regular recruits. Regular job rotation is observed, and we also find that the centralized personnel department integrates recruitment, personnel evaluation, and pay determination. At the same time, however, this firm also deviates from the stylized model. First of all, irregular recruits are a very important source of hiring, and this firm hires a significant share of its employees to fill vacancies in relatively high ranks. In essence, we find evidence of multiple ports of entry. Moreover, and in spite of nearly automatic promotion from the bottom rank, the selection process in this firm starts quite early, and there is evidence of fast-track effects.

Firm IKO

This firm is a subsidiary of a large US bank. As shown in table 5.14, this firm has little in common with other Japanese firms and much in common with a typical American firm, including a selection process that starts quite early (earlier than in ABO), the absence of automatic promotion even from the bottom rank, a share of irregular recruits higher than 50 percent in most recent years, and multiple ports of entry. This firm uses a variant of the Hey system for pay determination, and individual pay is primarily determined by (vertical) position and performance. One feature that deviates from the American norm is that recruiting, personnel evaluation, and pay hikes are controlled by the centralized personnel department.[52]

Discussion

An important feature of internal labor markets is recruitment. At the Japanese end of the spectrum we find a strong preference for new school graduates, emphasizing potential rather than tangible qualifications or tested skills and expertise. At the American end of the spectrum, we find that recruitment typically fills vacancies available for specific positions. The emphasis there is clearly on specific skills and experience. Not surprisingly, the behavior of employees is affected by hiring policies. Both in BGH and IKO, employees are highly mobile across firms, attrition rates are close to 10 percent per year, and exits and promotions are equally important instruments of labor allocation. On the other hand, exits are unavoidable anomalies in firms such as IH, and promotion is the dominant instrument of labor allocation. Emphasis on tangible qualifications and specific skills is also the hallmark of decentralized personnel policy. ABO, our sample firm, also exhibits some of these characteristics.

In chapter 2, we characterized late selection policy in promotion as a process where the internal labor market provides career opportunities to develop skill formation and human capital investment. The hallmark of such a policy is highly selective recruitment and uniform treatment of new entrants. Firms BGH and IKO do not meet this crucial condition, and there is clear evidence that new entrants are not treated equally, even from the beginning. The case study on IKO reports, for example, that new entrants with an MBA start their career as lower management, a rank that is almost out of reach for entrants with "only" a BA degree.

---

[52] IKO reports that the current system is the product of a large-scale institutional change that occurred in 1992. Before the change, each division had its own personnel department and HRM was highly decentralized.

Although ABO does hire a large share of workers with substantial previous work experience, who are immediately assigned to lower–middle management positions, we find no evidence that new school graduates are treated differently to the extent found in IKO.[53]

Given the observed differences, we believe that the best way to characterize the internal labor market in ABO is the dual-track system, with one track relatively close to the American model and the other close to the Japanese model. There are reasons to believe that such a dual-track system emerged as a compromise between the need to hire skilled employees in the high-growth period and the imperatives of long-term employment. Recall that ABO is a high-tech firm with a world-wide reputation, and that the majority of its employees are engineers who constitute the core skills of the firm. When ABO grew rapidly, the demand for skilled workers also grew so rapidly that it could not be met solely by internal promotion. At the same time, it is clear that the mixture of unique skills and knowledge could not easily be recruited from external labor markets. In the long run, the firm needed to develop its own internal labor market capable of training these workers internally.

While turnover is more important in the American end of the spectrum, firms do not rely exclusively upon external labor markets to fill managerial white-collar jobs. Even for BGH, outside hirings into higher levels of the hierarchy diminish rapidly as we move up the ladder: evidence from that firm suggests that only 10 percent of the employees in job levels 5–8 are hired into those levels, compared to 25–30 percent in lower levels (2–4).

These remarks suggest that the degree of internal training and promotion depends crucially upon the nature of skills and competency requirements in each job position. Japanese HRM policy is perhaps best viewed as an attempt to extend to other jobs methods and tools developed for white-collar managerial jobs. In this sense, late selection can be naturally interpreted as a hybrid promotion policy. In the lower layers of the hierarchy, promotion is a skill-development process, guided by a program of career progression. In the middle and higher layers, discretionary managerial capability dominates over skill development and the competition for higher positions is almost entirely performance/merit-based, even in firms such as IH.

---

[53] It is a standard practice among Japanese firms to allocate entrants to different initial ranks depending upon their education. In ABO, high school graduates start one rank immediately below the initial rank for college graduates.

Summary

In this chapter we have presented results on recruitment and promotion based upon personnel data of five Japanese firms. These data trade off the advantage of being a detailed representation of HRM policies with the disadvantage of being not representative of the universe of large Japanese firms. Since the quality of the available information is much superior in the case of firm ABO, the study of this firm has taken most of the space allotted in the chapter.

Our analysis partly confirms and partly casts some doubts on the well known stylized facts about career development in large Japanese firms, including late selection in promotion and a strong preference for regular recruits. In one firm where we have data, we have found both that irregular recruits are important and that there are multiple ports of entry and exit for such recruits.

In most of the firms studied in this chapter, firm-specific tenure matters for promotion, either because it affects the hazard to a higher rank or because it influences the probability of promotion. Merit, however, is also important, and in one case is the key determinant of promotion. Importantly, the relevance of seniority in the promotion decision does not imply that the speed of promotion is equal. Conditional on tenure and education, our evidence suggests that fast flyers in lower ranks are more likely to fly faster to higher ranks. The presence of fast promotion tracks suggests that individual performance, given seniority and other individual characteristics, is likely also to pay in large Japanese firms operating internal labor markets.

6 Product market competition and internal labor markets

Overview[1]

In this chapter we study the *interactions between competition within the firm and competition among firms* in the labor market. Our main objectives are: (1) to evaluate the degree of insulation of internal labor markets from competition in the external labor market; (2) to measure the interactions between internal labor market (ILM) arrangements and product market competition.

Perhaps the clearest picture that we can draw on these issues follows the logical implications of the *iron law of competition*. According to this law, a firm cannot enforce any arrangement that can be over-ruled by competition. Most of the arrangements discussed in this book so far cannot be implemented unless firms and employees are to some extent insulated from the discipline of the external labor market.

Take, for example, the *late selection approach* investigated in chapter 5. Unless the firm has an information advantage with respect to other firms over the quality of its employees, or there are frictions preventing employees from freely seeking their best employers, such a policy is clearly untenable. Given the fact that the large majority of white-collar workers in large Japanese firms tends to stay with one firm for an extended period of time, there is little doubt that firms do have at least some room to choose and design their employment and wage policy in order to meet specific needs and conditions. An important question to ask is thus to what extent these firms are insulated from the external labor market.

In a related perspective, there is a relatively large literature that argues that observed cross-sectional wage differences are the result of *rent-sharing*.[2] In a nutshell, the argument is that firms with higher than normal

---

[1] This chapter draws upon Ariga and Ohkusa (1997).
[2] See, for instance, Dickens and Katz (1987); Brunello and Wadhwani (1989); Blanchflower, Oswald and Sanfey (1996); Nickell (1998).

profits can afford to pay their employees higher than normal wages. While this hypothesis does not immediately imply that higher wages affect productivity, another well known strand of the literature suggests that causality runs from institutional arrangements to product market performance. In particular, the *efficiency wage hypothesis* suggests that firms pay higher wages to their employees in order to induce higher effort and/or loyal behavior.

The ability to compete in the *product* market is clearly important for a variety of arrangements that we observe in internal labor markets. For instance, generous rewards for good individual performance may not be possible unless firms can compete with their rivals and successfully sell their products in the market. At the same time, competition in the product market can be an effective means to discipline workers.

The *Lifeboat Principle* is based on such an idea. This principle states that competition inside the firm (among employees) and outside the firm (among firms) are *substitutes* in the following sense: keener competition in the product market acts as a disciplinary device against non-performing employees, and is a substitute for the internal incentives that firms facing relaxed competition must provide.[3]

As argued by Aoki (1988), institutional arrangements do not develop separately but are often bunched together. In the Japanese economic context, a firm with strong ties to a bank tends to have both close and long-term relationships with suppliers and arrangements with employees that emphasize long-term mutual commitment. *Institutional complementarity*, as it stands, cannot be observed when markets are complete and competitively organized.

In this chapter we look at these complex issues from a somewhat narrower angle and try to capture, from an empirical standpoint, the observed deviations of Japanese wage and employment policies from what we expect to prevail when labor markets are competitive. We also want to relate these deviations to the degree of product market competition. The plan of the chapter is as follows. We first introduce the data and present our cross-section evidence on inter-industry wage differentials, wage–tenure profiles, product market markups, and other variables that capture the institutional characteristics of the firms in our sample. We then investigate whether the wage paid by individual firms deviates in a significant way from the competitive baseline. The next section is devoted to the study of the correlation of wages and other key features of internal labor markets with product market competition. Here, we use

---

[3] See Williamson (1985) for a detailed discussion.

the estimates of individual firm markups obtained by Nishimura, Ohkusa and Ariga (1999). Finally, we present a critical assessment of the relative merits of alternative theories in the light of the findings of the previous sections. A brief summary concludes the chapter.

Inter-industry variations in wages and product market markups

Data and estimated markups

Our data are drawn from the financial statements and annual reports of all the non-financial firms listed in the major stock exchanges of Japan, organized in electronic archives by the Japan Development Bank. The selected sample period covers all the even years from 1972 to 1994. For each firm, these financial data are integrated with data on the number of employees and on average wages drawn from the Company Yearbook (*Kaisha Nenkan*), published annually by the *Nihon Keizai Shinbun*, the leading Japanese economic newspaper.

Our measure of the degree of competition in the product market is based upon the estimates of the markup of prices over marginal costs discussed by Nishimura, Ohkusa and Ariga (1999). The appendix (p. 183) presents a brief description of the model and of the estimation procedure used in the calculations. The information on labor available in our data is rather limited and includes the average wage in the firm, w, average *age*, and average *tenure*. We use these data to run the following three regressions for each firm and to estimate the slope of wage–tenure and wage–age profiles:

$$w_t^i = \alpha_0^1 + \alpha_1^1 tenure_t^i + \alpha_2^1 tenure_t^{i2} \qquad (6.1a)$$
$$w_t^i = \alpha_0^2 + \alpha_1^2 tenure_t^i$$
$$w_t^i = \alpha_0^3 + \alpha_1^3 tenure_t^i + \alpha_2^3 age_t^i$$

where α are parameters, i is for the firm, and t is for time. These regressions are run under the maintained assumption that the wage structure has remained constant during the sample period. Information on annual average wages is used to normalize wage data across the years. The dependent variable is thus measured relative to the average wage. We use the estimated intercepts in these regressions as our measures of the entrance wage, *iniw*. Hence we have

$$iniw1^i = \alpha_0^1$$
$$iniw2^i = \alpha_0^2$$
$$iniw3^i = \alpha_0^3 + \alpha_2^3 * 22$$

where we assume that average age when labor market entry occurs is 22. Our preferred measure of the slope of the wage–tenure profile, *wslop*, is α_1^1, and we define a dummy variable, *yslop*, equal to one if α_1^1 is positive and statistically significant and to zero otherwise.[4]

Some inter-firm and industry comparisons

Table 6.1 presents the summary statistics of the estimated product market markup, the initial wage, and the slope of wage profiles, all available at the firm level. Table 6.2 is devoted to an inter-industry comparison of the major variables used in the analysis below, the price markup, μ, a measure of the initial wage, *iniw2*, and the slope of the wage–tenure profile.[5]

The simple inspection of tables 6.1 and 6.2 suggests the following. First, there is evidence of a fairly strong negative correlation between the initial wage (*iniw*) and the price markup. Second, the correlation between the markup and either *wslop* or *yslop* is positive. Therefore, firms with higher price markups have steeper wage profiles and relatively low initial wages. While these correlations are relatively high at the micro level, they are close to zero when we aggregate at the two-digit industrial level.

The inter-industry variations in the price markups shown in table 6.2 are broadly in line with the results on inter-industry comparisons of price (average)–cost margins found in the literature (see Odagiri and Yamashita, 1987). In particular, we notice that industries with significant increasing returns to scale have higher price–cost margins. Examples include pharmaceuticals, petroleum, and ship-building. Markups are generally lower in assembly industries such as automobiles and mechanical engineering. Exceptions to these tendencies are electrical appliances (high markup) and pulp and paper (low markup).

Furthermore, initial wages are relatively low in the petroleum, foodstuffs, textiles, steel, and nonferrous metal industries, and relatively high among manufacturing sectors, in chemistry, pharmaceuticals, and ship-building. The numbers in table 6.2 are roughly comparable to the results of previous studies, including Tachibanaki and Ohta (1996). If we compare firms of different employment size (see panel (2) of table 6.2), we also find that larger firms (with more than 5,000 employees) have somewhat steeper wage profiles, significantly higher markups and higher initial

---

[4] In principle, we should include in this measure parameter α_2^1 as well. Since, however, the estimated coefficients for α_2^1 were not in many cases statistically significant, we decided to use only α_1^1.

[5] The results using *iniw1* and *iniw3* (not reported) are similar.

Table 6.1 *Summary statistics*

Variable	Mean	St.dev.	Min	Max	Median
Markup	1.55	0.48	0.83	2.66	1.28
*iniw*1	5.53	1.93	0.55	10.82	6.24
*iniw*2	5.81	0.52	3.96	6.34	5.93
*iniw*3	5.86	0.52	4.03	6.48	5.94
wslop	0.0077	0.035	−0.034	0.13	0.0032
yslop	0.175	0.087	0	0.436	0.158

Correlation matrix

	Markup	*iniw*1	*iniw*2	*iniw*3	*wslop*	*yslop*
Markup	1	–	–	–	–	–
*iniw*1	−0.199	1	–	–	–	–
*iniw*2	−0.301	0.666	1	–	–	–
*iniw*3	−0.292	0.690	0.983	1	–	–
wslop	0.431	−0.687	−0.966	−0.975	1	–
yslop	0.426	−0.318	−0.469	−0.474	0.558	1

wages.[6] In the manufacturing sector, the average markup of firms with more than 5,000 employees is 25 percent higher than that of smaller firms.[7]

External and internal labor markets

In this section we analyze to what extent individual firms can choose their wage policy freely – that is, without causing substantial inflows or outflows of their employees. This is equivalent to investigating in the Japanese institutional context to what extent the wage policy of individual firms is insulated from the pressure of the external labor market.

We start by pooling firms over time and by running the following regressions for average tenure and for the average wage rate

[6] Notice that most listed firms have more than 1,000 employees.
[7] A robust finding about wage differentials in Japan is the presence of strong firm size effects (see Tachinabaki and Ohta, 1996). Our results suggest that at least part of these wage differentials are associated with the higher price markups practiced by larger firms, not necessarily with firm size *per se*.

Table 6.2 *Inter-industry comparisons*
Panel (1) *Two-digit industries*

	Markup	iniw2	yslop		Markup	iniw2	yslop
Fishery	1.953	5.623	0.157	Shipbuilding	1.419	6.334	na
Mining	1.230	5.604	0.282	Automobiles	1.276	6.268	0.115
Construction	2.662	5.966	0.230	Other transp.	1.272	5.920	0.270
Foodstuffs	1.387	5.641	0.117	Precision mach.	1.280	5.863	0.315
Textiles	1.216	5.707	0.158	Other mfg.	1.530	5.990	0.114
Pulp and paper	1.188	5.801	0.106	Wholesale	2.167	3.961	0.321
Chemicals	1.230	6.074	0.070	Retail	1.290	6.172	0.214
Pharmaceuticals	1.825	6.214	0.307	Other land transp.	na	4.447	na
Petroleum	1.402	5.678	0.102	Merchant marine	na	5.748	na
Rubber	1.168	5.810	0.436	Aviation	na	6.043	0.171
Glass and cement	1.206	5.936	0.159	Storage	1.660	6.066	0.338
Steel	1.222	5.723	0.252	Communications	0.833	6.059	0.000
Non-ferrous metals	1.187	5.895	0.186	Electricity	1.853	6.032	0.000
Industrial mach.	1.263	5.975	0.139	Gas	1.555	6.179	0.234
Electric appl.	1.830	5.933	0.165	Other services	1.205	5.845	0.214

Note: na = Not available.

Table 6.2 (continued)

Panel (2) Inter-industry and firm-size comparisons

	Manufacturing		Services	
	Large[a]	Medium	Large[a]	Medium
iniw2	5.966	5.919	6.102	6.099
yslop	0.159	0.151	0.000	0.0057
Markup	1.627	1.256	1.338	1.396

Note: [a]Firms with more than 5,000 employees.

$$tenure_t^i = \alpha_0^i + \alpha_1 age_t^i + \alpha_2 n_t^i + \alpha_3 \mu_t^i + \alpha_4 mainb_t^i \qquad (6.1)$$

$$\log(w_t^{ik}) = \beta_0^i + \beta_1 age_t^i + \beta_2 tenure_t^i + \beta_3 \mu_t^i + \beta_4 mainb_t^i$$

$$+ \beta_5 \log\left[(va/n)_t^i\right] + \beta_6 \overline{wage}_t^k \qquad (6.2)$$

where i is for firm, k for industry and n, μ, va, $\overline{wage}^k$, and *mainb* are, respectively, the number of employees, the estimated markup, value added, the log of the industrial average wage, and a dummy taking the value one if the firm has a main bank relationship and zero otherwise.[8] Each regression includes both year and industry dummies. While (6.1) is estimated by ordinary least squares, (6.2) is estimated by instrumental variables, to take into account the potential endogeneity of both value added per head and the markup. Additional instruments are the lagged value of value added per head, the lagged markup, and the index of industrial productivity. The results are presented in table 6.3.

If longer average tenure can be taken as a measure of the degree of internalization of labor markets,[9] the regression results clearly show that firms with a higher price markup and/or a larger size, measured by the number of employees, are more likely to have well developed internal labor markets. The positive firm-size effect is not very surprising, as

---

[8] See Aoki and Patrick (1994) for a discussion of main bank relationships in Japan. In this chapter, a firm has a main bank if (a) the largest lender to the firm is a commercial bank; (b) the bank is one of the top 20 shareholders; (c) the bank has at least one of its employees on the executive board of the firm. By definition, there can be more than one main bank for a firm. Occasionally, the main bank changes for the same firm over time.

[9] The discussion in chapter 3 shows that this is an imperfect measure of the degree of internalization.

Table 6.3 *Regressions of tenure and average wages in individual firms, 1972–1994*

Dependent variable	Tenure		log(w)
Age	0.806***	0.800***	0.0046***
Markup	0.151**	0.162**	0.054***
log(*employment*)	0.297***	0.299***	–
Main bank	–	−0.171	−0.014
Tenure	–	–	0.010
log(*value added/emp.*)	–	–	$8.08e^{-8}$
log(*industry wage*)	–	–	0.928***
$\bar{R}^2$(*overall*)	0.74	0.71	0.45
Nobs (no. of firms)	892	892	934

Notes: ***Significant at the 1 percent level of confidence. **Significant at the 5 percent level of confidence.
Each regression includes year and industry dummies.

larger firms are known to have longer average tenure, in Japan and elsewhere. The positive and relatively strong effect of the markup on average tenure is less obvious. This result clearly demonstrates that firms with a more relaxed competition in the product market are better insulated from the pressures of the external labor market.

Turning to the average wage, our results suggest that, after controlling for the industry average wage, average age, and tenure, the firm-price markup has a significant and positive impact on the firm average wage. Compared to the relatively clear effect of the price markup, the main bank dummy is not statistically significant and its coefficient takes a negative sign in both regressions. Finally, and conditional on the price markup, *per capita* value added does not appear to affect average wages.

These findings are consistent with the *rent-sharing* view, in the sense that firms with higher price markups have stabler employment relationships (longer average tenure) and pay higher wages. They also suggest the presence of an important link between product market competition and the characteristics of the employment relationship in individual firms.

Interactions with product market competition and firm performance

In this section, we focus on the effects of internal labor markets on firm productivity. To do so, we estimate a translog production function after augmenting it with variables that capture the institutional arrangements typical of internal labor markets.[10] In particular, we define

$$\log(q_t^i) = \alpha_0 + F[\log(K_t^i), \log(L_t^i)] + \beta\mu_t^i + \gamma Z^i + \delta mainb_t^i \quad (6.3)$$

where $F(\cdot)$ is a translog production function, K_t^i is the capital stock, L_t^i is employment, μ_t^i is the estimated markup, Z^i is a vector that captures the wage policy of firms, including one of the following variables: the estimated initial wage (*iniw*), the estimated slope of the wage–tenure profile (*wslop*), and the dummy variable (*yslop*).

In this specification, both the wage policy, Z, and the degree of product market competition, μ, are considered as fixed effects and are treated as exogenous to firm output. Notice that output, q, is expressed at market prices, depending by definition on the markup, μ. We take this into account by dividing output, q, by the average markup. If real output is not correlated with the price markup, the coefficient β should be approximately equal to zero.

Table 6.4 uses the initial wage as the variable representing the wage policy of the firm, and shows unambiguously the following three points. First, the price markup has a large and highly significant negative effect on firm productivity. The effect is also quantitatively important, because a 10 percent increase in the average price markup can reduce value added by 1.7 percent. As the last three columns in table 6.4 show, the negative impact of the markup on value added is even stronger when we use as dependent variable the value added divided by the estimated markup.

Second, the main bank dummy attracts a positive and significant sign, suggesting that firms with a main bank relationship are likely to be more productive. Third, a higher initial wage reduces value added. The effect is negative and significant when we use definitions *iniw*1 and *iniw*2 for the initial wage, positive but not significant when we use definition *iniw*3.

Table 6.5 uses the dummy variable, *yslop*, as the measure of the degree of internalization of the employment relationship. In this case, the coefficients associated with the main bank dummy and with the price markup remain significant and the results are largely unchanged with respect to table 6.4. The estimated coefficient of the dummy *yslop* has a positive sign, but is not statistically significant.[11]

Next, table 6.6 shows the regression results based on a simpler Cobb–Douglas technology. In each regression, we split the sample period into two subperiods, prior to 1989 and after 1990, and, for each subsample,

---

[10] See for instance Wadhwani and Wall (1991) for a similar strategy in the context of efficiency wages.

[11] A similar result obtains when we use *wslop* instead of *yslop*.

Table 6.4 *Estimates of augmented production functions, using iniw*

Dependent variable	log(value added)			log(value added/markup)		
Wage policy variable	iniw1	iniw2	iniw3	iniw1	iniw2	iniw3
$\log(K_i^i)$	0.558*	0.558*	0.559*	0.555*	0.555*	0.553*
$\log(L_i^i)$	0.442*	0.442*	0.441*	0.445*	0.445*	0.447*
$\{\log(K_i^i)\}^2$	0.002	0.0018	0.0016	0.0008	0.0006	0.7×10^{-4}
$\{\log(L_i^i)\}^2$	0.002	0.0018	0.0016	0.0008	0.0006	0.7×10^{-4}
$\log(K_i^i) \cdot \log(L_i^i)$	−0.004	−0.0036	−0.0032	−0.0015	−0.0012	−0.00014
μ_i^i	−0.169*	−0.171*	−0.173*	−0.568	−0.571*	−0.561*
Z^i	−0.0091*	−0.0832*	0.0119	−0.010*	−0.089*	0.0114
$mainb_t^i$	0.353*	0.359*	0.356*	0.315*	0.322*	0.319*
$\overline{R}^2$ (overall)	0.326	0.326	0.326	0.289	0.288	0.289
Nobs (no. of firms)	4,757(876)	4,757(876)	4,757(876)	4,757(876)	4,757(876)	4757(876)

Notes: *The coefficient is significant at the 5 percent level of confidence.
Each regression includes year and industry dummies.

Table 6.5 *Estimates of augmented production functions, using yslop*

Dependent variable	log(value added)	log(value added/mark-up)
Wage policy variable		*yslop*
$\log(K_t^i)$	0.562*	0.559*
$\log(L_t^i)$	0.438*	0.441*
$\{\log(K_t^i)\}^2$	0.0026	0.0015
$\{\log(L_t^i)\}^2$	0.0026	0.0015
$\log(K_t^i) \cdot \log(L_t^i)$	0.0053	−0.0029
μ_t^i	−0.176*	−0.576*
Z^i	0.0508	−0.0642
$mainb_t^i$	0.367*	0.331*
$\overline{R}^2(overall)$	0.322	0.289
Nobs (no. of firms)	5,165(892)	5,165(892)

Notes: *The coefficient is significant at the 5 percent level of confidence.
Each regression includes year and industry dummies.

we use the values of *iniw* and *yslop*, estimated separately for each sub-period. The dependent variable in each regression is the growth rate of value added during the period. Our idea is that institutional arrangements involving the organization of labor within firms take time to produce noticeable effects, as can be seen more clearly by fixing the initial conditions and by looking at performance over an extended period of time.

Our results in table 6.6 show that, with a single exception, none of the wage policy variables is significant. We conclude that there is only weak evidence supporting the thesis that firms with a relatively steeper wage–tenure profile or with a relatively lower initial wage perform better than firms with a relatively flat wage profile and/or with a relatively higher initial wage.

At the beginning of this chapter, we discussed the possibility that institutions are bunched together, reflecting the presence of institutional complementarity. We check the empirical implications of institutional complementarity by adding to the regressions above the interactions of the main bank dummy with the price markup and the wage policy variables. The results (not shown) indicate that none of these interactions is significant. We thus find little support for the idea that having a combination of two or more institutional characteristics significantly contributes to firm productivity.

Table 6.6 *Estimates of augmented production functions, using growth rates*

Dependent variable	Period	Growth in value added			Growth in value added/markup		
Wage policy variable		iniw1	iniw2	iniw3	iniw1	iniw2	iniw3
Growth in $\log(K_t^i)$	1980s	0.198*	0.197*	0.197*	0.153*	0.149*	0.146*
Growth in $\log(L_t^i)$	1980s	0.252*	0.252*	0.253*	0.089	0.093	0.097*
$Z_1^i = iniwx$	1980s	−0.009	0.101	0.136	−0.016	0.215	0.402*
$Z_2^i = yslop$	1980s	−0.102	−0.087	−0.070	0.369	0.340	0.364
Growth in $\log(K_t^i)$	1990s	0.312*	0.314*	0.314*	0.276*	0.274*	0.272*
Growth in $\log(L_t^i)$	1990s	0.205*	0.203*	0.203*	0.080	0.076	0.078
$Z_1^i = iniwx$	1990s	0.0072	0.016	−0.0019	0.016	−0.023	0.123
$Z_2^i = yslop$	1990s	0.096	0.094	0.091	0.106	0.100	0.107

Notes: *The coefficient is significant at the 5 percent level of confidence.
Each regression includes year and industry dummies.

Discussion

Our strongest result in this chapter is the consistent negative effect of the estimated price markup on value added, even when value added is measured at market prices. Firms with higher markups are on average larger, at least in the manufacturing sector. Moreover, industries with higher markups tend to be mature or declining industries, with relatively high concentration and substantial increasing returns. At the risk of over-simplification, we infer from this that firms with higher markups tend to have larger size and to be located in either mature or declining industries. These are also the firms that use the typical Japanese human resource management (HRM) practices discussed at the beginning of chapter 5, including late promotion by seniority, extensive job rotation with internal transfers, and a strong preference for recruitment of school graduates.

Since wages increase and productivity declines with the price markup, our results are at odds with the view that firms pay higher wages to enhance internal efficiency. A more natural interpretation is that firms with higher market power pay higher wages (rent-sharing) and have higher degrees of X-inefficiency.

We have failed to find systematic evidence indicating that firms with steeper wage–tenure profiles have higher productivity. Although these results do not by themselves reject the view that steeper wage profiles can be an effective incentive device to elicit effort and strong attachment to the firm, they at least reject the view that inter-firm productivity differences are explicable in terms of variations in wage–tenure profiles.

A robust and strong result in our regressions is the consistent positive effect of the *main bank* dummy on firm productivity. In other work, some of us have shown that this effect is no longer significant or is in some cases even negative when firms are under financial distress.[12] Somewhat surprisingly, we do not find significant qualitative changes in the relationship between main bank affiliation and productivity when we limit the sample period to the 1990s, after the burst of the economic bubble.[13]

We have also failed to find evidence that initial wages consistently affect productivity in the direction suggested by the efficiency wage hypothesis. Quite the contrary, initial wages have often a *negative* and statistically significant effect on productivity. It is hard to find direct mechanisms that explain this negative relationship, and we are forced to speculate about indirect mechanisms. One possible explanation relies

---

[12] See Ariga and Ohkusa (1997).

[13] Ariga, Takehiro and Shima (1996) find a significant decline in the ability of main banks to monitor client firms, to prevent financial distress, and to provide rescue operations once firms get financially in trouble.

on the interactions among firms when recruiting new employees. As we have seen in detail in chapter 5, firms compete vigorously for new graduates in the external labor market, especially for new graduates of top-notch colleges, and a few prestigious and successful firms usually take the lion's share of the cream of the crop each year, without competing with other firms in terms of initial wage offers.

We suspect that the negative correlation between initial wages and productivity arises because of reputation mechanisms in the market for recruitment. Firms with a good reputation and also with a good observed performance generally have no problem in recruiting new graduates, and can afford to retain a relatively conservative wage policy with low initial wages. New graduates expect that, by accepting initial low wages, they will be compensated later by promotions and wage increases. On the other hand, firms with relatively unstable or poor performance and/or with poor future prospects must use more direct means of attracting new graduates, including higher initial wages.[14] If firms with a good reputation benefit from the recruitment of workers of higher quality, we expect that lower initial wages in these firms will be negatively correlated to productivity.

An alternative story is that the observed negative relationship reflects the relatively strong bargaining power of employees and their unions, who are capable of capturing an important share of the value added of the firm. Although the evidence is far from conclusive, our characterization of firms with higher markups is also consistent with the typical features of firms that have strong labor unions. According to this story, higher initial wages can be seen as the result of strong unions and poor management, with negative effects on productivity.[15]

Summary

In this chapter, we have investigated the interaction between internal labor markets, product markets, and the external labor market. Since this is a complex research problem, our findings are best viewed as a collection of relevant facts and our conclusions, summarized below, are mainly speculative.

[14] Ishikawa and Dejima (1994) use switching regression methods to estimate a dual labor market model in the Japanese context, and assume that entry into the primary sector is rationed for new employees. They find that the estimated male wage rate in the primary sector falls slightly short of the wage in the secondary sector for employees aged 25–29, but is much higher for employees aged 45–49.
[15] Empirical evidence on the negative impact of Japanese unions on firm productivity is presented by Brunello (1992).

We find evidence that major Japanese firms and their employees are insulated from the pressure of the external labor market. In particular, workers of firms with higher price markups have both longer average tenure and higher average wages.[16] At the same time, we find no evidence that the wage policy of firms significantly affects productivity, that is influenced instead negatively by price markups and positively by the presence of a main bank relationship. These results underline the importance of external monitoring and of discipline mechanisms that induce firms to maintain production efficiency.

Our results also suggest that inter-industry comparisons based on industrial data can be fairly misleading. Intra-industry variations in the markups of individual firms are typically larger than inter-industry variations in average markups.[17] Given the strong impact of price markups on firm wages and productivity, it is likely that intra-industry variations in wage and employment policies are at least as important as inter-industry variations.

Appendix   The estimation of the markups of prices over marginal costs

In Nishimura, Ohkusa and Ariga (1999) (hereafter, NOA), we assume that firms minimize costs and use the identity among output elasticity, factor shares, and price markup to estimate price markups at the firm level. In this appendix, we briefly outline NOA's approach. Let K_t^i and L_t^i be, respectively, the labor and capital services used by firm i for production during period t. The production function is

$$Q_t^i = F^i(K_t^i, L_t^i) \tag{6A.1}$$

where Q_t^i is output. We make two sets of assumptions. First, we assume that the production function is homothetic, and that the firm minimizes production costs, taking input prices as given. The elasticity of output with respect to capital and labor, ε_Q^i, can then be defined as

$$\varepsilon_Q^i \equiv \frac{K_t^i}{Q_t^i}[F_K^i]_t + \frac{L_t^i}{Q_t^i}[F_L^i]_t$$

that we can write also as[18]

---

[16] These findings are similar to those by Krueger and Summers (1988).

[17] See the discussion in Nishimura, Ohkusa and Ariga (1999).

[18] $\varepsilon_Q^i \equiv \frac{K_t^i}{Q_t^i}[F_K^i]_t + \frac{L_t^i}{Q_t^i}[F_L^i]_t = \frac{K_t^i}{Q_t^i}\frac{r_t^i}{\lambda_t^i} + \frac{L_t^i}{Q_t^i}\frac{w_t^i}{\lambda_t^i} = \frac{p_t}{\lambda_t^i}([\alpha_K^i]_t + [\alpha_L^i]_t) = \mu_t^i([\alpha_K^i]_t + [\alpha_L^i]_t).$

$$\varepsilon_Q^i = \mu_t^i([\alpha_K^i]_t + [\alpha_L^i]_t) \tag{6A.2}$$

In (6A.2), μ_t^i is the markup over marginal cost

$$p_t^i = \mu_t^i \lambda_t^i$$

where p_t^i is the price and λ_t^i is the marginal cost of firm i

$$\lambda_t^i = \frac{\partial C^i}{\partial Q^i}, \ C^i(r, w, Q) = \min \ r_t^i K_t^i + w_t^i L_t^i, \text{ subject to (6A.1)}$$

The term α_X^i ($X = K, L$) is the factor share, defined as

$$[\alpha_K^i]_t = \frac{r_t^i K_t^i}{p_t^i Q_t^i}; \ [\alpha_L^i]_t = \frac{w_t^i L_t^i}{p_t^i Q_t^i}$$

Notice that (6A.2) is an identity involving two unknowns [ε_Q^i and μ_t^i] and the factor shares, that are observable. Our strategy is to find a proxy for the output elasticity and to exploit (6A.2) and compute the markup. To find a proxy for ε_Q^i, we assume that production in the short run can deviate from constant returns to scale because of two reasons: (1) there exists a fixed cost of production; (2) the marginal cost is constant when production is normal: when production is expanding with respect to the normal level, marginal costs are increasing because of scarce managerial ability. Assumption (2) captures the Penrose effect.

To incorporate the above assumptions, we adapt the production function as follows:

$$F^i(K_t^i, L_t^i) = (1 + \gamma_0^i) f^i(K_t^i, L_t^i | \frac{\Delta S_t^i}{S_t^i}) - \gamma^i Q_t^{iN}$$

where S_t^i is the scale of production and f^i is homogeneous of degree $1 - \kappa^i (\Delta S_t^i / S_t^i)^2$ in its inputs, reflecting the Penrose effect. In this formulation, γ^i and γ_0^i are parameters and Q_t^{iN} is the normal output of firm i. Next, $\gamma^i Q_t^{iN}$ represents the magnitude of the fixed cost. Hence, there is no positive production until the firm inputs sufficient capital and labor.

Incorporating these two effects, we have

$$\varepsilon_Q^i = \left(1 + \gamma^i \frac{Q_t^{iN}}{Q_t^i}\right)\left(1 - \kappa^i \left(\frac{\Delta S_t^i}{S_t^i}\right)^2\right) \tag{6A.3}$$

Combining (6A.2) and (6A.3), we obtain

$$\mu_t^i\left([\alpha_K^i]_t + [\alpha_L^i]_t\right) = \varepsilon_Q^i = \left(1 + \gamma^i \frac{Q_t^{iN}}{Q_t^i}\right)\left(1 - \kappa^i \left(\frac{\Delta S_t^i}{S_t^i}\right)^2\right) \tag{6A.4}$$

This is the fundamental relationship that identifies the markup rate, μ_t^i. The term in the first bracket represents increasing returns caused by the fixed costs necessary for production, while the term in the second bracket represents decreasing returns caused by scarce managerial ability. When actual Q_t^i is sufficiently smaller than the normal output, Q_t^{iN}, the elasticity of output to capital and labor is greater than unity, showing increasing returns. As Q_t^i increases, the term in the first bracket becomes smaller, and is eventually dominated by the term in the second bracket, that is smaller than unity as long as the firm increases its size. In that case, the firm enters the region of decreasing returns to scale. Taking the first-order Taylor expansion of $\log(1 + x)$ around 1, we obtain

$$\log\left([\alpha_K]_t^i + [\alpha_L]_t^i\right) = -\log\mu_t^i + \gamma^i \frac{Q_t^{Ni}}{Q_t^i} - \kappa^i \frac{S_t^i - S_{t-1}^i}{S_{t-1}^i} + u_t. \quad (6A.5)$$

The markup is estimated using panel data of listed firms for the period 1970–94. (See NOA for detailed results.)

Part II
Recent changes in wage and employment structures

7 Institutional changes in Japanese internal labor markets

Overview

In the past few years there has been a growing concern over the future of the Japanese economy. Partly reflecting this concern, and partly because of the need to reshape their structure and organization, Japanese firms have been reconsidering their traditional employment policies.

The purpose of this chapter, that introduces part II of the book, is to describe the *key institutional changes* under way. We argue that these changes focus on three key aspects of the employment relationship. The first aspect is recruitment. Labor shortages in the late 1980s prompted firms to consider the possibility of expanding their pool of potential applicants by loosening up their strict adherence to the principle of hiring only new school graduates. The second aspect involves both the size and the composition of employment. Since the early 1980s, many firms have become increasingly concerned about the impact of demographic changes on horizontal and vertical hierarchies. The rapid ageing of the labor force and the shift in the mandatory retirement age from 55 to 60 have both contributed to the sharp increase of middle–senior aged employees in the Japanese workplace.[1]

Last but not least, there are organizational changes. There is a widespread concern about the effectiveness and competitiveness of the Japanese firm system in general – and, in particular, about its ability to swiftly organize and deploy resources in fast-growing and rapidly changing markets. This concern has led to attempts to reshape organizations into leaner and more flexible structures. Typical measures include flattening out hierarchies, creating loosely-knit flexible work units, and giving more discretionary managerial decision-making power to individual divisions.

---

[1] The implications of ageing for the Japanese labor market are discussed by Seike (1997).

We find that a substantial percentage of large Japanese firms is reshaping both compensation policy and the internal organization of jobs into career paths, while retaining most other aspects of the traditional employment system, in an attempt to reduce total labor cost and motivate incumbent workers. We also find that, in spite of the serious efforts to adjust the employment system, there has been no fundamental change in hiring policies, and most large firms still maintain both their preference for new school graduates and a human resources management (HRM) system that focuses on long-term internal training and promotion for all the incoming permanent employees.

We start by reviewing the major institutional changes that took place in the early 1980s and in the years of the big economic bubble. Next, we report the major changes occurring in the 1990s. Finally, we evaluate these changes. This chapter is descriptive and most of the evidence is drawn from case studies. We see it as a complement to chapter 8, where we describe changes in the wage and employment structure of Japanese firms by looking at the data from a well known national survey of establishments. A brief summary concludes the chapter.

The early 1980s and the bubble years

After going through the turbulent years of the first and the second oil crisis, the Japanese economy in the early 1980s was operating in an environment that differed markedly from the high-growth period. Here, we focus on two factors, which we believe were by far the most important in explaining the institutional changes occurring in Japanese internal labor markets. The first was the widespread recognition that the long-run growth rate of the economy had significantly slowed down. Perhaps of equal importance for the HRM of (large) Japanese firms was the rapid ageing of the Japanese labor force, that will continue well into the next century. The new environment stimulated firms to change some aspects of the traditional employment relationship. Two of these changes involved the mandatory retirement age and the reshaping of the organization of labor within firms.

Adjustment of the mandatory retirement age

Since the inception of the system, there had always been an important gap between the mandatory retirement age and the public pension and annuity system: in the late 1970s and in the early 1980s, the mandatory retirement age was 55 for the majority of large firms, and the pensionable age was 60.[2] Under the guidance and the encouragement of the Japanese government, firms started to change their mandatory retirement age from 55 to 60 (see table 7.1). The major concern, both for the government and for labor unions, was the financial security of retired workers.[3] The adjustment of the mandatory retirement age was completed by the mid-1980s for large firms and smaller firms followed suit within a few years.

As discussed later in the chapter, institutional changes in the mandatory retirement age did not automatically imply an increase in the average tenure of older workers. In 1989, for instance, the average tenure of male workers in Japanese firms declined sharply from age 55 onwards, and the difference in average tenure between the age group 50–54 (the age bracket where tenure peaks) and the age group 60–64 was close to 10 years. In 1996, this pattern changed only slightly: while average tenure was roughly 20 years in both the 50–54 and in the 55–59 age brackets, it was close to 13 years for the 60–64 and 65–69 age brackets.

In short, even today, the attrition of the senior labor force increases sharply from around age 50, despite changes in the mandatory retirement age. Firms used a variety of ways to reduce employees in these age brackets, ranging from offering special bonuses to those who volunteered for early retirement to setting internal age limits for managerial positions.

Reforming hierarchies

During the high-growth era, most large Japanese firms were organized in hierarchical systems with limited delegation of control from the center to the periphery. The introduction of new product lines was met typically by spinning off subsidiaries, rather than by setting up new divisions. Although the division system was widespread by the mid-1970s, the scope of managerial control allocated to divisions was relatively limited, at least compared with American firms. Among other things, the firm headquarters firmly retained control over employment issues. Typically, hirings were controlled by the personnel department in the headquarters, there were frequent inter-divisional transfers of white-collars, and per-

---

[2] See Rebick (1993) for a discussion of mandatory retirement in Japan.
[3] The current public pension and annuity system was introduced in 1973. At that time, government estimates of the share of the elderly (65 or over) in the population in 2025 was 16 percent. The current estimate is 25%, reflecting mainly the persistent decline in the birth rate. For a description of the Japanese pension system, see Oguchi, Kimura and Hatta (1994).

Table 7.1 Changes in mandatory retirement age, 1976–1997[a]

Year	Age	54	55	56	57	58	59	60	61–64	65+
1976	All firms	0.3	47.3	3.1	6.9	5.7	0.2	32.2	0.3	3.3
	5,000+[b]	0	39.2	14.4	14.4	11.6	1.7	18.2	0	0
1978	All firms	0.1	41.3	4.2	8.4	6.7	0.1	33.7	0.4	4.4
	5,000+	0	38.8	11.1	14.3	13.8	0.5	21.2	0	0
1982	All firms	0	26.6	5.1	16.0	10.6	1.2	39.7	0.6	0.3
	5,000+	0	13.8	2.8	16.4	11.2	1.2	54.6	0	0
1987	All firms	0.3	23.0	3.5	6.8	7.2	0.5	53.9	2.3	2.5
	5,000+	0	3.1	0	1.9	5.3	4.7	84.3	0.6	0
1992	All firms	0.2	11.5	0.8	5.3	5.1	0.5	71.4	1.7	3.5
	5,000+	0	0.4	0.7	0.4	1.1	1.5	95.2	0.4	0.4
1997	All firms	0	4.6	0.1	2.7	2.2	0.1	82.0	1.5	6.7
	5,000+	0	0	0	0	0	0	98.0	0.7	1.3

Notes:
[a] The numbers in the table are percentages of sampled firms.
[b] 5,000+ refers to firms with 5,000 or more employees.
Source: Ministry of Labor, Koyo Kanri Chosa (various years).

sonnel evaluations were managed at the center, which often over-ruled evaluations by immediate supervisors.

Several factors triggered the reorganization of hierarchies and the reduction of hierarchical levels. First of all, "baby-boomers" reached middle management levels in firms by the mid-1980s, requiring a serious adjustment in the hierarchical system. As discussed in chapter 5, most large Japanese firms use a dual-ranking system, with both horizontal and vertical ranks. The increased supply of middle-aged employees implied that available positions in vertical ranks were becoming increasingly scarce compared to the number of qualified candidates in the corresponding horizontal ranks.

The second factor was organizational efficiency. As firms expanded their scale and scope of operations, traditional hierarchies became increasingly slow to adjust and adapt. Above all, the system lacked the flexibility to quickly deploy the resources needed to meet immediate objectives. For example, the exploration of a new product line often required the approval of many different divisions and functionally separate departments. Reorganization centered upon flattening the hierarchy and shortening the line of control, so that one unit (most typically a department) could encompass a much wider set of functional responsibilities.

Last but not least, many firms had to redirect and reorganize their main operations, either because of permanent shifts in market shares or because of their changing competitive position in the market, associated with rapid appreciation of the yen after the 1985 Plaza Agreement. These reorganizations often involved scrapping and building major new divisions and departments.

Among the steps taken to simplify hierarchies, a typical measure was the elimination of sections, and the allocation of decision-making functions to the next hierarchical level (usually the department). This measure was typically accompanied by the introduction of more flexible, fluid, and often temporary units, called *teams*. The nature of these teams varied greatly from case to case. In some cases, teams were project oriented (task forces), organized across hierarchical units and dissolved once the task was completed. In other cases, these teams were nothing but new names for the old staff (sections) and played the same permanent role in the organization.

Another measure taken to flatten hierarchies was to make individual divisions more autonomous entities, and to endow them with more managerial decision-making power. A typical example is the company system adopted by Sony Corporation, where each *company*, corresponding roughly to a division, is given full power and responsibility in the recruit-

ment, promotion, and internal transfer of employees ranked below
department head.[4]

The bubble years and the aftermath

The years of the land and stock market boom were followed by the
deepest recession experienced by the postwar Japanese economy, which
had a serious impact on Japanese internal labor markets. Perhaps the
most visible consequence of the bubble years could be seen in the patterns
of recruitment, illustrated in figure 7.1. During the late 1980s and early
1990s, hirings increased substantially. While the pro-cyclical behavior of
hirings is an empirical regularity, the registered increase was remarkable,[5]
particularly for large firms and new college graduates. The recruitment of
new college graduates by large firms during the peak years (1990 and
1991) was about 60 percent higher than in the mid-1980s.[6] In 1991,
52.5 percent of the hirings of new college graduates in the private sector
were done by firms with more than 1,000 employees, compared to less
than 36.3 percent five years earlier.[7]

The sharp increase in the hiring rate had several important consequences. First of all, there was substantial labor hoarding when the economy started to slow down, especially in large firms. Chuma (1994) looks

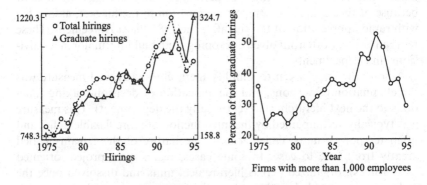

Figure 7.1 Total hirings and graduate hirings, 1975–1995

[4] See appendix (p. 204)
[5] The ratio of job offers to job seekers, a cyclical indicator of labor market slack, was equal
to 0.62 in 1987, after the *endaka* (yen appreciation) shock, reached 1.40 in 1990 and 1991,
only to fall back again to 1.08 in 1992 and to 0.63 in 1995, and to below 0.5 by 1998.
[6] The rate of employment of new college graduates also increased from 1987 to 1991 and fell
afterwards. See Rodosho (1997) for a detailed analysis.
[7] See Ministry of Labor (1997).

at employment adjustment in major firms and finds that, as early as the spring of 1993, many of the sampled firms were permanently laying off their core employees on an unprecedented scale. Often these firms started employment adjustment by cutting down the number of temporary workers and reducing new hirings. The next step was to accelerate retirement, most typically by offering additional severance pay to volunteers leaving before mandatory age. Transfers of employees to subsidiaries or to related firms were also a major tool to reduce labor costs. According to Chuma (1994), the three major steel companies alone spent more than 100 billion yen each year to compensate their dispatched workers for the reduction in the wage paid by the receiving (and smaller) companies.[8]

Another important consequence of the bubble years was that smaller firms had to increase their recruitment of workers with previous work experience. In the peak year of 1991, firms with more than 1,000 employees hired 145,600 new college graduates, corresponding to 64.7 percent of the total recruitment of college graduates. On the other hand, smaller firms in the same year could hire only 132,200 new college graduates, 26.3 percent of the total.

Even with larger than normal attrition rates, the substantial hirings during the bubble years implied that large firms now have a significant number of employees in their early 30s. In the recession following the burst of the bubble, firms that hired a large number of new college graduates faced a serious dilemma. On the one hand, the average quality of the recruits in the bubble years was likely to fall short of the average quality of the cohorts hired before and after the bubble, because of the lower recruitment standards. To retain a similar standard of quality among generations within each firm, the promotion rate of recruits in the bubble years should have been adjusted downward. On the other hand, the relatively large size of the cohort hired during the bubble meant that delaying the speed of promotion of these workers was going to seriously undermine the promotion prospects of the cohorts recruited afterwards.

The effects of ageing and of slower growth

It is well known that Japanese (large) firms rely mainly upon long-term firm-specific investment in human capital to develop the skills and

---

[8] Workers on dispatchment (*shukko*) remain employees of the original firm, and are thus entitled to receive standard pay. Usually firms taking in dispatched workers pay them according to their own pay rates and the dispatching firm makes up the difference. See Brunello (1988) for a detailed discussion.

increase the productivity of each permanent employee. As discussed in chapter 5, the promotion policy of these firms uses entry cohorts as the basic reference for promotion: personnel evaluation and promotion decisions sort out the relative ranking of each employee belonging to a given entry cohort, and there is limited competition for promotion across different cohorts.

When economic growth is strong, substantial recruitment of young cohorts of workers affects the age composition of employment within firms and increases employment in the lower ranks of the hierarchy, where most of the hirings occur. A significant (perceived) slowdown in the long-run growth of the firm reduces hirings without affecting in a substantial way the employment of incumbent core employees, because of the very high job security. With an unchanged promotion policy, the cohorts hired in a slowdown are bound to face on average lower promotion probabilities than the cohorts hired before the slowdown, because the sheer size of the latter reduces available vacancies in higher-ranked jobs within the firm. In this environment, a rigid application of the cohort oriented promotion policy is not sustainable unless the firm is prepared to sacrifice organizational efficiency and create additional jobs (positions) suitable for the promotion of the younger cohorts.

In chapter 8, we show that the adjustment of Japanese firms to the slowdown in the rate of growth involved both spans of control (that were reduced to partially accommodate the promotion expectations of the younger cohorts) and the promotion probability (that was adjusted downwards). With the reduction in spans of control, firms redistributed managerial responsibilities usually held by a single manager to several positions in comparable ranks. For example, the decision-making power usually held by a department head was partially delegated to the heads of loosely-knit units newly created within a department. Changes in overall promotion prospects also required additional changes. Many firms, for instance, restructured the relationship between the vertical and horizontal ranks by introducing non-managerial positions for higher-ranked (in terms of horizontal ranks) employees, without attaching to them any managerial responsibility.

As documented in chapter 9, the slowdown in the rate of growth is also likely to induce firms to flatten their wage–tenure profiles in an effort to save labor costs. This adjustment, however, is difficult to implement for incumbent employees without breaching the implicit long-term contract and changing expected promotion and compensation policies.

As mentioned at the beginning of this chapter, the Japanese labor force is ageing at a pace faster than predicted by most government forecasts. Table 7.2 shows the changing composition of employment by age from

Table 7.2 *Age composition of employment, 1975–1995*

Age	1975	1985	1995
15–24 years	20.2	15.5	15.7
25–39 years	42.6	39.4	33.4
40 years and older	37.2	45.1	50.9
Total	100	100	100

Source: Japanese Ministry of Labor, *Rodoryoku Chosa*, (several issues).

1975 to 1995 in favor of the age group older than 40. The impact of ageing on internal labor markets has two aspects. First, ageing operates on the promotion prospects of the younger cohorts much in the same way as a deceleration in the rate of growth. Second, it reduces the supply of new school graduates and could lead firms to switch their recruitment policy increasingly in favor of workers with previous labor market experience.

This shift could have important side effects if experienced workers are not hired at the start of the career ladder, as happens in the case of new school graduates. In the model presented in chapter 1, firms adopting internal labor markets hire unskilled new school graduates and train and upgrade them to fill vacant skilled jobs. When the pool of new school graduates shrinks, however, it becomes increasingly costly to fill skilled vacancies from within and firms can switch to filling part of their skilled vacancies by hiring experienced workers from the market. In this case, the morale of incumbent employees could be negatively affected by the implied reduction in their probability of promotion and the whole incentive structure of the firm could be threatened.

Institutional changes in the 1990s

We document institutional changes in the 1990s by drawing our data from *Rousei Jihou*, a HRM weekly magazine. We scan this magazine for reports on firms that have gone through important changes in their employment policy during the past 20 years, and exclude from this search reports covering economy-wide labor market developments and government policy affecting employment and pay. The result of the search consists of about 300 reports covering 776 firms.[9] We classify the contents

[9] The appendix (p. 204) presents the details and a few selected case studies of major institutional changes reported in *Rousei Jihou*.

Table 7.3 Distribution of firms, by major institutional change, reported in Rousei Jihou, 1979–1998, percent

	1979–98	1979–84	1985–89	1990–94	1995–98
Recruitment	4.17	6.41	3.68	1.67	4.81
Job demarcations, horizontal ranks	25.24	30.03	27.70	22.41	19.79
Promotion policy and evaluation	27.84	31.78	28.19	29.77	22.19
Wage policy (excl. annual salary system)	22.78	20.99	22.55	20.74	27.01
Annual salary system	3.90	1.17	0.25	4.35	8.56
Rationalization, employment adjustment	2.33	2.92	3.19	3.01	0.54
Mandatory retirement and pensions	3.08	4.08	2.70	1.67	4.01
Dispatchment	0.27	0	0.49	0	0.54
Fringe benefits (excl. pensions)	0.82	0.29	1.47	0.33	1.07
Female employment	0.75	0.58	1.23	1.00	0.27
Organizational changes	1.16	0	1.96	0	2.41
Training, skill qualifications	5.75	1.75	6.62	12.71	3.21
Other institutional changes	1.92	0	0	2.34	5.61
Total	100	100	100	100	100

of these reports in 13 subjects, with each subject being a major institutional change, and assign firms to these subjects. Since each report often encompasses more than one subject, we allow for multiple entries. Overall, the total number of entries is 1,406.[10]

The distribution of firms by subject is presented in table 7.3. First, we notice that, although *promotion policies and personnel evaluation* has been the most frequent subject during the last 20 years, its share has sensibly diminished during the most recent period. We find a similar trend for the subject dealing with *job demarcations and horizontal ranks*. On the other hand, *wage policy and system of pay* have become the most popular subjects in the last few years. The remaining subjects have relatively small shares, with peaks in particular subperiods. For example, *training and skill qualifications* were a relatively frequent subject during 1990–4.

In the rest of this section, we illustrate more in detail three areas of change, involving, respectively, career ladders, retirement policy, and the compensation system.

Multiple career tracks

The horizontal ranking system described in chapter 5 is relatively new and was adopted by most firms during the 1970s or even later. Before the introduction of the *Shokuno Shikaku Seido* (SSS: Skill-based job qualification system), individual pay was based upon vertical ranks and functions. The SSS system separates vertical positions in the hierarchy from pay determination, and uses instead horizontal ranks as the basis for both pay and career development. The most important innovation to this system in recent years has been the introduction of multiple career tracks. In the SSS system, all regular employees share the same career ladder as a sequence of horizontal and vertical ranks. With multiple career tracks, horizontal ranks are organized into two or three separate career ladders. Most typically, employees allocated to different career ladders face a different promotion policy, and some ladders can be climbed without an increase in managerial responsibility.[11]

---

[10] One cautionary note is needed in interpreting these reports. Very often, concerns and proposed changes never materialize into hard facts, or often end up as cosmetic changes. For example, we see waves of reports in the *Rousei Jihou* concerning reforms in training and promotion policies that aim at enhancing professional skills. The hard evidence shows, however, that internalization was the main trend, at least until the mid-1990s.

[11] See for example the case of *Nichirei Ltd.*, described in *Rousei Jihou*, 3325 (1997); *TOA Ltd.* and *Matsuya Foods Ltd.* in *Rousei Jihou*, 3325 (1997); and *Daiei* (the largest national supermarket chain), in *Rousei Jihou*, 3304 (1997).

There are two basic reasons for introducing multiple career tracks. First of all, it is a way to promote individuals to higher horizontal ranks without associating managerial responsibility with these promotions. Multiple tracks thus increase the separation between the horizontal and the vertical ranking hierarchies described by Aoki (1988) as typical of large Japanese firms. Second, a unique ranking system can bias promotion speed because of the differences in the nature and scope of job assignments and functions. If vacancies for managerial positions open up faster in one division, the need to fill these vacancies can accelerate promotion speed compared to divisions where vacancies turn out more slowly. Multiple career tracks, tailored to the specific needs of a division, can avoid this problem.

The major shortcoming of multiple career tracks is that the system is not designed to hire and train workers for careers that are different from the traditional managerial career track. The reason is that career tracks are separated into different ladders after a threshold rank and employees cannot choose which ladder to enter. Since the separation of ladders is typically set at age 40–45, the system cannot be an effective means of internally training specialized professionals. Most likely, it is a disguised way of separating fast flyers from the rest of the pack.[12]

Accelerated retirement and age limits for managerial positions

As discussed above, changes in the mandatory retirement age from 55 to 60 were supposed to increase the percentage of individuals in the age bracket staying on with the firm. In practice, when age 60 became the normal mandatory retirement age, many firms started to introduce measures to soften the impact of the new limit on the age composition of employees. In some cases, firms negotiated with labor unions a temporary exemption from the agreement on mandatory retirement. In some other cases, the transition to age 60 was postponed. In some extreme cases, such as at *Ohkuma*, an industrial machinery firm, the mandatory retirement age was pushed back to 55 from 60.[13] Many firms experiencing

---

[12] In some cases, branching out takes place much earlier (see, for instance, the system adopted by *Hankyu Department Store*). In some other cases, employees can choose their preferred career path (see the case of *Noritake*, a ceramics firm). It is still true, however, that none of these multiple-track systems recruit employees separately (*Rousei Jihou*, 3258, 1996). Hence, there is limited scope for the system to operate as a substitute for the external market for professionals.

[13] Chuma (1994) reports that *Hitachi Shipbuilding, Ishikawajima Harima Heavy Machinery*, and *Osaka Kikou* have also reduced the mandatory retirement age to deal with excess employment.

excess employment, however, preferred to discharge senior employees rather than to change the mandatory age.

The reduction of excess employment is not the only reason why firms have tried to soften the impact of a higher mandatory age. In many white-collar jobs, firms have set up age limits for specific positions. Under these limits, employees cannot retain managerial positions beyond a certain age (usually 50 or 55) unless they are promoted to become members of the board. Although the mandatory retirement age is honored, senior employees are *de facto* demoted from managerial positions at the specified age and allocated to non-managerial positions until retirement. The age limit is typically set three–five years before mandatory retirement. This system is close to the *up or out* rule used, for instance, in American academia.

Restructuring compensation

A trend in the adjustment of compensation policy has been to reduce age-related (*nenko*) elements in pay and place more weight both on individual performance and on the horizontal rank that is linked to performance evaluation. Changes in compensation policy have often involved changing promotion rates and wages attached to ranks. Some firms have, however, started to introduce more drastic changes.

The key innovation is the so-called Annual Salary System (ASS) (*Nenpo-sei*), that can be summarized as follows: (a) annual pay for each employee depends only on job assignment and performance; (b) supervisors in charge of performance evaluation are given substantial discretion in individual pay determination; (c) age-related pay is virtually absent. This new system not only rules out automatic wage increases but in principle introduces nominal wage reductions.[14] According to a recent survey conducted by *Romu Kasei Kenkyujo* (1997) covering nearly 600 firms, the percentage of firms adopting this new compensation system is slightly higher than 20 percent.[15] Notice that the system applies only to workers in middle–upper horizontal ranks, with the rank corresponding to section chief as the most common threshold.[16]

Apparently, the introduction of the ASS calls for fundamental changes, not only in the compensation and evaluation of employees, but also in dual-ranking structure typical of the SSS system, because pay is linked to the job and the functional position, rather than to the

[14] See the discussion in *Rousei Jihou*, 3276 (1996).
[15] The same survey finds that the percentage of firms involved in flattening ranking hierarchies is 19.9 percent.
[16] See the cases of *Komatsu Ltd.* and *JTB Ltd.*, in *Rousei Jihou*, 3276 (1996).

horizontal rank.[17] Most of the firms that have introduced ASS, however, still retain the dual-ranking system. Most typically, the compromise between the two systems is obtained by widening the wage range in pay schedules to accommodate performance-based adjustment of individual wages.

Summary

Every organization experiences periodic adjustments that cumulatively and over time bring about evolution and change. The Japanese employment system has gone through such a periodic reassessment and adjustment. We have tried to document above the latest episodes of this recurring story. Our view is that the ageing of the labor force and the slowdown in the rate of growth of the economy have generated problems that cannot be fully addressed by piecemeal adjustments involving only parts of the employment system.[18] An exceptionally deep and long recession in the 1990s added difficulty and immediacy, especially in reducing labor cost in an effort to retain/recover competitive advantage in the market place.

We believe that recent waves of institutional changes do differ in important ways from previous attempts, mainly because management in major firms is hard pressed by the need to make organizations leaner, cost efficient, and more flexible. At the same time, however, there is also strong inertia in the current system, especially in the dual-ranking system (SSS), that remains the basis of the employment relationship in most of these firms.[19]

At the risk of simplifying things, two distinct options appear to emerge in the discussions about the future of the Japanese employment relationship. One is to more or less completely abandon the current employment system and move towards the more market oriented Anglo-Saxon system (see the case of *Takeda Pharmaceuticals*). The other is to preserve the current system by minimizing its costs, for instance by eliminating age-related elements (*nenko*) in individual pay (see the case of *Sony*). In the short run, such a change is going to reduce wage costs substantially, because employment is heavily concentrated in the middle and senior

[17] *Takeda Pharmaceuticals*, the largest pharmaceutical firm in Japan, has switched to a job-related pay system for managerial employees. For these employees, performance is evaluated using the Hey system and pay is based upon this evaluation. See *Rousei Jihou*, 3306 (1997).
[18] See also the discussion in Economic Planning Agency (1997).
[19] We do not necessarily subscribe to the view that such organizational inertia is the major problem facing large firms. Notice that the speed of change is not uniform, as illustrated by the case of *Shin Nippon Steel* detailed in the appendix (p. 000).

age brackets, who are paid more relative to productivity than younger age groups. It is yet to be seen, however, whether changing pay is suffi-cient to maintain the core of the current employment system. There is no clear sign that long-term employment contracts are becoming less impor-tant. If anything, average tenure is increasing among employed workers, as shown in chapter 8.

We believe that there is a third option that Japanese firms can follow without jeopardizing the merits of the current employment system. This system, based upon internal labor markets, is fundamentally a very sound and effective way to organize, allocate, and train employees.[20] Internalization, however, has gone too far. It has gone too far because firms used to train employees even for jobs that are best organized in external professional labor markets. It is only in the last few years, for example, that the major security houses and commercial banks have started recruiting specialists, including bond traders, strategists, and economists, from the external labor market. We find no particular reason to insist upon training workers internally for these jobs.

We also believe that excessive internalization and the preference for new school graduates shown by large Japanese firms are closely related. If these firms want to use the external labor market to recruit highly spe-cialized professionals, they need to have multiple career tracks *from the start* of the employment relationship and to offer competitive compensa-tion opportunities to newcomers.[21]

At the same time, we fail to find any compelling reason for changing in a fundamental way the current employment system for blue-collars and managerial employees. We see no real alternative for these workers to the current internal labor markets, facilitating both long-run skill formation and the effective allocation of workers to positions within the firm. Notice that, with the exception perhaps of top executives, managerial employees are often trained internally in most developed countries.

Some institutional changes could benefit the current organization of labor in internal labor markets. For instance, we see no need to continue the current policy of hiring mainly new school graduates that still char-acterizes recruitment in large firms. Extending recruitment to individuals with a few years of previous experience would also dramatically increase the pool of available applicants, avoiding the bottlenecks of an ageing society. In 1996, the number of male workers with previous labor market

---

[20] The attempts to simplify and flatten hierarchies can be seen as attempts to retain the current dual-ranking system, while minimizing the mismatch between the demand and the supply of skills.
[21] See the case of *Panasonic* in the appendix (p. 205).

experience and aged less than 30 was 650,000, more than the 560,000 new school graduates hired in the same year. By extending their hiring to young job changers, firms can more than double the size of their potential pool of applicants without necessarily changing in a substantial way their policy of long-term employment and internal training.

Appendix   Case studies from the *Rousei Jihou*

Table 7A.1 (p. 205) shows the number of firms that appeared in the *Rousei Jihou* each year from 1979 to 1998. Our data indicate that, in the past 20 years, there were three periods of major concern about institutional change in the employment relationship: 1980–1, 1986–8 and 1994–6. All of these years were recession years.

Case studies

In this appendix we illustrate in more detail three case studies, referring to well known companies, *Sony*, *Panasonic* and *Shin Nippon Steel*.

Sony: introducing the company system
    Sony has changed its organization to the so-called "company system." In a sense, this reorganization can be seen as the attempt to further decentralize and delegate decision-making power to each division, which is renamed as a "company." Each company is headed by its own president and is structured much in the same way as an independent firm. Moreover, a company is free to reshuffle its personnel and change its internal organization, and can also decide on important investment plans in an independent way (at least up to a certain limit in terms of the money involved).
    The company system is also meant to centralize decision-making within each company.[22] One of the reasons for strengthening the controlling function of each division (company) is to allow flexible adjustment of the employment relationship that was traditionally controlled by headquarters, including working conditions and the wage system.[23]
    Another relevant aspect of the company system is the simplification of the hierarchical structure. The layers of the hierarchy are reduced, and so

---

[22] In accordance with the change, Sony also reduced the number of board members to almost a third.
[23] If the company system is pushed towards its logical limit, each company becomes close to a spun-off subsidiary, and Sony's strategy becomes more similar to that pursued by large Japanese firms attempting to diversify their activities.

Table 7A.1 *Cases reported in Rousei Jihou,*
1979–1998

Year	No. of cases	Percent
1979	35	2.4
1980	107	7.3
1981	99	6.8
1982	49	3.4
1983	35	2.4
1984	18	1.2
1985	68	4.7
1986	67	4.6
1987	143	9.8
1988	88	6.0
1989	42	2.9
1990	38	2.6
1991	41	2.8
1992	93	6.4
1993	59	4.0
1994	106	7.3
1995	84	5.7
1996	141	9.6
1997	116	7.9
1998	33	2.3

is the number of divisions. By reorganizing divisions into companies, Sony slashed the number of departments from 580 to 380, and the number of sections from about 2,000 to 1,500.

The introduction of the company system can also be found in several other large electrical appliances firms and in major trading companies. In some cases, the ultimate goal of the reform is to reorganize the hierarchy in such a way that the headquarters becomes a holding company, something at one time prohibited by law.[24]

Panasonic (Matsushita): front-loading severance pay[25]

Panasonic has introduced a dual-compensation system that allows each new recruit to choose her preferred course. The first option is the traditional pay schedule, with each employee receiving severance

[24] *Hitachi* and *Daiei* are leading examples of firms that publicly announced plans to set up a holding company, following the lifting of regulations preventing such companies.
[25] *Nihon Keizai Shinbun* (daily newspaper), March 28 and July 3, 1998.

pay upon retirement, or the company-funded pension income, that adds to the compulsory social security system. The second option is a pay schedule where severance pay is front-loaded.

The compensation policy of many large Japanese firms is designed to motivate employees to stay with the firm until mandatory retirement. Such a policy has the side effect of discouraging applicants who are not happy with committing themselves to life with a single employer. Panasonic's dual system can be seen as an attempt to attract the talented applicants whom it missed before because of the structure of compensation. Rather surprisingly, the percentage of new recruits who have joined Panasonic since April 1998, when the dual system was introduced, and chose the new compensation package, was higher than expected and equal to 44 percent of the total. Panasonic then announced that in October 1998 all incumbent employees would be given the opportunity to choose one of the two options explained above.

Shin Nippon Steel: way behind, but moving

Shin Nippon Steel is the oldest and largest steel firm in Japan. After a number of organizational changes during the past 20 years, employment was cut by half, from over 80,000 to less than 40,000. Shin Nippon Steel then introduced a new compensation system. There are three major points in the new system. First, it merges the horizontal ranking system and the pay schedule of blue- and white-collars into a single career and pay track. One reason for this change is that reorganizations and diversifications of the output mix had resulted in a major reshuffle of personnel from blue- to white-collar jobs. In spite of the changed job allocations, many of these workers, before the new system was introduced, were still evaluated and paid according to their original blue-collar classification.

The second major point is the simplification of pay and the move towards the SSS system, with horizontal ranks at the basis of pay for all employees. The last point is that the number of horizontal ranks has been reduced to obtain a leaner and flatter hierarchy. Overall, Shin Nippon Steel's attempt to reshape its pay system can be interpreted as a step towards the system that most large Japanese firms adopted during the late 1960s and early 1970s.

8 Changes in the employment and wage structure of Japanese firms, 1976–1996

Overview[1]

In this chapter we describe the changes in the wage and employment structures of large and medium-sized Japanese firms during the 20 years from the mid-1970s to the mid-1990s, using the data contained in volume 3 of the Survey on the Wage Structure (*Chingin Kouzou Kihon Chosa*), published annually by the Japanese Ministry of Labor, including information on wages, age, tenure, and employment classified by age group, rank, industry, and firm size. Our purpose is to summarize these data into stylized facts, and use these facts to guide the analysis in the final part of the book.

Data and definitions

As already mentioned in chapter 4, the data published in the Basic Survey are classified in such a way that the information on educational attainment is available only for the aggregate of all industries. This information is not available in the industrial data. Since we are interested in how wages and employment vary not only over time but also across industries, we use industrial data and select the following three sectors: manufacturing, finance and retail, and wholesale distribution.[2]

While manufacturing has attracted considerable international attention because of its innovative practices and competitiveness, the distribution sector has often been blamed for being protected and hostile to foreign competition[3] and the finance sector was particularly affected by the burst of the bubble in the early 1990s. By using industrial data, we gain a broader perspective on the changes occurring in the Japanese labor

---

[1] This chapter builds on Ariga *et al.* (1992).
[2] The selected data include only male employees.
[3] See the discussion in Ito (1992).

market that cannot be fully captured by focusing only on the aggregate data or on the manufacturing sector.

Firm size in these data is classified into three categories: large (1,000 employees or more), medium (500–999), and small (100–499). Since these categories change over time, we reclassify the available information into two categories – *large*, for firms with more than 1,000 employees, and *medium-sized*, for firms with 100–999 employees. The exclusion from the data of small firms with fewer than 100 employees, that constitute the large majority of Japanese firms, reduces the scope of our analysis to the primary sector of the economy.

There are nine age groups used in this study, encompassing individuals aged 18–59.[4] Job ranks are: unranked (rank 0), foreman (*shokucho*), subdivision director (*kakaricho*: rank 1), division director (*kacho*: rank 2), and department director (*bucho*: rank 3). Using the distinction made in chapter 5, these ranks correspond to functions in the vertical ranks and should be distinguished from horizontal ranks that are important for status and pay.

Denoting as t, i, s, j, and a, respectively, year, industry, firm size, job rank, and age, we compute relative wages (RW) and spans of control (SPC) from the original data on wages (W) and the number of employees (N), as follows

$$RW(t, i, s, j, a) = w(t, i, s, j, a)/w(t, i, s, 0, a)$$

$$SPC(t, i, s, j) = \sum_{k<j}\sum_{a} n(t, i, s, k, a)/\sum_{a} n(t, i, s, j, a)$$

$$t = 1976\text{--}96; i = 1, 2, 3; s = 1, 2; j = 1, 2, 3; a = 1, 2\ldots 9$$

Since the rank foreman is available only in manufacturing industry, we treat this rank in this chapter as equivalent to rank 1 and average out the information available in these two ranks. Notice that, according to our definition, the span of control, SPC, is the number of employees in lower ranks per each worker in a supervisory position. For example, SPC (76, 1, 1, 3) = 20 means that each rank 3 employee in a medium-sized firm in the manufacturing industry had 20 subordinates in 1976.

Growth deceleration

After the first oil crisis, the growth rate of the Japanese economy declined substantially and during the last twenty years the three selected industries

---

[4] These age groups are: 18–19, 20–24, 25–29, 30–34, 35–39, 40–44, 45–49, 50–54, and 55–59.

(manufacturing, distribution, and finance) grew at an average annual rate of 4–5 percent. Although the average growth rate was relatively similar over the sample period, short-term fluctuations differed markedly. Figures 8.1 and 8.2 plot both the annual rates of growth of real output and employment and the five-year moving averages of these rates.

In manufacturing industry, real output grew on average 5.9 percent a year during 1976–90 and only 0.9 percent a year during 1991–5, after the burst of the bubble. As shown in panel a of figure 8.1, output growth was negative in 1986, during the downswing triggered by the appreciation of the currency, grew fast in the late 1980s, and was negative again in the early 1990s. At the same time, employment growth (panel b of figure 8.1) was positive in the 1980s and negative in the early 1990s.

In the distribution sector, real output growth fell from 5.6 percent a year during 1976–90 to 1.5 percent in the 1990s (panel a of figure 8.2), but employment growth was faster in the 1990s (1.7 percent a year) than before (1.4 percent). Rapid output growth in the late 1970s reflected the rapid expansion of national chains of supermarkets. The deceleration in the early 1980s and the acceleration in the second part of the 1980s were partly the consequences of the "stop–go" policies adopted by the government in the regulation of entry of large retail stores.

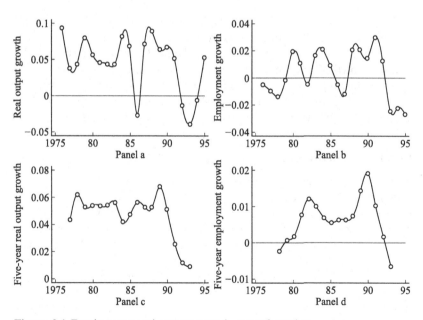

Figure 8.1 Employment and output growth, manufacturing

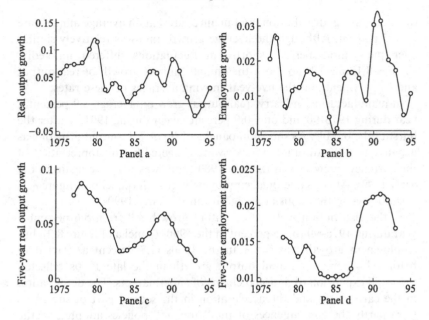

Figure 8.2 Employment and output growth, distribution

The finance industry grew most rapidly from the early 1980s to the end of the decade (panels a and c of figure 8.3) and was hit most badly by the downswing associated with the burst of the land and stock price bubble. Output growth during the whole period was equal to 5.4 percent a year, with a high 7.6 percent a year from 1976 to 1990 and a low −1.1 percent in the 1990s. Employment also grew fast during the 1980s (panels b and d of figure 8.3), but its rate of growth declined sharply after 1990.

Changes in relative wages and spans of control

The evolution of relative wages by rank during the period 1976–96 is shown for each of the three industries in figures 8.4–8.6. Each figure has three panels, one each for rank 1, 2, and 3, and each panel displays rank-specific relative wages, for both large and medium-sized firms.

Consider first manufacturing. Figure 8.4 shows that relative wages exhibit a clear negative trend, especially pronounced in the late 1970s and for large firms. The steep declining trend among large firms implies increasing convergence in the wage structure of large and medium-sized firms. A comparison of relative wages by rank and firm size at the beginning and at the end of the sample period is presented in table 8.1.

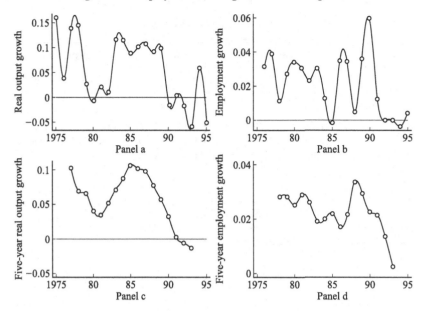

Figure 8.3 Employment and output growth, finance

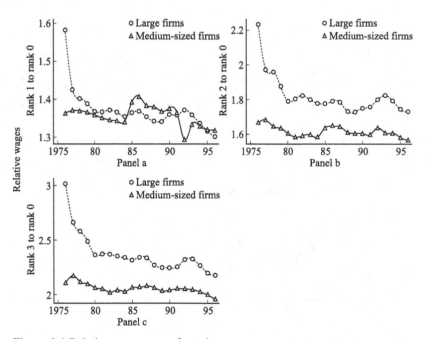

Figure 8.4 Relative wages, manufacturing

Table 8.1 *Changes in relative wages, 1976–1996*

	Manufacturing		Finance		Distribution	
	1976	1996	1976	1996	1976	1996
Large firms						
Rank 1	1.58	1.30	1.55	1.33	1.37	1.25
Rank 2	2.24	1.73	1.94	1.75	1.92	1.66
Rank 3	3.02	2.18	2.34	2.22	2.48	2.06
Medium firms						
Rank 1	1.36	1.32	1.43	1.31	1.38	1.24
Rank 2	1.67	1.57	1.87	1.69	1.72	1.54
Rank 3	2.11	1.96	2.20	2.09	2.29	1.97

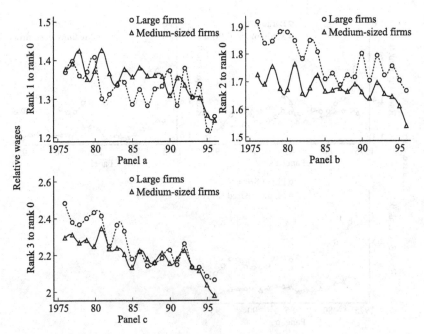

Figure 8.5 Relative wages, distribution

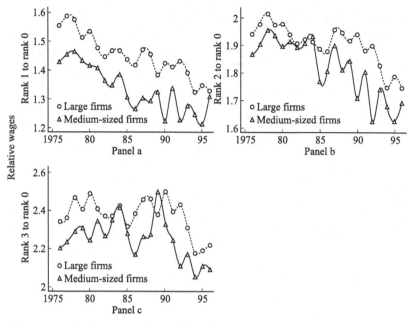

Figure 8.6 Relative wages, finance

Next, consider distribution (figure 8.5). Compared to manufacturing, the negative trend in relative wages is less pronounced, especially among large firms. There are signs of convergence in the wage structures of large and medium-sized firms in this sector, too. Finally, consider the finance industry (figure 8.6). While this industry shares with the distribution sector both a mild negative trend and some convergence in the wage structure by firm size, it is also characterized by rather sharp relative wage fluctuations, especially pronounced for ranks 2 and 3, that could be correlated to business cycle fluctuations, as discussed in detail in chapter 10.

The dynamics of spans of control are illustrated in figures 8.7–8.9. Starting again from the manufacturing sector (figure 8.7), we notice that spans of control share with relative wages both a clear negative trend and signs of convergence between large and medium-sized firms. A negative trend in spans of control characterizes also the distribution and the finance industries (figures 8.8 and 8.9), with the sole exception of the span of control for subsection chiefs in the latter industry, which exhibits a positive trend. A comparison of spans of control at the beginning and at the end of the sample period, by rank, firm size, and industry is presented in table 8.2.

Table 8.2 *Changes in spans of control, 1976–1996*

	Manufacturing		Finance		Distribution	
	1976	1996	1976	1996	1976	1996
Large firms						
Rank 1	6.4	5.0	7.7	9.5	8.2	5.9
Rank 2	28.6	11.4	9.8	6.2	9.1	6.3
Rank 3	71.4	30.2	25.1	21.8	28.4	23.6
Medium firms						
Rank 1	12.3	9.1	7.5	4.5	9.2	8.4
Rank 2	15.3	9.7	9.6	6.0	9.1	8.5
Rank 3	40.4	24.1	19.1	15.0	24.4	22.4

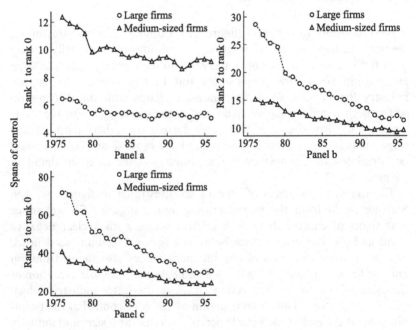

Figure 8.7 Span of control, manufacturing

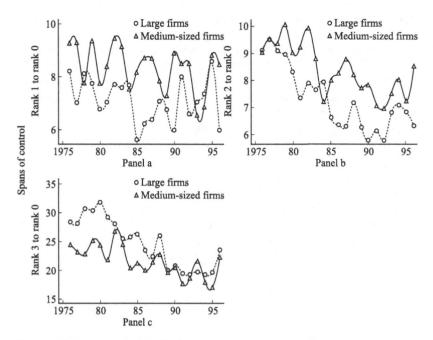

Figure 8.8 Span of control, distribution

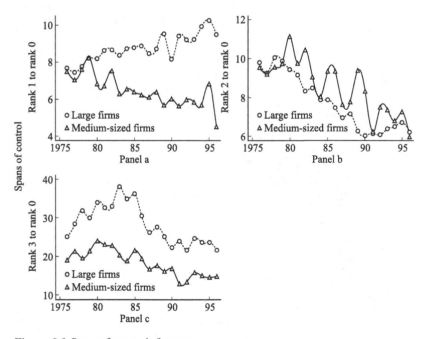

Figure 8.9 Span of control, finance

The declining trend in both relative wages and spans of control suggests the presence of a stable relationship linking these two variables. In figure 8.10 we plot average relative wages and spans of control for all ranks, industries, firm sizes, and years, and show that relative wages are an increasing and concave function of spans of control. This relationship implies that the decline in relative wages by rank should be analyzed as a facet of the change in the hierarchical structure of firms that has occurred during the past 20 years.

This declining trend has been accompanied by an upward trend in the average age and tenure of employees, independently of firm size, rank, and industry. In our data, average age and tenure have increased between 1976 and 1996, respectively, from 34.17 to 37.99 and from 10.36 to 14.79. As shown in tables 8.3 and 8.4, this increase has been across the board but relatively stronger in medium-sized firms. As a result, there are clear signs of convergence in the average age and tenure of large and medium-sized firms.

Changes in promotion rates

In chapters 1, 2, and 10 of this book we show how relative wages and spans of control in hierarchical firms are related to promotion rates. We expect that the changes in the wage and employment structures described

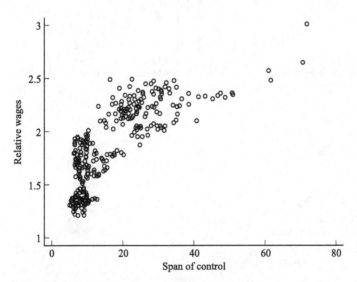

Figure 8.10 Relative wages and spans of control

Table 8.3 *Changes in average age, 1976–1996*

	Manufacturing		Finance		Distribution	
	1976	1996	1976	1996	1976	1996
Large firms						
Rank 0	33.1	37.1	33.5	35.5	30.2	34.0
Rank 1	40.7	43.2	37.9	39.0	36.3	40.5
Rank 2	43.5	47.2	42.8	44.1	41.6	46.2
Rank 3	49.4	51.7	47.6	49.8	47.4	50.3
Medium firms						
Rank 0	33.5	35.8	29.2	32.6	29.1	33.3
Rank 1	38.2	42.5	34.8	38.8	34.8	39.7
Rank 2	42.2	46.7	41.8	46.0	39.9	45.5
Rank 3	46.7	51.1	46.3	51.0	45.2	50.6

Table 8.4 *Changes in average tenure, 1976–1996*

	Manufacturing		Finance		Distribution	
	1976	1996	1976	1996	1976	1996
Large firms						
Rank 0	10.8	15.5	9.1	10.6	7.3	10.9
Rank 1	20.1	22.8	17.1	16.8	14.0	18.1
Rank 2	19.8	24.9	20.8	21.9	18.5	23.6
Rank 3	24.3	28.3	23.8	26.8	23.5	25.7
Medium firms						
Rank 0	8.6	11.5	6.4	9.6	5.7	9.3
Rank 1	14.5	18.7	12.8	17.0	11.2	15.4
Rank 2	16.6	21.7	18.1	21.7	14.8	21.4
Rank 3	18.2	24.1	20.2	25.6	17.4	24.4

above will also have affected promotion rates and career opportunities of incumbent workers. Data on promotion rates are not immediately available from national surveys and need to be estimated using the available information. The details of our estimation method are given in the appendix (p. 223). The underlying idea, however, is quite simple and can be summarized as follows.

First, suppose that all available vacancies in upper-ranked jobs are filled exclusively by internal promotion. Although this is an extreme assumption that cannot be literally true, the data on average tenure for each cell suggests that we are not too far from reality. For example, while average tenure of department heads in the manufacturing industry in 1996 was 28.3 years, average age was about 52 years. Potential labor market experience of workers aged 52 can be at most 30 years for college graduates and 34 for high school graduates, quite close to average tenure. Long tenure spells and shallow previous labor market experience at the top of the hierarchy clearly indicate that internal upgrading is very important.

Next assume that employees are not demoted, as implied by the model in chapter 2. Given these two assumptions, outflows from each cell are either promotion flows or separations. Total outflows from each cell are computed by simply tracking cohorts over time. For example, section heads aged 30–34 in year T either remain in their rank in year $T + 5$, moving to the age bracket 35–39, or are promoted to department heads or separate from their current firm.

For each cell in the data, we estimate separation outflows and obtain promotion outflows as total outflows *minus* separations. Next, we compute rank-specific promotion rates by adding promotion outflows over the available cells and by dividing the sum by total employment at the beginning of the time interval (five years). Since each cell is defined by a five-year age range, this procedure implies that we can compute only five-year promotion rates.

Table 8.5 shows the weighted averages of computed promotion rates over the period 1981–95, by rank of origin and destination, by industry, and by firm size.[5] We find that, on average, estimated promotion rates are highest for promotion from rank 1 to rank 2, and lowest for promotion from rank 0 to rank 1.

An important question is whether estimated promotion rates vary with changes in real output growth. If firms adopt internal labor markets and

[5] In the computation of promotion rates, we exclude the rank of foreman, which is available only in the manufacturing sector. Since our data are from 1976 onwards and promotion rates are computed over a five-year interval, we can start only from 1981.

Table 8.5 *Average five-year promotion rates, by industry and firm size*[a]

Industry	Size	Rank 0–1	Rank 1–2	Rank 2–3
Manufacturing	Medium	0.0484 (0.0424)[b]	0.439 (0.193)	0.216 (0.111)
	Large	0.0553 (0.0544)	0.511 (0.215)	0.295 (0.156)
Distribution	Medium	0.0573 (0.0519)	0.512 (0.207)	0.219 (0.147)
	Large	0.0675 (0.0619)	0.511 (0.200)	0.208 (0.107)
Finance	Medium	0.0728 (0.0577)	0.442 (0.226)	0.275 (0.189)
	Large	0.0459 (0.0383)	0.462 (0.219)	0.173 (0.121)

Notes:
[a]Promotion rates in table 8.5 are employment-weighted averages of five-year rates.
[b]Standard deviations in parentheses.

internal promotion, an increase in real output growth that increases the number of available positions in upper-rank jobs will also increase promotion opportunities for incumbent workers in lower ranks, as discussed in detail in the theoretical model of chapter 10. Figure 8.11 plots for each industry both the five-year average real output growth rate and the five-year average promotion rate, obtained as the weighted average of rank-specific promotion rates, using employment shares as weights.[6]

We notice three things. First, promotion rates exhibit significant fluctuations over time. Second, these fluctuations are positively correlated with current and lagged real output growth in the industry. In manufacturing industry, the correlation between the average promotion rate and current five-year real output growth is 0.55, while the correlation between average promotion and lagged five-year real output growth is equal to 0.16. In the distribution sector, these correlations are, respectively, 0.33 and 0.52. In the finance sector, they are 0.08 and 0.46. Third, promotion rates significantly declined in the 1990s, after the burst of the economic bubble.

Figures 8.12 and 8.13 plot, respectively, average promotion rates by firm size and by industry. Mainly because of the large drop in average promotion among large firms in the early 1980s, the correlation between promotion rates by firm size is negative. On the other hand, the correlation between promotion rates across different industries is positive. Next, figure 8.14 shows the empirical distribution of promotion rates, by age and

[6] To avoid losing information, five-year real output growth rates are computed for each year, t, by using the information from year $t - 4$ to year t. This procedure is different from that used in figures 8.1–8.3, where five-year averages are centered in year t.

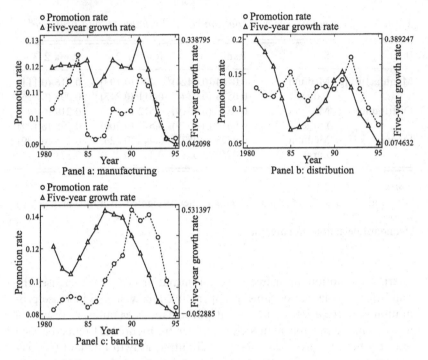

Figure 8.11 Promotion and growth

rank. In each panel of the figure, we compare two distributions, one for 1981, at the beginning of our sample, and the other for 1995, and show that the latter distribution is consistently below the former. This implies that, on average, promotion rates have declined for each age group and rank. The downward shift in the distribution of promotion by age is accompanied by an increase in the average age of promotion. Starting from promotion to rank 1, average age at promotion was 37.3 in 1981 and 37.4 in 1995. The average age at promotion from rank 1 to rank 2 was 41.45 in 1981 and 42.10 in 1995. Finally, promotion to rank 3 occurred at the average age of 46.59 years in 1981 and 47.73 years in 1995.

We use the estimated promotion and separation rates to compute the present discounted value of earnings in each rank, firm size, industry, and year. Denote by

$$V_a^r(t) = w_a^r(t) + \rho[p_a^r(t) \cdot V_{a+1}^{r+1} + q_a(t) \cdot V_{a+1}^N(t)$$
$$+ \{1 - p_a^r(t) - q_a(t)\}V_{a+1}^r(t)] \tag{8.1}$$

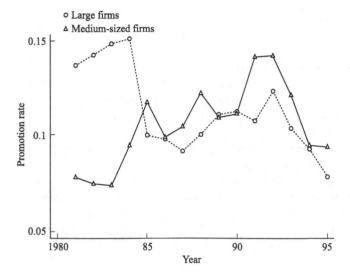

Figure 8.12 Promotion rates, by firm size

the asset value of employment in rank r at age a, where w is the real wage, q is the separation rate, p is the probability of promotion, t is time and the superscript N refers to labor market opportunities available in other firms. The asset value, V, depends on the current wage *plus* the expected gain from a change in state, including both promotion and separation from the firm. Next, define

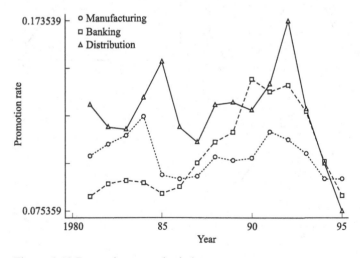

Figure 8.13 Promotion rates, by industry

$$S_a^r(t) \equiv \frac{(V_a^{r+1} - V_a^r)}{V_a^r} \tag{8.2}$$

as the (expected) promotion premium.

We compute asset values by assuming stationarity, implying that the expected asset value V_{a+1} for an individual in the age range a is exactly equal to the current asset value of individuals in the age group $a + 1$. We also assume that the real rate of interest is equal to 3 percent, implying that the five-year discount factor is approximately 0.85. Average promotion premia, by rank, are obtained as weighted averages of promotion premia, by age group, using as weight employment in each age cell. Table 8.6 presents estimated promotion premia, by rank, for both the 1980s and the 1990s. It turns out that, with the exception of promotion from rank 1 to rank 2, promotion premia have declined over time, especially for employees who expect to be promoted to rank 1.

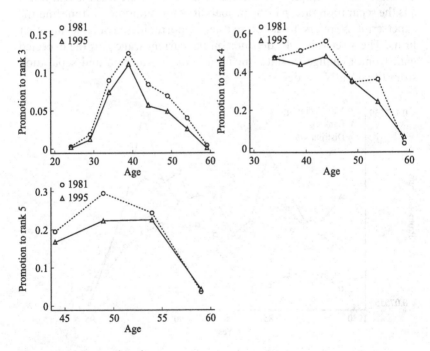

Figure 8.14 Promotion, by age

Table 8.6 *Promotion premia, by rank,*
1980s and 1990s

	1980s	1990s
Rank 0–1	0.347	0.315
Rank 1–2	0.062	0.080
Rank 2–3	0.101	0.098

Summary

We summarize our major findings in this chapter as follows:

(1) With the deceleration of output and employment growth, there is evidence of a long-term decline both in relative wages, RW, and in spans of control, SPC
(2) There is evidence of convergence in the wage and employment structure of large and medium-sized firms, indicating that these firms are becoming increasingly similar in terms of hierarchical structure and compensation system
(3) Average age and tenure have increased over time, especially among medium-sized firms
(4) Both promotion rates and promotion premia have declined in the 1990s, and the average promotion age has slightly increased
(5) Fluctuations in average promotion rates are positively correlated to fluctuations in five-year real sectoral output growth.

Appendix

We compute promotion flows for each age cohort by imposing on the data the following assumptions:

(a) promotions can be only one rank per period
(b) there are no demotions
(c) all entrants start from the bottom rank.

Given these assumptions, a worker in rank j at time t can be in any of the following states at time $t + 5$: rank j, rank $j + 1$, separated from the firm. Hence, we can retrieve promotion flows from rank j to rank $j + 1$ by estimating separation flows.

Letting a be the age group, j the rank, s the firm size, i the industry, and t time, we define

$$P(t, t + 5, i, s, j, a) = \frac{D(t, t + 5, i, s, j, a)}{N(t, i, s, j, a)}$$

where D are promotion flows from t to $t + 5$, N is employment at time t, and P is the promotion rate. Suppose that there are only three job ranks. In this case, we compute promotion flows as follows:

$$D(t, t + 5, i, s, 1, 1) = N(t + 5, i, s, 2, 2)$$

$$D(t, t + 5, i, s, 2, 2) = N(t + 5, i, s, 3, 3)$$

$$D(t, t + 5, i, s, 2, a + 1) = N(t + 5, i, s, 3, a + 2)$$

$$-\{1 - Q(t, t + 5, i, s, a + 1)\} \times N(t + 5, i, s, 3, a + 1)$$

$$D(t, t + 5, i, s, 1, a) = N(t + 5, i, s, 2, a + 1)$$
$$- \{1 - Q(t, t + 5, i, s, a)\} \times N(t + 5, i, s, 2, a)$$
$$- D(t, t + 5, i, s, 2, a + 1) \text{ for } a \geq 2$$

where $Q(t, t + 5, i, s, a)$ is the separation rate.

Data on employment, N, are from the third volume of the Survey on the Wage Structure. Separation rates are computed from the data published in the annual Survey on Employment Trends (*Koyo Doko Chosa*). The original data include separation rates by industry, age, gender, group and firm size, but not by rank. We are thus forced to assume that these rates do not vary with rank. We used regression analysis to decompose age/gender/industry/firm-size effects on separation rates and to obtain our estimate for $Q(t, t + 5, i, s, a)$. The details are available upon request.

Given the estimated promotion probabilities, we can compute the distribution of employees in each rank according to the age of promotion to their current rank. Denoting by $m(j, y, a)$ the number of employees of age a who have been promoted to job rank j at age y, with $a \geq y$, we have

$$m(j, y, a) = m(j - 2, y - 1, a - 1) \times p(j - 2, a - 1)$$
$$\text{for } y = a \text{ and } j = 3$$

$$m(j, y, a) = m(j, y - 1, a - 1) \times [1 - q(a - 1)] - p(j, a - 1)$$
$$\text{for } y < a \text{ and } j = 3$$

$$m(j, y, a) = m(j - 1, y - 1, a - 1) \times p(j - 1, a - 1)$$
$$\text{for } y = a \text{ and } j = 4, 5$$

$$m(j, y, a) = m(j, y - 1, a - 1) \times [1 - q(a - 1)] - p(j, a - 1)$$
$$\text{for } y < a \text{ and } j = 4, 5$$

where we use ranks 1, 3, 4, and 5; q and p are the average quit and promotion probabilities for each cell. These equations are recursive and the number of promoted employees, m, can be computed for each rank and age by starting from the average age distribution of rank 1 employees. The empirical distribution of employees in each rank by age of promotion is then given by

$$m(j, y) = \frac{\sum_{a \geq y} m(j, y, a)}{\sum_a \sum_{a \geq y} m(j, y, a)}$$

9 Changes in Japanese earnings profiles

Overview

As described in chapters 7 and 8, Japanese internal labor markets are undergoing important changes under the pressures of slower growth and an ageing labor force. Some of these changes have affected the compensation system, and several measures have been taken to reduce the importance of age and tenure in individual pay.

The purpose of this chapter is to study from an empirical perspective whether the changing economic environment has affected Japanese earnings profiles – and, in particular, the returns to tenure in the firm. Using two datasets and different estimation strategies, we present evidence that the slope of wage–tenure profiles has declined. We then relate this decline to the slowdown in the rate of economic growth and to the ageing of the Japanese labor force. A brief summary concludes the chapter.

Previous literature

In an exchange in the *American Economic Review*, Clark and Ogawa (1992) and Hashimoto and Raisian (1992) discussed whether Japanese earnings profiles had changed from the early 1970s to the mid-1980s. Clark and Ogawa (1992) concluded that the value of an extra year of tenure had declined substantially from 1971 to 1986. They explained this finding by the progressive ageing of the Japanese labor force and the increase of the mandatory retirement age from 55 to 60. Hashimoto and Raisian (1992) examined a selected number of years in the 1980s and found that, while there could be some cyclical effects, there was no evidence of a substantial decline in the slope of wage–tenure profiles.[1]

---

[1] Higuchi (1988) also studied changes in earnings profiles.

Changes in the rate of economic growth can affect the slope of wage–tenure profiles in at least two ways. First, if technical progress and (firm-specific) human capital are complements, as assumed by Mincer (1989), a slowdown in the rate of economic growth, driven by a slower rate of technical progress, reduces the accumulation of human capital. When wage profiles reflect human capital accumulation in the firm, slower technical progress reduces their slope by reducing growth.[2] Mincer and Higuchi (1988) use this argument and the lower rate of productivity growth in the United States to explain why the slope of wage–tenure profiles is steeper in Japan than in the United States.[3]

An alternative argument, that does not rely on human capital considerations, is discussed in detail in chapter 10, and runs as follows: a slowdown in productivity growth reduces individual effort required by workers in firms. If individual effort is elicited by internal promotion tournaments, as is often the case in internal labor markets, lower effort can be obtained by reducing either the promotion probability to a job paying a higher wage, or the wage premium upon promotion, or both. With internal promotion, such measures reduce the slope of (expected) wage–tenure profiles.

Even with unchanging growth, flatter wage–tenure profiles can simply reflect a shift in the relative supply of junior and senior workers. The progressive ageing of the Japanese labor force, documented in chapter 7, has increased the supply of older workers. Unless this supply shift is compensated by a relative demand shift that increases the demand for senior workers, relative wages by age and tenure have to fall, either because of market pressure or because firms are forced to change the internal wage structure to cut expanding labor costs.[4]

Data

We study changes in Japanese earnings profiles by using data from the Survey on the Wage Structure covering two subperiods, 1980–4 and

---

[2] Mincer (1989) argues that

> the effects [of productivity growth induced by technical change] . . . on the demand for human capital are more predictable if we assume complementarity between technology and human capital in the production functions. Under this assumption, rapid technical change raises the return on human capital attracting educated workers as well as encouraging training in the newer technologies . . . To the extent that trained workers bear some of the costs of investment in training, their wages grow during training as their productivity is raised. Steeper wage profiles in the firm should be observable when productivity growth persists over longer periods. (1989, p. 10).

[3] Chapter 4 of this book shows that earnings profiles are steeper in Japanese than in British manufacturing.

[4] Relative demand shifts in favor of senior workers are unlikely with the rapid diffusion of information-related technologies during the past 10 years.

1990–4, and including all industries. These are the same data used in chapter 4, where our focus was on estimating the relationship between earnings and tenure. As in that chapter, we consider only male employees and construct our data by pooling cross-sections over time.

It is often argued that estimates based upon cross-sectional data are not an adequate representation of individual earnings profiles when the economic environment is not stationary. In the absence of individual data, when the original data consist of cells with average information on groups of individuals, an alternative to cross-sectional data is to construct cohort data by following these cells over time. In the second part of this chapter, we build cohort data using the industrial data described in chapter 8, covering the period 1976–96. We do so for six cohorts and three subperiods, 1976–86, 1981–91, and 1986–96. Each cohort is identified by year of birth. We use these data to check the robustness of the results obtained from pooled cross-sections.

Pooled cross-sections

Our dataset covers all industries and the years 1980–4 and 1990–4. An advantage of using data for all industries is that we have information on educational attainment. Compared to the first period, which registered an average real GNP growth rate of 3.08 percent a year, real growth in the second period was lower and equal to 2.18 percent a year. Moreover, the percentage of employees older than 40 was 43 percent in 1980 and 50 percent 10 years later. The second subperiod is thus characterized both by a lower average rate of economic growth and by an older labor force.

The empirical model is the same model used in chapter 4, and consists of the following two equations

$$\ln W_{it} = \lambda_0 + \lambda_1 T_{it} + \lambda_2 T_{it}^2 + \lambda_3 X_{it} + \lambda_4 X_{it}^2 + \sum_j \lambda_{5j} E_{ij} + \lambda_6 R_{it} \quad (9.1)$$

$$+ \lambda_7 SHARE_t + \sum_k \lambda_{8k} YD_k + \lambda_9 D90 * T_{it} + \lambda_{10} D90 * T_{it}^2$$

$$+ \lambda_{11} D90 * X_{it} + \lambda_{12} D90 * X_{it}^2 + \sum_j \lambda_{13j} D90 * E_{ij} + \eta_{it}$$

$$R_{it} = \beta_0 + \beta_1 T_{it} + \beta_2 X_{it} + \sum_j \beta_{3j} E_{ij} + \beta_4 Z_{it} + \beta_5 D90 * T_{it} \quad (9.2)$$

$$+ \beta_6 D90 * X_{it} + \sum_j \beta_{7j} D90 * E_{ij} + \beta_8 \mu_i$$

where X is net labor market experience, computed as age *minus* tenure *minus* years of education *minus* 6, E_j is an educational dummy, R is rank, $SHARE$ is the number of employees in the rank relative to total employment, YD is a vector of year dummies, $D90$ is a dummy equal to one for the period 1990–94 and to zero for the previous period, and η_{it} and μ_j are error terms.

Compared to chapter 4, we have augmented both equations with the interactions between $D90$, net experience, tenure, and educational dummies. These interactions are meant to pick up changes in the relationship between earnings, rank allocation, tenure, education, and net experience. Using the terminology introduced in chapter 4, this empirical framework allows us also to distinguish between conditional and unconditional earnings differentials, where the conditional variable is rank allocation, R.

Tables 9.1 and 9.2 show average tenure, net experience, education, age, and real monthly pay by rank in 1980 and in 1994, for both large and medium-sized firms. While average age and tenure have increased during the sample period in both types of firm, the increase in tenure has been larger among medium-sized firms. Since tenure has increased more than age, net labor market experience has declined in either type of firm. The ratio between average wages in the top and in the bottom rank has declined, from 1.96 to 1.62 in large firms and from 1.64 to 1.53 in medium-sized firms. At the same time, the shape of the hierarchical pyramid has changed: in 1980, the percentage of unranked employees was 83.4 percent in large firms and 81.1 percent in medium-sized firms; in 1994, it was 78.9 percent in large firms and 78.5 percent in medium-sized firms.[5] The relative decline in the share of unranked employees has been compensated by an increase in the share of individuals in the top two ranks: in 1980, this share was 8.7 percent in large firms and 11 percent in medium-sized firms; in 1994, it was 12.5 percent in large firms and 13.8 percent in medium-sized firms.

Table 9.3 shows the ordinary least squares estimates of (9.1), for both large and medium-sized firms. In either case, we test whether the interactions with $D90$ are jointly significantly different from zero, and find that a likelihood ratio test never rejects the alternative hypothesis of significant interactions.[6] Next, we test whether the interactions of $D90$ with each group of variables (e.g. tenure and tenure squared) are significant, and find that, with the single exception of the interactions with

---

[5] Foremen are excluded from this dataset. We use the definition of ranks given in chapter 4.
[6] The χ^2_7 statistic is equal to 51.27 in large firms and to 139.6 in medium-sized firms.

Table 9.1 *Weighted means and standard deviations, large firms, 1980 and 1994*

Means and std. deviations	1980	1994
Tenure unranked	13.45 (5.8)[a]	15.86 (8.7)
Tenure rank 1[d]	18.82 (7.6)	19.59 (10.1)
Tenure rank 2[d]	20.32 (7.0)	21.65 (8.8)
Tenure rank 3[d]	21.70 (7.9)	21.86 (9.7)
Age unranked	39.93 (11.5)	39.99 (11.5)
Age rank 1	41.92 (9.9)	41.19 (10.8)
Age rank 2	43.78 (9.1)	43.72 (9.4)
Age rank 3	45.40 (8.4)	45.60 (8.6)
Monthly wage unranked[e]	377.2 (133.6)	634.3 (194.8)
Monthly wage rank 1	456.2 (75.2)	722.4 (163.2)
Monthly wage rank 2	588.8 (103.5)	869.4 (196.8)
Monthly wage rank 3	742.3 (129.7)	1025.9 (253.9)
Education unranked (years)[c]	10.75 (2.6)	10.75 (2.6)
Education rank 1	10.50 (2.5)	11.06 (2.5)
Education rank 2	10.88 (2.6)	11.11 (2.5)
Education rank 3	11.13 (2.6)	11.39 (2.5)
Experience unranked[b]	9.73 (6.9)	7.38 (3.7)
Experience rank 1	6.28 (4.3)	4.52 (2.1)
Experience rank 2	6.57 (4.1)	4.96 (1.9)
Experience rank 3	6.56 (2.7)	6.31 (2.8)

Notes:
[a]Standard deviations in parentheses.
[b]Experience is net of tenure.
[c]Education is measured by expected years of schooling.
[d]Rank 1 is for subdivision directors, rank 2 for division directors, and rank 3 for department directors.
[e]Monthly earnings are in 000 yen.

educational dummies in large firms, they always are.[7] Our data thus suggest that the relationship between earnings, tenure, net experience, and education is significantly different in the early 1990s compared to the early 1980s.

In particular, there is evidence that the conditional returns to tenure have declined. Using the results in table 9.3, we can compute these returns

[7] Interactions with tenure: $\chi_2^2 = 40.54$ in large firms and 87.1 in medium-sized firms. Interactions with experience: $\chi_2^2 = 12.9$ in large firms and 27.0 in medium-sized firms. Interactions with educational dummies: $\chi_3^2 = 0.84$ in large firms and 19.96 in medium-sized firms.

Table 9.2 *Weighted means and standard deviations, medium-sized firms, 1980 and 1994*

Means and std. deviations	1980	1994
Tenure unranked	9.22 (3.6)[a]	11.15 (5.4)
Tenure rank 1[d]	12.45 (5.1)	15.96 (7.5)
Tenure rank 2[d]	14.94 (5.4)	17.68 (7.2)
Tenure rank 3[d]	14.85 (6.8)	17.51 (8.4)
Age unranked	39.36 (11.3)	39.99 (11.6)
Age rank 1	40.09 (11.1)	40.69 (10.9)
Age rank 2	42.40 (10.1)	43.21 (9.4)
Age rank 3	41.99 (10.4)	43.25 (9.6)
Monthly wage unranked[e]	312.7 (108.1)	523.9 (147.2)
Monthly wage rank 1	337.4 (69.1)	572.1 (104.6)
Monthly wage rank 2	427.5 (69.2)	674.5 (101.7)
Monthly wage rank 3	512.8 (110.7)	804.6 (145.3)
Education unranked (years)[c]	10.58 (2.6)	10.75 (2.6)
Education rank 1	10.75 (2.6)	10.71 (2.7)
Education rank 2	10.75 (2.6)	10.92 (2.6)
Education rank 3	11.03 (2.5)	10.92 (2.6)
Experience unranked[b]	13.56 (8.6)	12.09 (6.7)
Experience rank 1	10.89 (8.6)	8.01 (4.1)
Experience rank 2	10.70 (6.7)	8.60 (3.5)
Experience rank 3	10.10 (5.5)	8.82 (3.6)

Note: For definitions see table 9.1.

by keeping education, net experience, and rank allocation constant and letting tenure vary. As shown in table 9.5, 10 years of tenure in large firms increased earnings by 88.7 percent in the 1980s and by 63.4 percent in the 1990s. On the other hand, 20 years of tenure increased earnings in these firms by 157.9 percent in the 1980s and by 130.1 percent in the 1990s. In medium-sized firms, returns to tenure are lower: after ten years of tenure earnings were 88.6 percent higher than at zero tenure in the 1980s and 42.3 percent higher in the 1990s; 20 years of tenure increased earnings by 106.6 percent in the 1980s and by 75.2 percent in the 1990s. Overall, these numbers suggest that the expected returns to tenure, conditional on rank, declined significantly in the early 1990s.

As discussed at length in chapter 4, tenure affects earnings both directly and indirectly, by influencing the allocation of individuals to ranks. The evaluation of the unconditional returns to tenure requires that we estimate also (9.2). In this chapter, we use the instrumental vari-

Table 9.3 *Estimated earnings equations, Japanese men*

	Large firms	Medium-sized firms
	(9.1)	(9.1)
T	0.074**	0.079**
T^2	−0.0011**	−0.0016**
$D90 \times T$	−0.017**	−0.036**
$D90 \times T^2$	0.0003**	0.0009**
X	0.003	0.018**
X^2	−0.0001	−0.0005**
$D90 \times X$	0.023**	0.022**
$D90 \times X^2$	−0.0016**	−0.0009**
E_1	0.133**	0.173**
E_2	0.219**	0.299**
E_3	0.424**	0.468**
$D90 \times E_1$	−0.014	−0.057**
$D90 \times E_2$	−0.021	−0.080**
$D90 \times E_3$	−0.018	−0.065**
$SHARE$	0.186**	0.205**
R	0.201**	0.182**
R^2	0.91	0.93
Nobs[a]	1105	1175

Notes: Dependent variable: $\ln W$; method: ordinary least squares.

**The estimated coefficient is significant at the 5 percent level of confidence. Heteroskedasticity-consistent standard errors.
Each regression includes a constant and nine year dummies.
[a]In all tables in this chapter: number of observations.

ables approach and instrument tenure and its interaction with $D90$ with a third-order polynomial in age, the interaction of $D90$ with age and year dummies. Results are in table 9.4.

Notice first that both the Sargan Criterion, SC, and the Lagrange Multiplier test of the over-identifying restrictions, $TEST$, cannot reject the null hypothesis of no mis-specification for both firm sizes. Next, the Gallant–Jorgenson test for the joint significance of interaction terms clearly rejects these terms: the χ_5^2 statistic has a p-value to 0.465 in the case of large firms and to 0.136 in the case of medium-sized firms. While the interactions of $D90$ with educational dummies are never significant, the interaction with tenure is significant at the 10 percent level of confidence in the case of large firms and not significant in the case of medium-sized firms. The interaction with net experience is also never

Table 9.4 *Estimates of the rank function, by instrumental variables*

	Large firms	Medium-sized firms
T	0.041**	0.037**
$D90 \times T$	−0.01*	0.0005
X	−0.014*	−0.014**
$D90 \times X$	0.023	−0.011
E_1	0.083	0.101
E_2	0.123	0.117
E_3	0.254**	0.191**
$D90 \times E_1$	0.062	−0.009
$D90 \times E_2$	0.068	−0.036
$D90 \times E_3$	0.041	−0.091
$SHARE$	−2.366**	−2.40**
R^2	0.63	0.65
SC	0.93 (11)	0.76 (11)
$TEST$	0.11 (12)	0.33 (12)
Nobs	1105	1175

Notes: For definitions, see table 9.3.
Additional instruments are year dummies and a third-order polynomial in age net of tenure.
SC is the Sargan Criterion for instrument validity; $TEST$ is a Lagrange Multiplier test for the over-identifying restrictions (see Main and Reilly, 1993).
Probability values of the tests in the table.
Degrees of freedom in parentheses.
*The estimated coefficient is significant at the 10 percent level of confidence.

significant. We conclude from this that there is little evidence of a significant change of the rank allocation function in the early 1990s, compared to the early 1980s.

We can use the estimates of the rank allocation function to compute the unconditional returns to tenure in the two subperiods. Table 9.5 presents the results and figures 9.1 and 9.2 illustrate them for large and medium-sized firms. The ratio between unconditional and conditional returns is illustrated in figures 9.3 and 9.4, respectively, for large and medium-sized firms. While this ratio has remained more or less unchanged for medium-sized firms, it has decreased in large firms, because of the smaller impact of tenure on rank allocation. Overall, the estimates of unconditional earnings profiles confirm that returns to tenure declined in the early 1990s.

Table 9.5 *Estimated earnings growth^a caused by tenure, Japanese men, 1980–1994*

Tenure	Condit. 1980–4	Uncondit. 1980–4	Condit. 1990–4	Uncondit. 1990–4
Large firms				
0	100	100	100	100
5	141.1	147.0	130.2	134.2
10	188.7	201.9	163.4	173.6
15	229.6	263.9	197.6	216.4
20	257.9	295.8	230.1	259.8
Medium-sized firms				
0	100	100	100	100
5	142.9	147.9	121.5	125.7
10	188.6	166.3	142.3	152.5
15	187.4	197.2	164.1	183.3
20	206.6	221.2	175.2	201.2

Notes: ^{a}Entries are hourly earnings at various years of tenure.
Hourly wages at zero tenure and experience are normalized to 100.

Table 9.6 *Estimated unconditional earnings growth^a caused by net experience, Japanese men, 1980–1994*

	Large firms		Medium-sized firms	
Net experience	1980–4	1990–4	1980–4	1990–4
0	100	100	100	100
5	99.8	110.0	106.5	114.9
10	98.8	111.0	110.4	122.9
15	97.1	102.5	111.6	122.2
20	94.6	86.7	109.9	112.9

Note: ^{a}Entries are hourly earnings at various years of tenure.
Hourly wages at zero tenure and experience are normalized to 100.

While the returns to tenure have fallen, the returns to net experience have significantly increased in both types of firm. Table 9.6 simulates

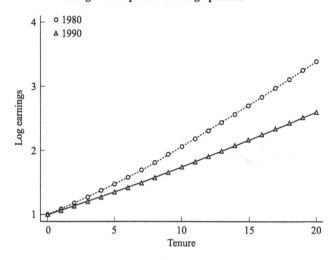

Figure 9.1 Unconditional wage–tenure profiles, large firms

earnings growth when net experience is allowed to vary from zero to 20 years and tenure and education remain unchanged and figures 9.5 and 9.6 illustrate the associated earnings–experience profiles. Consider first large firms. In the early 1980s, an increase in labor market experience, given education and tenure, reduced earnings; in the early 1990s, an increase in experience yielded a wage premium, but very long experience (20 years)

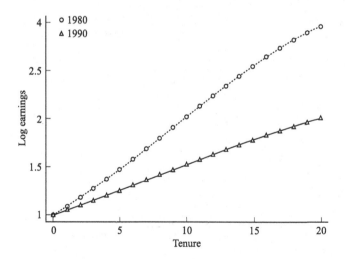

Figure 9.2 Unconditional wage–tenure profiles, medium-sized firms

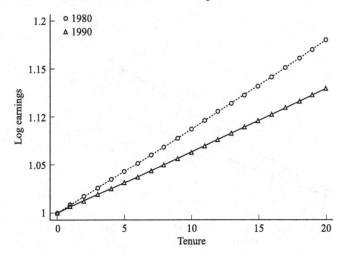

Figure 9.3 Unconditional over conditional profiles, large firms

penalized net earnings. In medium-sized firms, experience always increases earnings, especially in the early 1990s, when an individual with 10 years of previous labor experience earned on average 23 percent more than an individual without any previous market experience.

Finally, while we find no evidence of changes in the returns to education among large firms, there is evidence of a decline in the returns to education among medium-sized firms.

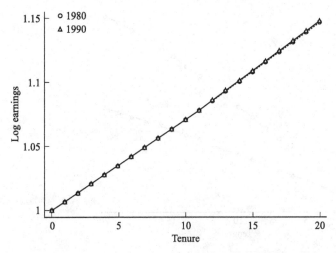

Figure 9.4 Unconditional over conditional profiles, medium-sized firms

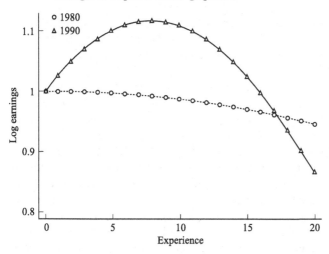

Figure 9.5 Wage–experience profiles, large firms

Cohort data, 1976–1996

An important question is whether the results in the previous section are robust. As mentioned earlier in the chapter, estimates of wage–tenure profiles based upon cross-sectional data have problems when the economic environment is not stationary, as was obviously the case for the period of interest. For example, if labor force ageing pushes up the entry

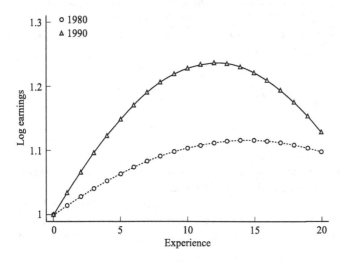

Figure 9.6 Wage–experience profiles, medium-sized firms

wage of increasingly scarce cohorts of young workers, these shifts in the entry wage contribute to flatten earnings profiles estimated from cross-section data, even though the slope of the actual profiles do not differ across cohorts.

Since we are interested in changes of earnings profiles, we select three partially overlapping subperiods, 1976–86, 1981–91, and 1986–96, and construct data for six cohorts in each subperiod. Notice that average real GNP growth was 3.84 percent per year during the first subperiod, 4.07 percent during the second subperiod, and 3.02 percent during the last subperiod. Furthermore, the share of workers in total employment aged 40 years or older was 40 percent in 1976 and 50 percent in 1995. Hence, while ageing has increased during the whole period, growth accelerated during the second subperiod and decelerated afterwards.

The construction of each cohort is detailed in table 9.7, where we show both age groups and cohorts for the two subperiods.[8] The first cohort in the first subperiod, for instance, includes the age group 20–24 years in 1976, the age group 25–29 years in 1981, and the age group 30–34 years in 1986. The same cohort in the last subperiod picks the same age groups, respectively, for 1986, 1991, and 1996. Intervals between two consecutive data points span five years, the length of each age group. Since our last time observation is 1996, we choose for symmetry to select three periods for each cohort, corresponding to 10 years in the labor market.

We can build cohort data for the three industries and the two firm sizes. Educational attainment, however, is not available in the industrial data. Since education is not time-varying, however, we can pick up differences in education and labor market experience across cohorts by using cohort dummies and by controlling for tenure and year dummies. The empirical model is written as follows:

$$\ln W_{it} = \sum_{i=1}^{6} \alpha_i COHORT_i + \beta_1 T_{it} + \beta_2 T_{it}^2 + dummies + u_{it}$$

$$(9.3)$$

where W is the real consumer wage, i is for the cohort, $COHORT$ is a cohort dummy, T is tenure, t is for time, $dummies$ refer to industrial, firm-size, and year dummies, and u is the error term.

As discussed in chapter 4, ordinary least squares estimates of (9.3) are likely to be biased by the correlation of tenure with the error term, u, that includes cell- and match-specific quality. Following Altonji and Shakokto

---

[8] See Hart and Kawasaki (1995) for a similar method applied to Japanese bonus pay.

Table 9.7 *Age groups and cohorts, 1976–1996*

Cohort	1976/81/86	1981/86/91	1986/91/96
1	20–24	25–29	30–34
2	25–29	30–34	35–39
3	30–34	35–39	40–44
4	35–39	40–44	45–49
5	40–44	45–49	50–54
6	45–49	50–54	55–59

(1987), we instrument tenure and tenure squared with the deviation of tenure from its mean $\overline{T}_i$, defined as

$$\overline{T}_i = \frac{1}{N} \sum_t T_{it}$$

and with the deviation of tenure squared from $\overline{T}_i^2$. By construction, these variables are orthogonal to the error term.

Our results are presented in table 9.8, separately for each subperiod. We notice that tenure and tenure squared both have significant coefficients, and that the relationship between (log) wages and tenure has the usual concave shape. Moreover, the coefficient of tenure is highest in the second subperiod, when the average rate of growth was 4.07 percent a year, and lowest in the last subperiod, when output grew by 3.02 percent a year. This evidence confirms that the returns to tenure are higher when the rate of growth of the economy is faster.

Summary

Compared to the early and mid-1980s, the early and mid-1990s in Japan were characterized by both an older employed labor force and slower economic growth. In this chapter, we have compared earnings profiles in the two subperiods and found that:

(a) The shape of vertical hierarchies in both large and medium-sized firms have changed, with more people being allocated to the top rungs of the vertical hierarchy

Table 9.8 *IV estimates of (9.3), 1976–1996; dependent variable:* ln W_{it}

	1976–86	1981–91	1986–96
T	0.106**	0.117**	0.098**
T^2	−0.0017**	−0.0019**	−0.0017**
R^2	0.96	0.96	0.95
Nobs	108	108	108

Notes: **The coefficient is significantly different from zero at the 5 percent level of confidence.
Heteroskedasticity-consistent standard errors.
Each regression includes cohort, industry, firm size, time dummies, and a constant term.

(b) Average tenure has increased more than average age; with small changes in educational attainment, previous labor market experience has fallen, especially among medium-sized firms
(c) The returns to tenure, both conditional and unconditional, have fallen in both large and medium-sized firms, and the reduction has been sizeable, especially for longer tenure spells
(d) The returns to previous labor market experience have increased.

Our results confirm some of the findings by Clark and Ogawa (1992) (who compared the early 1970s with the mid-1980s and showed that the returns to tenure declined over time) and extend them to the early 1990s. In partial contrast with these authors, however, we also find that the returns to previous labor market experience increased significantly in the early 1990s.

In this chapter, we have associated the decline in the returns to tenure with the slowdown in the rate of economic growth and the progressive ageing of the Japanese labor force. As shown in chapter 1, sustained economic growth is key to the development of internal labor markets. By increasing the ratio of vacancies to unemployment, higher growth makes labor market matching relatively more difficult and motivates firms both to use internal upgrading and to establish long-term employment relationships by rewarding tenure. When growth slows down, however, the required skills can be more easily obtained from the labor market. In such circumstances, internal labor markets are partly replaced by occupational labor markets.

Similarly, the progressive ageing of the labor force has reduced the pool of young labor market entrants, who are expected to fill the lower rungs of promotion hierarchies in internal labor markets, increasing the relative wage of new entrants and making internal upgrading more costly compared to market procurement of skilled employees.

As discussed in chapter 2, labor market experience matters more in occupational labor markets and tenure is more important in internal labor markets. The decline in the returns to tenure and the increase in the returns to labor market experience found in this chapter can thus also be explained by the increased importance of occupational labor markets among large and medium-sized firms, induced by the slowdown in the rate of economic growth and by the ageing of the Japanese labor force.

10 The impact of growth and business cycles on Japanese corporate hierarchies

Overview[1]

In chapter 9, we showed that the slope of Japanese wage–tenure profiles declined in recent years, and we explained this decline by the slowdown in economic growth and the ageing of the labor force. In this chapter we show that the slowdown in economic growth has also been a key factor behind the long-run changes in relative wages by rank, spans of control, and promotion rates described in chapter 8. These changes can be summarized as follows: during the past 20 years, relative wages and spans of control have declined, whereas promotion rates have shown large fluctuations around a negative trend.

We start by presenting a simple theoretical model that highlights the *interaction between growth* (measured by employment growth), *relative wages*, *spans of control*, and *promotion probabilities* in firms that adopt internal labor markets. Next, we turn to the discussion of *cohort effects on average wages*, distinguishing between changes in the size and in the average quality of a cohort of newly hired employees. Our empirical investigation, based upon the data described in chapter 8, clearly supports the implications of the theoretical model.

In the second part of the chapter we turn to the analysis of the *effects of business cycle fluctuations* on the wage structure of Japanese firms. We show that, while average wages are clearly pro-cyclical, relative wages are sensitive to the cycle only in the finance industry. We find no evidence that the responsiveness of wages to short-run fluctuations varies with the seniority of employees. A brief summary concludes the chapter.

---

[1] This chapter builds on Ariga *et al.* (1992) and Brunello *et al.* (1995).

A model of internal labor markets, incentives, and growth

In chapter 1, we presented a model of internal labor markets where the main emphasis was on training versus matching costs. In chapter 2, we considered the optimal assignment problem of firms that use career paths to induce workers to accumulate skills that vary in their degree of proximity. In both chapters, we assumed perfect and symmetric information. While this working assumption can be justified as a way of simplifying and focusing matters, it rules out relevant issues that have been extensively explored in the literature on contracts and agency relationships within firms.

To illustrate, consider internal promotion. While accumulated human capital and matching costs are important facets of the decision to promote, another relevant aspect is the evaluation of individual performance. When information is asymmetric, either because the action is hidden (*moral hazard*) or because the quality of the individual is unknown to the principal (*adverse selection*), promotion tournaments can be used as an incentive device.[2]

In this chapter, we develop a simple model of internal labor markets where the promotion decision is based upon promotion tournaments among equally able participants. This is equivalent to assuming that moral hazard is the only problem generated by asymmetric information between the principal and the agents. An alternative approach, that focuses on adverse selection and on promotion as a signaling game, can be found in Prendergast (1990, 1992).[3]

Setup

Consider an economy composed of identical workers and of price-taking firms that organize labor in internal labor markets (ILM firms). Prices are normalized to one. Each firm in this economy has a hierarchical structure, composed of two levels or ranks. Subordinate employees are in the lower rank and supervisors are in the upper rank. Promotion to supervisor is restricted to incumbents.[4]

Each worker lives and works for two periods, and each firm offers to potential hires a two-period contract, designed to exclude mid-career quits. There are no exogenous separations. During her first period with the firm, the newly hired employee (entrant) is assigned to an unskilled

---

[2] See the review of the related literature in chapter 5.
[3] Malcomson and McLeod (1988) look at both moral hazard and adverse selection problems in their theory of corporate hierarchies.
[4] See chapter 1 for a model that also includes OLM firms.

job slot and works at the fully observable minimum effort level $e^{\min}$. By the end of the first period, the worker is an incumbent and can participate to a tournament for promotion to supervisor in her second and final period.[5] Promotion is achieved if individual measured performance is at least equal to the given promotion standard. Since performance depends on effort, the likelihood of promotion depends on individual effort, e. Each participant in the tournament plays a non-cooperative Nash game and there is no collusion.[6]

Each worker has private information on effort spent during the tournament. Effort generates human capital that becomes perfectly observable after the tournament is over. This assumption rules out information problems in the second and final stage of the contract. After the tournament, workers are allocated to ranks, effort is embodied in human capital, and production takes place.

At the beginning of each period of time, firms hire new workers, allocate incumbents to ranks, and produce and sell output. Each firm produces output by using the following technology

$$Y = sef\left[\frac{(m + m_{-1} - s)}{se}\right] \tag{10.1}$$

where Y = real output, f is the production technology, and s, m, and m_{-1} are, respectively, the number of supervisors, new entrants, and incumbents, who were hired in the previous period.

This constant returns to scale technology implies that firms produce output by organizing labor into production units headed by a supervisor (see Rosen, 1982). The output of each unit depends on the productivity of each supervisor, e, and on the output of subordinates in each unit, f.

Growth of the firm and the incentive structure

Since we are interested in the relationship between growth, incentives, and the design of corporate hierarchies, we shall make the bold simplifying assumption that the rate of employment growth in firms is determined by the exogenous rate of economic growth. By doing so, we retain the scale effects of output growth on employment, but eliminate the possibility both that firms can substitute employment for individual effort and that changes in the span of control affect total employment. Letting employment growth be μ, it follows that

[5] See Lazear and Rosen (1981); McLaughlin (1988) for a discussion of rank-order tournaments.
[6] See McLeod (1986) for a discussion of collusion in a similar setup.

$$m = (1 + \mu)m_{-1} \tag{10.2}$$

Next, define

$$k = \frac{s}{m + m_{-1}} = \frac{s}{(2 + \mu)m_{-1}} \tag{10.3}$$

as the share of supervisors in total employment and

$$\theta = \frac{s}{m_{-1}} = (2 + \mu)k \tag{10.4}$$

as the probability of internal promotion faced by incumbents. Notice that, by definition, this probability depends in a natural way on the rate of employment growth, μ.

Let promotion be determined by a promotion tournament, and assume that each individual participating in the tournament is evaluated on the basis of the noisy test statistic

$$z = e + u \tag{10.5}$$

where e is individual effort that is not observed by the principal and u is a random variable with a uniform distribution $H = \int_{-\xi}^{\xi} (1/2\xi)du$ and mean equal to zero.

Supposing that workers are risk-neutral,[7] a two-period contract offers expected income equal to

$$V = w_0 + w_1 + \theta(w_2 - w_1) - c(e) \tag{10.6}$$

where V is the value of the contract, w_0, w_1, and w_2 are the wages paid, respectively, to entrants, incumbents, and supervisors, the discount factor is equal to one, and c is the cost function, an increasing and strictly convex function of effort.

Since incumbents are homogeneous and play a symmetric Nash non-cooperative game, their choice of effort, e^*, must be identical. When each firm promotes s incumbents to supervisors, the required promotion standard is

$$z^s = e^* + u^s \tag{10.7}$$

where

$$H(u^s) = 1 - \frac{s}{m_{-1}} = 1 - \theta \tag{10.8}$$

For each incumbent, promotion occurs if the outcome of the test is at least as high as the standard, z^s, and the probability of promotion is equal to

[7] We assume risk-neutrality to separate incentive issues, that we focus upon, from insurance issues.

$$\text{Prob}(e^* + u \geq e^* + u^s) = 1 - H(u^s) = \theta \tag{10.9}$$

With no corner solutions, the level of effort that maximizes expected utility in (10.6) is given by the following first-order condition

$$c'(e^*) = (w_2 - w_1)\frac{\partial \theta}{\partial e^*} = (w_2 - w_1)h\big[H^{-1}(1 - \theta)\big] \tag{10.10}$$

where h is the density function of H and the principal (firm) can elicit this level of effort by setting the wage premium $p = (w_2 - w_1)$ to satisfy the following incentive compatibility constraint

$$(w_2 - w_1) = p = \frac{c'(e^*)}{h\big[H^{-1}(1 - \theta)\big]} \tag{10.11}$$

Plugging (10.11) into (10.6), we obtain that

$$V = w_0 + w_1 + \theta p - c(e^*) \tag{10.12}$$

Since the market for new entrants is competitive, contracts must offer the reservation level of utility, V_0, and the participation constraint is $V \geq V_0$. If they are to avoid mid-term quits, contracts must also satisfy the no-quit constraint, given by

$$w_1 + \theta p - c(e^*) \geq V_1 \tag{10.13}$$

where V_1 is the (expected) level of utility offered by one-period contracts available in the market. In partial equilibrium, both V_0 and V_1 are given for each firm.

Firms choose the optimal values of k and e by maximizing profits subject to the participation, the no-quits, and the incentive compatibility constraints. By choosing the optimal value of k, k^*, firms also choose the optimal promotion probability offered in their contracts, θ^*.[8] Since employment growth is exogenous, this is equivalent to maximizing profit per head

$$\pi = ekf\left[\frac{(1-k)}{ke}\right] - \frac{(1+\mu)}{(2+\mu)}\left[w_0 + \frac{w_1}{1+\mu} + \frac{\theta p}{1+\mu}\right] \tag{10.14}$$

Using (10.12) and (10.13) to substitute wages out, and letting f be the first derivative of f, the first-order conditions of this maximization exercise are

$$f\left(\frac{(1-k)}{ke}\right) - \frac{1}{ke}f'\left(\frac{(1-k)}{ke}\right) = 0 \tag{10.15}$$

---

[8] In this chapter, "optimal" refers to profit-maximizing values, not to the social optimum.

$$kf\left(\frac{(1-k)}{ke}\right) - \frac{1-k}{e}f'\left(\frac{(1-k)}{ke}\right) = \frac{c'(e)}{2+\mu} \qquad (10.16)$$

The differentiation of these first order conditions yields the following.

Lemma 10.1 *If ϕ, the elasticity of substitution associated with the production function f, is less than or equal to one, the promotion probability, θ^*, the optimal effort level, e^*, and output per head $Y/m + m_{-1}$ in ILM firms are all increasing in the rate of employment growth, μ. Moreover, the optimal span of control, $SPC = 1 - k^*/k^*$, is also increasing in μ if $\phi <$ one.*

Proof: See the appendix (p. 264).

Next, we can establish the following result.

Lemma 10.2 *The (privately) optimal wage premium, p^*, is increasing in the rate of growth, μ.*

Proof: See the appendix (p. 265).

These results depend critically on the assumption that there is internal promotion. Promotion from within provides the link between employment growth and optimal effort. If required effort is unchanged by growth, there is no need to vary the wage premium.[9]

Extension I: production efficiency and promotion

With α and β measuring the fully observable production efficiency of supervisors and subordinates, the production technology can be written as

$$Y = \alpha sef\left[\frac{\beta(m+m_{-1}-s)}{\alpha se}\right] \qquad (10.17)$$

Defining the span of control in efficiency units as

$$\tilde{n} = \frac{\beta(1-k)}{\alpha ek} \qquad (10.18)$$

---

[9] The relationship between growth and promotion is studied in a different framework by Ohashi and Matsushige (1994).

Table 10.1 *The effects of technological progress, growth, and supply shocks*

	$d\alpha > 0$	$d\beta > 0$	$(d\alpha/\alpha) = (d\beta/\beta) > 0$	$t = \tau+1$	$t = \tau$	$t = \tau+1$
	Long-run effects			$d\lambda_\tau > 0$		$dm_\tau > 0$
e^*	+	+	+	?	+	−
$\tilde{n}$	−	−	+	−	−	+
$1 - k^*/k^*$	+	+	−	+	+	−
θ^*	+	−	+	−	+	−
p^*	+	+	+	?	+	−

Note: We use + and − when an increase in the variable heading each column leads, respectively, to an increase and a decrease in the variable heading each row. A question mark is used when the direction of the effect cannot be signed.

Equations (10.15) and (10.16) become

$$e\alpha f(\tilde{n}) - (\alpha e\tilde{n} + \beta)f'(\tilde{n}) = 0 \tag{10.19}$$

$$\alpha\beta^2(2 + \mu)f(\tilde{n}) = (\alpha e\tilde{n} + \beta)^2 c'(e) \tag{10.20}$$

In the appendix (p. 264), we compute the effects of changes in α, β, and μ on individual effort, e, the share of supervisors, k, the promotion probability, θ, and the wage premium, p. The qualitative results are summarized in table 10.1.

First, given our assumptions on the elasticity of substitution, ϕ, an increase in employment growth, μ, increases individual effort, e^*, the span of control, $SPC = 1 - k^*/k^*$, the promotion probability, θ^*, and the wage premium, p^*. An increase in α, the efficiency of supervisors, given β, reduces the relative demand for supervisors relative to subordinates, thus reducing k^* and increasing the span of control, SPC. Given employment growth, the decline in the share of supervisors reduces the probability of promotion, θ^*. Since the marginal efficiency of supervisors increases as α increases, so do individual effort, e^*, and the wage premium, p^*.

Next, consider an increase in β, given α. Given that the efficiency of subordinates increases while employment growth remains constant, the relative demand for subordinates falls, leading to an increase in k^* and to a decline in the span of control. The probability of promotion thus increases. As in the case of an increase in α, individual effort increases because the efficiency of the production unit run by each supervisor increases. As a consequence, both e^* and the wage premium, p^*, increase because of the higher β.

Finally, consider the case when both α and β increase at the same proportional rate. In this case, the relative efficiency of supervisors and subordinates remains unchanged, and the same level of effort brings about a larger increase in efficiency. In this sense, the proportional change is equivalent to a proportional reduction in the cost function. Table 10.1 shows that the effect of a symmetric increase in α and β is qualitatively similar to the effects of an increase in α.

The message of this comparative statics exercise is that the effects of higher production efficiency on corporate hierarchies differ from the effects of (employment) growth because only in the second case do we observe a contemporaneous increase in spans of control, promotion probabilities, and relative wages.

Extension II: cohort effects

In our setup, each period of time corresponds to half of an employee's career and our analysis has been confined to the study of long-run changes that spread over many generations. Temporary changes in the economic environment, however, are also important for corporate hierarchies. Below we consider two such changes, that affect both the quality and the quantity of labor supply in each particular period.

Consider first a change in the average quality of the cohort of new recruits. Assume that workers belonging to the same cohort are homogeneous, but that average quality changes across generations. In particular, let λ_τ be the quality of cohort τ and e_τ be the investment in human capital by individuals in that cohort. Then $\tilde{e}_\tau \equiv \lambda_\tau e_\tau$ is the quality adjusted human capital of cohort τ.

The effects of a temporary increase in average quality are shown in the fifth column of table 10.1. By construction, the impact of this increase is felt when the cohort invests in firm-specific human capital, by the end of the first period in the firm. Since the relative efficiency of supervisors increases, the relative demand for supervisors falls, leading to an increase in the span of control. Given the size of the cohort at recruitment, the promotion probability must fall. Notice that the effect of a temporary improvement in quality on individual effort, e^*, cannot be signed because of the presence of two counteracting effects. On the one hand, when the cost of effort is sufficiently elastic with respect to variations in the level of effort, there is substitution away from costly effort. On the other, when the marginal productivity of supervisors is sufficiently larger than the marginal productivity of subordinates, higher quality increases effort. One consequence of this is that the effects of a change in quality on the wage premium also cannot be signed.

Next, consider a temporary increase in the size of the cohort of new hires, given quality. As shown in the last two columns of table 10.1, this is equivalent to a temporary increase in m, given m_{-1}. The immediate effect is similar to that induced by a temporary increase in μ. Since the current size of the hierarchy increases, incumbents face a higher probability of promotion and effort, the span of control, and the wage premium all increase. In the next period of time, entrants become incumbents and invest in human capital. Since the size of the corporate hierarchy shrinks back to its original level, the promotion probability falls, because there are more incumbents for a smaller number of upper-rank positions. The reduction in promotion probability is accompanied by lower effort, a smaller span of control, and a smaller wage premium.

Empirical evidence

In the simple model discussed above, we have studied the interactions between growth and the design of corporate hierarchies in internal labor markets. Growth influences relative wages, spans of control, and promotion probabilities in corporate hierarchies because firms operate internal labor markets and promote employees internally to fill vacancies in upper-rank position.

The model generates the following sequential structure

$$w_2 - w_1 \equiv p = \sigma_1(k, \mu) \tag{10.21}$$

$$e = \sigma_2(k, \mu) \tag{10.22}$$

$$k = \sigma_3(\mu) \tag{10.23}$$

Given μ, optimal k is determined by (10.23). Given μ and k, both p and e are determined by (10.21) and (10.22). In this section, we use the data described in chapter 8 to test some of the implications derived above. We focus on three key variables – relative wages, spans of control, and promotion rates – all defined in chapter 8, and on the relationship of these variables with economic growth, measured either by five-year real output growth or by five-year real *per capita* output growth.

Growth, relative wages, spans of control, and promotion rates

We start our empirical analysis by pooling the available cross-section data over time (1976–96), and by regressing rank-specific relative real wages – that is, real wages in ranks 1, 2, and 3 relative to real wages in rank 0^{10} – on the age and tenure of employees in rank 0, age and tenure squared, firm size, industry and rank dummies, the rank-specific spans of control, and our measures of economic growth. Table 10.2 presents the results and shows that relative wages significantly increase when both the span of control and the rate of economic growth increase.

One potential shortcoming of the results in table 10.2 is that relative wages are disaggregated by age group while spans of control and output growth are both invariant across age groups. As remarked by Moulton (1990), the regression of data at a lower level of disaggregation on data at a higher level of disaggregation tends to under-estimate the true standard errors of the coefficients attached to the more aggregated variables. We check whether our results are robust by aggregating relative wages over

---

[10] We exclude foremen from the empirical analysis, because this rank is available only in manufacturing industry. The data used in this section are described in detail in chapter 8.

Table 10.2 *Relative wages and growth, pooled cross-sections*

	RVA[a]	RVA per head
Age	0.035**	0.036**
Age^2	-0.251×10^{-3}	-0.252×10^{-3}
Tenure	$-0.045**$	$-0.045**$
Tenure^2	$0.128 \times 10^{-3}**$	$0.128 \times 10^{-3}**$
SPC	0.008**	0.008**
Growth	1.111**	1.160**
Nobs[b]	2749	2749
R^2	0.56	0.56

Notes:
[a]RVA is real value added.
[b]In all tables in this chapter: number of observations.
Each regression includes a constant and industry, firm-size and rank-specific dummies.
**The coefficient is significantly different from zero at the 5 percent level of confidence.

age groups, using employment in the cell as weights. As shown by table 10.3, regressions based upon more aggregate data confirm our previous results, in that both the span of control and long-run economic growth have a highly significant and positive effect on relative wages.

Next, table 10.4 shows the results from regressing the spans of control on industry, firm size and rank dummies, and the five-year rate of growth of output (or, alternatively, *per capita* output). As predicted by our model, economic growth has a large positive and significant effect on spans of control.

Finally, tables 10.5 and 10.6 focus on promotion rates. Table 10.5 is based on pooled cross-sections and table 10.6 on data aggregated over age groups. The evidence suggests that, while the span of control has a negative effect on promotion rates, the rate of economic growth has a positive and significant effect on promotion. These results are consistent with the model discussed above. An increase in the span of control reduces the share of supervisors, k, thus reducing the probability of promotion. On the other hand, higher growth increases the size of the corporate hierarchy, thereby improving the promotion outcomes of incumbent employees.

These results suggest that the slowdown in the rate of economic growth experienced by the Japanese economy has been an important reason

Table 10.3 *Relative wages and growth, data aggregated over age groups; dependent variable: relative wages*

	RVA	RVA per head
Age	−0.008	−0.007
Age^2	−0.227 × 10^{-3}	0.217 × 10^{-3}
Tenure	−0.007	−0.006
Tenure^2	−0.94 × 10^{-3}	−0.125 × 10^{-3}
SPC	0.009**	0.009**
Growth	0.828**	0.797**
Nobs	266	266
R^2	0.94	0.93

Note: For definitions, see table 10.2.

Table 10.4 *Span of control and growth, data aggregated over age groups; dependent variable: spans of control*

	RVA	RVA per head
Growth	1.713**	2.495**
Nobs	266	266
R^2	0.87	0.87

Note: For definitions, see table 10.2.

Table 10.5 *Promotion rates and growth, pooled cross-sections*

	RVA	RVA per head
Age	0.033**	−0.007
Age^2	−0.501 × 10^{-3}**	0.217 × 10^{-3}
SPC	-0.003**	−0.009**
Growth	0.241*	0.197**
Nobs	1855	1855
R^2	0.53	0.54

Table 10.6. *Promotion rates and growth, data aggregated over age groups*

	RVA	RVA per head
Age	−0.030	−0.029
Age^2	0.447×10^{-3}	0.435×10^{-3}
SPC	−0.003	−0.003
Growth	2.185**	1.995**
Nobs	270	270
R^2	0.82	0.82

Note: For definitions, see table 10.2.

behind the observed reduction in relative wages, spans of control, and promotion rates. The joint decline in these three variables over the past few years also confirms that shifts in productive efficiency, measured by parameters α and β, cannot explain the stylized facts as well as a decline in the rate of overall economic growth.[11]

Cohort effects

In the theoretical model, we have argued that both the size and the average quality of newly hired cohorts can have important implications for wages and promotion within firms. First of all, the size of the cohort of entrants affects promotion rates because recruits of larger cohorts face, *ceteris paribus*, stronger competition for upper-rank jobs. Since promotion yields a wage premium, and the size of this premium declines as the size of the cohort of new recruits increases, larger cohorts that face lower promotion probabilities experience over time lower average wages, conditionally on tenure, age, and economic growth.

To test for the presence of cohort size effects on wages, we use our data for the period 1976–96 to build a cohort dataset that tracks over time groups of individuals belonging to the same range of years of birth. We start with the cohort of individuals aged 20–24 in 1976, whom we can follow for 15 years (age 25–29 in 1981, age 30–34 in 1986, and age 35–39 in 1991), continue with the cohorts aged 20–24 in 1977, 1978, 1979, and

[11] Chuma and Higuchi (1995) explain recent trends in the Japanese employment system by assuming that technical progress has been biased towards enhancing the productivity of skilled workers.

Table 10.7 *Cohort effects on average wages, pseudo panel data*

	(1)	(2)
Age	1.047**	0.690**
Age^2	−0.022**	−0.014**
Tenure	0.104**	0.100**
$Tenure^2$	−0.0014**	−0.0018**
Growth	0.163*	0.142**
Cosize	−0.796**	–
QUA	–	−0.009**
Nobs	168	227
R^2	0.85	0.83

Note: **The coefficient is significantly different from zero at the 5 percent level of confidence.

1980 and end with the cohort aged 20–24 in 1981 that is aged 35–39 in 1996, our last available year in the data.

For each cohort, we compute the average real wage and regress this wage on average age, tenure, age and tenure squared, five-year output growth, and *Cosize*, where *Cosize* is obtained by associating to each cohort the relative share of employment in the age range 20–24 over total employment. Assuming that employees aged 20–24 are mainly new entrants, *Cosize* measures the size of each cohort relative to total employment in the year of recruitment.

Column (1) in table 10.7 shows the results. It turns out that average real wages increase both with age and tenure, as expected, and with the five-year real output growth rate. At the same time, there are significant cohort effects, and cohorts with a higher value of *Cosize* experience lower wages, conditional on age, tenure, and growth.

Next, we investigate whether the average quality of newly recruited cohorts affects average wages. It is well known that new school graduates in Japan strongly prefer jobs in large firms. One crude but effective measure of the average quality of a new cohort of recruits is the percentage of new graduates hired by large firms. Suppose that the distribution of new graduates by quality and ability is stationary. Since large firms have the first pick in the labor market, when the percentage of new graduates they hire increases, average quality declines, for both large and medium-sized firms. Cohorts with lower average quality should be paid, *ceteris paribus*, lower wages.

Column (2) in table 10.7 presents the results of the regression of average real wages in medium-sized firms on age, tenure, output growth, and QUA, a cohort-specific variable obtained by assigning to each cohort the percentage of new graduates hired by large firms. We expect that the larger this percentage, the lower the average quality of the cohorts hired by medium-sized firms, and the lower the average real wage. It turns out that our predictions are supported by the data, because QUA attracts a negative and significant coefficient.[12]

Relative wages and business cycle fluctuations

In this section, we investigate whether the wage structure of Japanese firms has been responsive to the business cycle fluctuations experienced by the Japanese economy in the past 20 years. Comparative analysis carried out at the macro level has shown that aggregate real wages in Japan are more sensitive to business cycle fluctuations than wages in other developed economies (see, for instance, Ito, 1992; Layard, Nickell and Jackman, 1991; Brunello, 1990).

Whether this higher flexibility extends to the wage structure within firms has attracted so far little attention. There are two main economic approaches to the analysis of the short-run behavior of relative wages within firms. The standard competitive approach views firms as collections of heterogeneous jobs that are traded in the labor market. According to this approach, changes in the wage structure are the outcome of the interaction between the relative demand and the relative supply of heterogeneous jobs. To illustrate, suppose that firms consist of skilled supervisors and unskilled laborers and that we observe that the relative wages of supervisors are pro-cyclical. With relative labor supply sluggish in the short run, this outcome can be explained by aggregate shocks that have asymmetric effects on the relative demand for skills and shift the relative demand for supervisors outwards during a business expansion and inwards during a contraction (Katz and Revenga, 1989, and Bound and Johnson, 1992, are useful examples of this approach).

An alternative approach is based upon the internal labor market theory. While this theory was born as a rich descriptive set of propositions about wages and employment within firms, many of its predictions have

---

[12] The sample size is larger than in the previous case because the data on hirings are available from 1971. This allows us to track a larger number of cohorts.

now been encapsulated into more formal setups, based upon learning and incentive models or upon efficiency wage models.

In the tradition of Doeringer and Piore (1971), firms have specific ports of entry to career ladders, and the pricing of labor and its allocation within firms is regulated by administrative rules and customs rather than by market forces. Insulation from market forces and from temporary aggregate shocks hitting the economy occurs away from these ports. When ports of entry are located at the bottom of career ladders and there is internal promotion, a testable implication of this view is that the real wages of workers allocated to the lower ranks of the corporate hierarchy should be more sensitive to business cycle fluctuations than the wages of other workers. In the previous example, suppose that laborers and supervisors are, respectively, at the bottom and at the top of the career ladder and that the ports of entry are in the bottom rank. Internal labor market theory suggests in this case that a business expansion should affect wages near the port of entry more than wages away from the port of entry, thus modifying the internal wage structure of firms.

Baker and Holmstrom (1995) have found that "the average wage of entrants varies considerably over time and in a manner consistent with general industry trends. Once inside, however, cohort average wages progress more or less in unison; and whatever differences prevailed upon entry, tend to persist over time" (1995, p. 258). They conclude that market forces have an impact on wages at the time of entry, but much less so inside the firm they study, and interpret this evidence as support of internal labor market effects. When time of entry matters, the wages of workers with short tenure spells should be more responsive to economic fluctuations.[13]

Descriptive analysis

Since our focus is on the effects of business fluctuations on the employment and wage structure of firms belonging to both the manufacturing and the non-manufacturing sector of the Japanese economy, we choose measures of economic fluctuations at the sectoral rather than at the aggregate level. The reason is that sectoral indicators reflect both common and idiosyncratic factors that are averaged out in aggregate measures. We select sectoral real value added per head in manufacturing, distribution, and finance and obtain our cyclical indicators by taking

---

[13] Beaudry and DiNardo (1991) and Bertrand (1998) study the relationship between current wages, current unemployment, and the unemployment rate at the time of labor market entry.

the residuals from regressions of real value added on a constant, a linear, and a quadratic trend. The resulting series, *GAPM*, *GAPD*, and *GAPF*, are shown in figures 10.1–10.3.

Notice that the identification of the long run with a deterministic trend is open to question, since real value added per head is likely to be non-stationary. Given that the available time-series observations are few, however, we believe that running the (by now) standard battery of unit root tests is more or less useless in our context.[14]

The figures below show that both the size and the timing of expansions and contractions are somewhat different in the three industries under study. The sectoral cycles do share, however, a common pattern, and the simple correlation of each sectoral indicator with a widely used aggregate indicator, the job offer/job seekers ratio (*kyujin bairitsu*) is equal, respectively, to 0.747 for *GAPM*, to 0.604 for *GAPD*, and to 0.549 for *GAPF*.

In the manufacturing sector (figure 10.1), the upswing in the second part of the 1980s and the downswing in the early 1990s dominates the short-run behavior of sectoral output per head. In wholesale and retail trade (figure 10.2), the sample period is characterized by two similar cycles, one peaking in 1980 and the other in 1991, when the economic

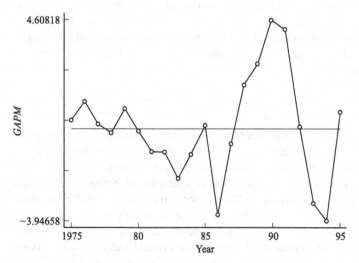

Figure 10.1 Cyclical indicator, manufacturing

[14] See also the discussion in Yoshikawa (1995).

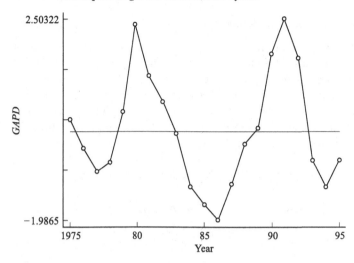

Figure 10.2 Cyclical indicator, distribution

bubble burst. Finally, the finance industry (figure 10.3) has gone through a period of substantial expansion (starting in 1982) and a period of sharp contraction (in the early 1990s). The relative size of sectoral fluctuations differs across industries, and is highest in finance and lowest in wholesale and retail trade.

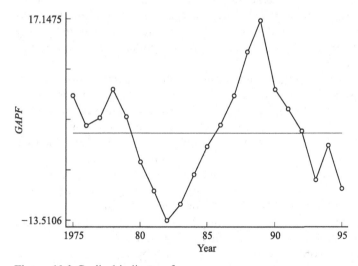

Figure 10.3 Cyclical indicator, finance

The wage structure and the business cycle

There are two important and complementary aspects to the dynamics of real wage differentials within firms over the business cycle: rank and seniority. Consider first rank. If ports of entry in internal labor markets are located in lower hierarchical ranks, because of the importance of internal promotion, we expect wages in those ranks to be less shielded from economic fluctuations and to vary more with short-term changes in output per head. We look at this hypothesis by estimating the following equation

$$\ln W_{ijt} = \alpha_0 + \sum_j \alpha_{1j} R_{ijt} + \sum_k \alpha_{2k} AD_{ijkt} + \alpha_3 T_{ijt} + \alpha_4 T_{ijt}^2$$

$$+ \alpha_5 GAP_t + \alpha_6 TIME + \alpha_7 TIME^2$$

$$+ \sum_j \alpha_{8j} GAP_t * R_{ijt} + \sum_j \alpha_{9j} TIME * R_{ijt}$$

$$+ \sum_j \alpha_{10j} TIME^2 * R_{ijt} + \alpha_{11} L + \varepsilon_{ijt} \qquad (10.24)$$

where W are real consumer wages, i is the age group, with $i = 1, 9$, j is rank, with $j = 0, 1, 2, 3$, t is time, R are rank dummies, AD are age dummies, T is tenure, GAP is the sector-specific cyclical indicator, $TIME$ is a linear trend, L is a firm-size dummy, and average real wages are cell means by rank, age group, industry, and firm size.

We control for long-run changes in the wage structure with a linear and a quadratic trend. By interacting the cyclical variable, GAP, with rank dummies, we check whether there are significant variations in rank-specific real wages over the cycle. These interactions are tested jointly with a likelihood ratio test, where the null hypothesis is the absence of rank-specific effects.

Table 10.8 presents our results. When we pool together industries (column (1)), we find that, while real wages are pro-cyclical, the wage structure is a-cyclical. The likelihood ratio test, with a p-value equal to 0.11, rejects the joint significance of interaction terms between rank dummies and GAP, thus suggesting that wage differentials by rank do not vary with fluctuations in output per head. There are also interesting differences among industries. In the manufacturing and distribution sectors (columns (2) and (3)), for instance, rank-specific wages are pro-cyclical but the wage structure is a-cyclical. In the finance industry, only the real wages of top-ranked employees (ranks 2 and 3) are pro-cyclical. Because of this, wage differentials by rank are also pro-cyclical.

We check the robustness of the above results by aggregating (log) real wages and tenure in the firm over the available age groups and by run-

Table 10.8. *Rank-specific wages and the cyclical indicator GAP; dependent variable: log real wages*

	All industries (1)	Manufacturing (2)	Distribution (3)	Finance (4)
GAP	0.17**	0.50**	0.60**	0.07
GAP* rank 1	−0.04	0.00	−0.02	0.00
GAP* rank 2	0.18*	−0.20	0.41	0.25**
GAP* rank 3	0.23	−0.20	0.49	0.29*
Nobs	5900	2308	1829	1763
TEST (p-value)^a	0.106	0.65	0.76	0.04

Notes:
^{a}*TEST* is the likelihood ratio test.
Each regression includes age and size dummies and a constant term.
Sectoral dummies are included in the pooled data.
**The coefficient is significant at the 5 percent level of confidence.
The standard errors are White-consistent.
Each coefficient in the table is a semi-elasticity and is multiplied by 100.

ning (10.24) in the new sample. The results, summarized in a compact form in table 10.9, confirm that, in the finance industry, wage differentials by rank are pro-cyclical.[15] They also confirm that, in manufacturing industry, real wages are pro-cyclical.

Another important aspect in the short-term dynamics of real wages is seniority. If newcomers are more exposed than incumbents to changes in the business climate, independently of rank, we expect the real wages of workers with short tenure spells to be more responsive to economic fluctuations than the wages of more senior employees. We check this hypothesis by running the following regression

$$\ln W_{ijt} = \alpha_0 + \sum_j \alpha_{1j} R_{ijt} + \sum_k \alpha_{2j} AD_{ijkt} + \alpha_3 T_{ijt} + \alpha_4 T_{ijt}^2$$

$$+ \alpha_5 GAP_t + \alpha_6 TIME + \alpha_7 TIME^2$$

$$+ \alpha_8 GAP_t * TD_i + \sum_h \alpha_{9h} TIME * TD_{ih}$$

$$+ \sum_h \alpha_{10h} TIME^2 * TD_{ih} + \alpha_{11} L + \varepsilon_{ijt} \qquad (10.25)$$

---

[15] The likelihood ratio test of the joint significance of interactions between *GAP* and rank dummies cannot reject the alternative at the 10 percent level of confidence.

Table 10.9 *Rank-specific wages and the cyclical indicator GAP;*
dependent variable: log real wages, data aggregated over age groups

	Manufacturing	Distribution	Finance
GAP	0.61**	0.63	0.19**
GAP* rank 1	0.22	0.22	0.02
GAP* rank 2	−0.21	0.61	0.12**
GAP* rank 3	−0.41	0.61	0.01
TEST (*p*-value)	0.53	0.75	0.08

Notes: **The coefficient is significant at the 5 percent level of confidence.
The standard errors are White-consistent.
Number of observations in each regression: 80.
Each coefficient in the table is multiplied by 100.

where TD is a dummy equal to one if average tenure in the cell is lower
than a given threshold and equal to zero otherwise. Since average tenure
in our sample is close to 16 years, with a substantial number of workers
having long average tenure spells, we experiment with three alternative
thresholds given, respectively, by 5, 10, and 15 years of tenure.

We present results for both the full sample and by industry in table
10.10. The findings in the table show that the real wages of workers with
shorter seniority spells are more sensitive to sector-specific economic
fluctuations only in the pooled data (column (1)) and in the finance
industry (column (4)). We check again the robustness of these results
by selecting two age groups, 18–19 years and 40–44 years, and by aver-
aging the original data over ranks. While average tenure in the former
group is close to one year, it is about 19 years in the latter group. The
results from running (10.25) on data that share the same level of aggregation are reported in table 10.11. It turns out that real wages are pro-
cyclical in manufacturing and in the finance industry, but that there is
no significant difference in the responsiveness of real wages to business
fluctuations between the younger (and short-tenured) and the older (and
long-tenured) age group.

Summary

We have started this chapter with a simple theoretical model, that clarifies
the interactions between economic growth and the structure of wages and
employment in firms that organize labor in internal labor markets. The

Table 10.10 *Rank-specific wages and the cyclical indicator GAP, by tenure group; dependent variable: log real wages*

	All industries (1)	Manufacturing (2)	Distribution (3)	Finance (4)
$TD = 1$: tenure < 5				
GAP	0.24**	0.40*	0.80**	0.18**
$GAP \times TD$	0.10	0.40	−0.60	−0.30
$TD = 1$: tenure < 10				
GAP	0.18**	0.40**	0.65**	0.12**
$GAP \times TD$	0.26*	0.30	0.47	0.20*
$TD = 1$: tenure < 15				
GAP	0.15**	0.50**	0.58**	0.06
$GAP \times TD$	0.24**	−0.09	0.40	0.28**
Nobs	5900	2308	1829	1763

Note: For definitions, see table 10.8.

model predicts that a slowdown in the rate of growth that reduces the growth in the size of corporate hierarchies should also reduce relative wages, promotion rates, and spans of control. An implication of the model in our context is that the combined decline of relative wages, spans of control, and promotion rates described in chapter 8 as typical of the Japanese experience during the past 20 years, could be explained by the slowdown in the rate of economic growth that occurred from the early 1970s onwards and in the early 1990s. These predictions are supported by our empirical analysis.

We have also shown that cohort effects matter for wages. Given growth, age, and tenure, the larger the size or the lower the quality of a newly hired cohort, the lower the average wage. Finally, we have looked at the relationship between relative wages and business cycle fluctuations. We have found limited support in our data for the view that wages paid to workers in lower ranks or with shorter seniority spells are more responsive to short-term variations in output per head. We have found instead interesting differences among industries. In manufacturing industry, real wages are pro-cyclical but the wage structure is a-cyclical. In the finance industry, wage differentials by rank vary with the ups and downs of the sectoral cycle. In particular, it is the wages of employees in higher ranks that are more responsive to business fluctuations.

Table 10.11 *Rank-specific wages and the cyclical indicator GAP, by tenure group; dependent variable: log real wages, data aggregated over ranks*

	Manufacturing	Distribution	Finance
GAP	0.58**	−0.34	0.46**
GAP × *Dummy*	0.22	1.26	−0.24

Notes: For definitions, see table 10.9.
Dummy is a dummy variable equal to one for the group aged 40–44 and to zero for the group aged 18–19.
Each coefficient in the table is multiplied by 100.

Appendix

Proof of lemma 10.1

Define $n = (1 - k)/ek$ and differentiate both first-order conditions with respect to μ to get

$$e\frac{\partial n}{\partial \mu} = \frac{f'}{f''(1 + ne)}\frac{\partial e}{\partial \mu}$$

$$\left[\frac{nf''}{1 + ne} + \frac{e(f - nf')}{(1 + ne)^2}\right]\frac{\partial n}{\partial \mu} = -\left[\frac{n(f - nf')}{(1 + ne)^2} + \frac{c''}{(2 + \mu)}\right]\frac{\partial e}{\partial \mu} + \frac{c'}{(2 + \mu)^2}$$

where c' and c'' are, respectively, the first and the second derivative of the function c and f'' is the second derivative of f. Substitution yields

$$\frac{\partial e}{\partial \mu} = \frac{\dfrac{c'}{(2 + \mu)^2}}{\left\{\dfrac{nf}{(1 + en)^3}(1 - \phi) + \dfrac{n(f - nf')}{(1 + en)^2} + \dfrac{c''}{2 + \mu}\right\}}$$

where

$$\phi = \frac{-f'(f - nf')}{nff''}$$

is the elasticity of substitution associated to f.

The numerator on the RHS of this expression is positive and the denominator is also positive if $\phi \leqslant 1$. In this case the whole expression is positive and $\partial n / \partial \mu < 0$.

Next, notice that the probability of promotion, θ, can be written as

$$\theta = (2 + \mu)k = \frac{2 + \mu}{ne + 1} = \frac{c'(e)}{f(n) - nf'(n)}$$

because of (10.16). Differentiating this expression with respect to μ we obtain

$$\frac{\partial \theta}{\partial \mu} = \frac{1}{(f - nf')^2} \left\{ c''(e)(f - nf') \frac{\partial e}{\partial \mu} + c'(e)nf'' \frac{\partial n}{\partial \mu} \right\} > 0$$

Finally, we consider the span of control and show that

$$\frac{\partial \left(\frac{1-k}{k} \right)}{\partial \mu} = \frac{\partial en}{\partial \mu} = n(1 - \phi) \frac{\partial e}{\partial \mu} > 0$$

if $\phi < 1$. ∎

Proof of lemma 10.2

Differentiation of (10.11) yields

$$\frac{\partial p}{\partial \mu} = -ph' \frac{1}{H^2} \frac{\partial k}{\partial \mu} + c''(e) \frac{\partial e}{\partial \mu} > 0$$

Since H is uniform, h' is zero. ∎

Derivations of the results in table 10.1

Full differentiation of (10.19) and (10.20) yield:

$$\frac{de}{e} + \frac{1}{\phi} \frac{d\tilde{n}}{\tilde{n}} = -\frac{d\alpha}{\alpha} + \frac{d\beta}{\beta} \tag{10A.1}$$

$$\epsilon_1 \frac{de}{e} + \epsilon_2 \frac{d\tilde{n}}{\tilde{n}} = \epsilon_3 \frac{d\alpha}{\alpha} + \epsilon_4 \frac{d\beta}{\beta} + \epsilon_5 \frac{d\mu}{\mu} \tag{10A.2}$$

where

$$\epsilon_1 = 2\psi\{\alpha(1 + \eta)e\tilde{n} + \eta\beta\} > 0$$

$$\epsilon_2 = \psi\alpha e\tilde{n} > 0$$

$$\epsilon_3 = \psi(\beta - \alpha e\tilde{n}) \lessgtr 0$$

$$\epsilon_4 = 2\psi\alpha e\tilde{n} > 0$$

$$\epsilon_5 = \alpha\beta^2 f(\tilde{n}) > 0$$

$$\eta \equiv \frac{ec''(e)}{c'(e)} > 1$$

$$\psi \equiv (\alpha e\tilde{n} + \beta)c'(e) > 0$$

Effects of an increase in α, β or μ

To compute the effect of an increase in α, β, or μ, substitute out de/e in (10A.1) to get:

$$(\phi\epsilon_2 - \epsilon_1)\phi^{-1}\frac{d\tilde{n}}{\tilde{n}} = (\epsilon_3 + \epsilon_1)\frac{d\alpha}{\alpha} + (\epsilon_4 - \epsilon_1)\frac{d\beta}{\beta} + \epsilon_5\frac{d\mu}{\mu} \qquad (10A.3)$$

We also have:

$$(\phi\epsilon_2 - \epsilon_1) < 0$$

$$\epsilon_3 + \epsilon_1 = (2\eta + 1)\psi > 0$$

$$\epsilon_4 - \epsilon_1 = -2\psi\{(\eta - 1)\alpha e\tilde{n} + 2\eta\beta\} < 0$$

These results are sufficient to establish the following:

$$\frac{d\tilde{n}}{d\mu} < 0, \frac{de}{d\mu} > 0$$

$$\frac{d\tilde{n}}{d\alpha} < 0, \frac{de}{d\alpha} > 0$$

$$\frac{d\tilde{n}}{d\beta} > 0, \frac{de}{d\beta} < 0$$

To derive the effects on spans of control and on promotion probabilities, notice that

$$\frac{d\left(\frac{k}{1-k}\right)}{\frac{k}{1-k}} = \frac{d\tilde{n}}{\tilde{n}} + \frac{de}{e} + \frac{d\alpha}{\alpha} - \frac{d\beta}{\beta} = \left(\frac{\phi - 1}{\phi}\right)\frac{d\tilde{n}}{\tilde{n}} \qquad (10A.4)$$

Therefore, assuming that the elasticity of substitution (ϕ) is less than unity, the effects on spans of control are opposite to the effects on $\tilde{n}$. Next, to compute the effects on the promotion probability $\theta \equiv (2 + \mu)k$, notice that, in the case of an increase in α or β, the effect on θ is the same as the effect on k – that is, the opposite of the effect on the span of control. In the case of an increase in μ, simply use the relation below

$$\theta = \frac{c'(e)}{\alpha(f - nf')} \tag{10A.5}$$

Temporary changes in quality and quantity of new recruits

As we noted in the main text, the effect of a temporary increase in the size of entering cohorts is exactly the same as the change in μ. This is the case because in our model the only inter-temporal link is that each employee works for two periods. Other endogenous variables are determined by solving the within-period profit-maximization problem.

To obtain the changes in quality, replace e by $\tilde{e}$. Next fully differentiate the first-order conditions (10.19), and (10.20) to obtain

$$\frac{d\hat{n}}{\hat{n}} = \frac{-\phi(1 + \eta)f(\hat{n})}{nf(\hat{n}) + (1 + \eta - \phi)\hat{n}f'(\hat{n})} \frac{d\lambda}{\lambda} < 0$$

$$\frac{de}{e} = \frac{f(\hat{n}) - (1 + \eta - \phi)\hat{n}f'(\hat{n})}{nf(\hat{n}) + (1 + \eta - \phi)\hat{n}f'(\hat{n})} \frac{d\lambda}{\lambda} \lessgtr 0$$

$$\hat{n} \equiv \frac{(1 - k)}{\lambda ke}$$

Epilog

As remarked in chapter 5, both Ronald Dore and Masahiko Aoki used *Hitachi* as a typical example of the Japanese employment system. Hitachi, a major electrical machinery firm, employs roughly 70,000 workers and its sales are over 4 trillion yen. Hitachi's home town is Hitachi City, located in the north of Tokyo, one of the most well known examples of a company town, together with Toyota City and Kadoma (*Matsushita*'s home town). Hitachi is well known for its paternalistic employment system, and a typical Hitachi worker employed in a Hitachi factory located in Hitachi City is likely to be married to an ex co-worker and to live in company housing built by one of Hitachi's subsidiaries and furnished with a large variety of Hitachi electrical appliances. Even after retirement from Hitachi, the worker is going to have a second job at one of Hitachi's subsidiary firms before starting to receive generous company pension benefits. In many cases, sons and/or daughters are also employed by Hitachi.

Hitachi announced that, for the first time in its history, it would register a loss of 260 billion yen for the 1998–9 fiscal year. The company is clearly in deep trouble, and there are several reports that it is now in the middle of wholesale restructuring, including long-term management strategy, the hierarchical structure, and the compensation and recruitment systems.

Is the employment system at least partially responsible for the trouble that Hitachi (and many other major Japanese firms) are facing? The analysis carried out in this book suggests that the line of causality runs in the opposite direction, with the decline in economic growth strongly affecting the employment and pay system.

The employment system is clearly changing, albeit with inertia, and adapting to the changing economic environment. What are the main directions of change? We end this book with two warning messages and one simple proposition. As pointed out in chapter 7, two distinct options seem to emerge from the analysis of case studies on institutional changes taking place in Japanese internal labor markets. The first option is more or less to abandon completely the current system and move decisively toward the Anglo-American system. Two important features of this system are: (a) position-based job rating and (b) pay for performance. Such a change would involve a complete restructuring of compensation policy from the dual-ranking (SSS) system, where pay is based primarily upon horizontal rank. The second option is to retain the basis of the current system by minimizing its cost, especially by eliminating tenure-related pay to a large extent.

Our first warning is that *neither option is likely to work well.* Independently of the option chosen, firms adopting important changes *de facto* renege on implicit promises made to their employees at the time of recruitment, thus seriously undermining their reputation and credibility and consequently affecting in an adverse way their position in the hiring market. At worst, these changes can severely affect the work attitude of incumbent employees, who are either unwilling or unable to quit, and make it more difficult to hire good new school graduates.

Our second warning is that any serious effort to develop a new employment system must entail *major changes in hiring policies.* If hiring policies are kept intact, feasible changes in career development and training are bound to be limited and unlikely to be effective. The cases studied in chapter 7 are good examples. One reason for starting major changes in the employment system from recruitment is that firms can offer new types of employment contracts only to new entrants.

Designing new hiring and training policies requires a major reappraisal of the stock of skills and of the competitive advantage that each firm owns. Our proposition is concerned with such a reappraisal. We believe that the internalization of Japanese labor markets in large firms went too far. As shown in chapter 6, the market mechanism can be a powerful incentive and screening device for some jobs, and not all jobs developed within the firm are essential to competitive advantage or strategically indispensable. The trend to the outsourcing of secretarial jobs in large firms is a clear example in this direction. One important advantage of Japanese firms is their flexible use of supplier firms; strategic use of competition among rival supplier firms contributed not only to important cost reductions but also to the development of important process innovations and new products. We believe that the analogy is useful in developing more flexible employment systems.

Kazuo Koike once observed that Japanese corporate hierarchies are similar to Japanese chess pieces in that hierarchies also have a "choke point" beyond which the race for promotion becomes increasingly fierce and only the selected few can survive. Clearly, corporate hierarchies in other countries also have such a choke point, but the difference is that in Japanese large firms the great majority of employees reaching that point are incumbents, whereas in Anglo-Saxon firms those reaching the critical point are more heterogeneous in terms of background and previous work experience.

To paraphrase Koike's observation, Japanese hierarchies should perhaps be more similar to squids than to chess pieces, and the employment system should be able to freely pick elements inside and outside of the firm, without giving up its potential for skill development in a changing economic environment.

References

Abraham, K. and Farber, H. (1987). "Job duration, seniority, and earning," *American Economic Review*, 77, 278–97

Abraham, K. and Medoff, J. (1980). "Experience, performance and earnings," *Quarterly Journal of Economics*, 95, 701–35

(1985). "Length of service and promotions in union and nonunion work groups," *Industrial and Labor Relations Review*, 38, 408–20

Acemoglu, D. and Pischke, S. (1997). "Why do firms train?" *NBER Working Paper*, 5605, Cambridge, MA

(1999). "The structure of wages and investment in general training," *Journal of Political Economy*, 107, 539–72.

Altonji, J. and Shakotko, R. (1987). "Do wages rise with seniority?" *Review of Economic Studies*, 54, 437–59

Altonji, J. and Williams, N. (1996). "The effects of labor market experience, job seniority and job mobility on wage growth," *NBER Working Paper*, 4133

Aoki, M. (1982). "Equilibrium growth of a hierarchical firm: shareholder-employee cooperative game approach," *American Economic Review*, 72, 1097–1110

(1988). *Information, Incentives and Bargaining in the Japanese Economy*, Cambridge: Cambridge University Press

Aoki, M. and Patrick, H. (eds.) (1994). *The Japanese Main Bank System*, Oxford: Oxford University Press

Ariga, K. and Ohkusa, Y. (1997). "*Kigyo Sisan no Chikuseki to Nihon-teki Koyo System*" (Corporate asset accumulation as an incentive device in the Japanese employment system), in K. Asako *et al.* (eds.), *Gendai Makuro Keizai Bunseki* (Contemporary Macroeconomic Analysis), Tokyo: University of Tokyo Press

Ariga, K., Brunello, G. and Okhusa, Y. (1997). "Promotions, skill formation and earnings growth in a corporate hierarchy," *Journal of the Japanese and the International Economies*, 11, 347–84

Ariga, K., Ohkusa, Y. and Brunello, G. (1999). "Fast track: is it in the genes? The promotion policy of a large Japanese firm," *Journal of Economic Behavior and Organization*, 38, 385–402.

271

Ariga, K., Takehiro, R. and Shima, K. (1996). "Rescuing firms in financial distress," *KIER Discussion Paper*, 446

Ariga, K., Brunello, G., Nishiyama, K. and Ohkusa, Y. (1992). "Corporate hierarchy, promotion and firm growth: the Japanese internal labor market in transition," *Journal of the Japanese and the International Economies*, 6, 440–71

Baker, G. and Holmstrom, B. (1995). "Internal labor markets: too many theories, too few facts," *American Economic Review*, 85, 255–65

Baker, G., Gibbs, M. and Holmstrom, B. (1994a). "The internal economics of the firm: evidence from personnel data." *Quarterly Journal of Economics*, 109, 881–919

(1994b). "The wage policy of a firm," *Quarterly Journal of Economics*, 109, 921–55

Baker, G., Jensen, M. and Murphy, K. (1988). "Compensation and incentives: theory versus practice," *Journal of Finance*, 43, 593–616

Barro, R. and Lee, J. (1992). "Source of economic growth," *Carnegie–Rochester Conference on Public Policy*, 40, 1–46

Beaudry, P. and DiNardo, J. (1991). "The effect of implicit contracts on the movement of wages over the business cycle: evidence from micro data," *Journal of Political Economy*, 99, 665–88

Bertola, G. and Caballero, R. J. (1994). "Cross-sectional inefficiency and labour hoarding in a matching model of unemployment," *Review of Economic Studies*, 61, 435–56

Bertrand, M. (1998). "From the invisible handshake to the invisible hand? How product market competition changes the employment relationship," Harvard University, mimeo

Blanchard, O. and Diamond, P. (1992). "The flow approach to labor markets," *The American Economic Review*, 82, 354–59

Blanchflower, D., Oswald, A. and Sanfey, P. (1996). "Wages, profits and rent-sharing," *Quarterly Journal of Economics*, 107, 227–51

Blinder, A. and Krueger, A. (1992). "International differences in labor turnover: a comparative analysis with emphasis on the US and Japan," Princeton University, mimeo

Booth, A. and Frank, J. (1996). "Seniority, earnings and unions," *Economica*, 63, 673–86

Bound, J. and Johnson, G. (1992). "Changes in the structure of wages in the 1980s: an evaluation of alternative explanations," *American Economic Review*, 82, 371–91

Bourguignon, F. and Chiappori, P. A. (1995). "Executives' promotion in an internal labor market: an econometric analysis," in P. Champsaur (ed.), *Essays in Honor of Edmond Malinvaud*, Cambridge, MA: MIT Press

Brunello, G. (1988). "Transfers of employees between Japanese manufacturing enterprises: some results from an enquiry on a small sample of large firms," *British Journal of Industrial Relations*, 26, 119–32

(1990). "Hysteresis and the 'Japanese unemployment problem': a preliminary investigation," *Oxford Economic Papers*, 42, 483–500

(1992). "The effect of unions on firm performance in Japanese manufacturing," *Industrial and Labor Relations Review*, 45, 471–87

(1996). "Equilibrium unemployment with internal labor markets," *Economica*, 63, 19–35

Brunello, G. and Ariga, K. (1997). "Earnings and seniority in Japan: a reappraisal of the existing evidence and a comparison with the UK," *Labour Economics*, 4, 47–69

Brunello, G. and Ishikawa, T. (1999). "Elite schools, high tech jobs and economic welfare," *Journal of Public Economics*, 72, 395–419

Brunello, G. and Medio, A. (1996). "A job competition model of workplace training and education," *FEEM Working Paper*, 75.96, Milan

Brunello, G. and Wadhwani, S. (1989). "The determinants of wage flexibility in Japan: some lessons from a comparison with the UK using micro data," *Centre for Labour Economics Discussion Paper*, 362

Brunello, G., Ariga, K., Ohkusa, Y. and Nishiyama, Y. (1995). "Recent changes in the internal structure of wages and employment in Japan," *Journal of the Japanese and the International Economies*, 9, 105–29

Carmichael, L. (1983). "Firm specific human capital and promotion ladders," *Bell Journal of Economics*, 14, 251–8

Carmichael, L. and McLeod, B. (1993). "Multiskilling, technical change and the Japanese firm," *Economic Journal*, 103, 142–60

Card, D. and Vella, F. (1997). "Testing the validity of instruments in models with censored treatments and outcomes," Princeton University, mimeo

Chan, W. (1996). "External recruitment vs. internal promotion," *Journal of Labor Economics*, 14, 555–70

Chuma, H. (1994). *Kensho: Nihongata Koyo Chosei*, Tokyo: Shueisha

(1997). "Keizai Kanyo no Henka to Chukonenko no Chokinzokuka," in H. Chuma and Y. Tsuruga (eds.), *Koyo Kanko no Henka to Joshi Rodo*, Tokyo: Daigaku Shuppankai

Chuma, H. and Higushi, Y. (1995). "Keizai Kankyono Henka to Choki Koyou System," in T. Inoki and Y. Higuchi (eds.), *Nihon no Koyo System to Rodou Shijo*, Tokyo: Nihon Keizai Shinbunsa, 23–56

Clark, R. and Ogawa, N. (1992). "Employment tenure and earnings profiles in Japan and the United States: comment," *American Economic Review*, 82, 336–45

Cole, R. (1979). *Work, Mobility and Participation*, Berkeley: University of California Press

Collier, P. and Knight, J. (1985). "Seniority payments, quit rates and internal labour markets in Britain and Japan," *Oxford Bulletin of Economics and Statistics*, 47, 19–32

Contini, B. and Filippi, M. (1995). "A study of job creation and job destruction in Europe," *RP Working Paper*, Turin

Crafts, N. (1992). "Productivity growth reconsidered," *Economics Policy*, 15, 44–78

Demougin, D. and Siow, A. (1994). "Careers in ongoing hierarchies," *American Economic Review*, 84, 1261–77

Devine, T. and Kiefer, N. (1991). *Empirical Labour Economics*, Oxford: Oxford University Press

Dickens, W. and Katz, L. (1987). "Inter-industry wage differences and industry characteristics," in K. Lang and J. Leonard (eds.), *Unemployment and the Structure of Labor Markets*, Oxford: Blackwell

Doeringer, P. and Piore, M. (1971). *Internal Labour Markets and Manpower Analysis*, Lexington: Lexington Books

Dore, R. (1987). *Taking Japan Seriously*, London: Athlone Press
  (1973). *British Factory, Japanese Factory*, Berkeley: University of California Press

Dore, R. and Sako, M. (1988). "Teaching or testing: the role of the state in Japan," *Oxford Review of Economic Policy*, 4, 72–81

Economic Planning Agency (1997). *Keizai Hakusho*, Tokyo

Farber, H. and Gibbons, R. (1996). "Learning and wage dynamics," *Quarterly Journal of Economics*, 111, 1007–47

Freeman, R. (1995). "Does it fit? Drawing lessons from differing labor practices," *CEP Discussion Paper*, 230

Freeman, R. and Weitzman, M. (1987). "Bonuses and employment in Japan," *Journal of the Japanese and the International Economies*, 1, 168–94

Garen, W. (1988). "Empirical studies of the job matching hypothesis," *Research in Labor Economics*, 9, 187–224

Genda, Y. (1998). "Job creation and job destruction in Japan 1991–95," *Journal of the Japanese and the International Economies*, 12, 1–24

Gibbons, R. (1996). "Incentives and careers in organisations," *NBER Working Paper*, 5705

Gibbons, R. and Waldman, M. (1999). "A theory of wage and internal promotion dynamics in internal labor markets," *Quarterly Journal of Economics*, 114, 1321–58

Gregory, M. and Thomson, A. (1990). *A Portrait of Pay*, Oxford: Clarendon Press

Hanada, H. (1987). "Jinji Seido ni okeru Kyoso Genri no Jittai – Shoshin, Shokaku System kara mita Nihon no Jinji Senryaku," *Soshiki Kagaku*, 21 (2)

Harris, M. and Holmstrom, B. (1982). "A theory of wage dynamics," *Review of Economic Studies*, 49 (3), 315–33

Hart, R. and Kawasaki, S. (1995). "The Japanese bonus system and human capital," *Journal of the Japanese and the International Economies*, 9, 225–44

Hashimoto, M. and Raisian, J. (1985). "Employment tenure and earnings profiles in Japan and the United States," *American Economic Review*, 75, 721–35
  (1992). "Employment tenure and earnings profiles in Japan and the United States: a reply," *American Economic Review*, 82, 346–54

Hatvany, N. and Pucik, V. (1981). "An integrated management system: lessons from the Japanese experience," *Academic Management Journal*, 6, 23–47

Hersch, J. and Reagan, P. (1990). "Job match, tenure and wages paid by firms," *Economic Inquiry*, 28, 488–506

Higuchi, Y. (1988). "Japan's changing wage structure," *Journal of the Japanese and the International Economies*, 3, 481–99

Imada, S. and Hirata, S. (1995). *Howaito Cara no Shoshin Kiko*, Tokyo: Nihon Rodo Kenkyu Kiko

Inoue, S. (1982). "Naibu Rodo Shijo no Keizaiteki Gamen," *Nihon Rodo Kyokai Zasshi*, 2–16

Ishikawa, T. and Dejima, K. (1994). "Rodo Shijou no Niju Kozo," in T. Ishikawa, *Nihon no Shotoku to Tomi non Bunpai*, Tokyo: Tokyo University Press

Ito, T. (1992). *The Japanese Economy*, Cambridge, MA: MIT Press

Itoh, H. (1991). "Japanese human resource management from the viewpoint of incentive theory," in M. Aoki and G. Brunello (eds.), *Current Topics on the Japanese Economy*, Special issue of *Ricerche Economiche*, Venice

Itoh, H., Kumagai, S. and Ohtake, F. (1998). "Satei, Shosin, Chingin Kettei: aru Gaishi kei Kinyu Kikan no Kesu," ISER, Osaka, mimeo

Jonsson, A. and Klevmarken, A. (1978). "On the relationship between cross-sectional and cohort earnings profiles," *Annales del l'INSEE*, 12, 30–51

Jovanovic, B. (1979). "Job matching and the theory of turnover," *Journal of Political Economy*, 87, 972–90

Jovanovic, B. and Nyarko, Y. (1996). "Stepping stone mobility," New York University, mimeo

Katz, L. and Revenga, A. (1989). "Changes in the structure of wages: the US versus Japan," *Journal of the Japanese and the International Economies*, 3, 522–53,

Kremer, M. (1993). "The O-ring theory of economic development," *Quarterly Journal of Economics*, 108, 551–76

Koike, K. (1981). *Nihon no Jukuren*, Tokyo: Yuhikaku
(1988). *Understanding Industrial Relations in Japan*, London: Macmillan
(1991). *Shigoto no Keizaigaku*, Tokyo: Toyo Keizai Shinposha
(1995). *The Economics of Work in Japan*, LTCB International Library Foundation, Tokyo: Toyo Keizai

Krueger, A. and Summers, L. (1988). 'Efficiency wages and the inter-industry wage structure," *Econometrica*, 56, 259–93

Lancaster, T. (1990). *The Econometric Analysis of Transition Data*, Cambridge: Cambridge University Press

Layard, R., Nickell, S. and Jackman, R. (1991). *Unemployment*, Oxford: Oxford University Press

Lazear, E. (1995). *Personnel Economics*, Cambridge, MA: MIT Press

Lazear, E. and Rosen, S. (1981). "Rank-order tournaments as optimal labor contracts," *Journal of Political Economy*, 89, 841–64

Lincoln, J. and Kalleberg, A. (1990). *Culture, Control and Commitment*, Cambridge: Cambridge University Press

276   Internal Labor Markets in Japan

Lincoln, J., Hanada, M. and McBride, K. (1986). "Organizational structures in Japanese and US manufacturing," *Administrative Science Quarterly*, 31, 338–64

Lynch, L. (ed.) (1993). *Training and the Private Sector*, Chicago: Chicago University Press

Main, B. and Reilly, B. (1993). "The employer size–wage gap: evidence from Britain," *Economica*, 60, 130–42

Malcomson, J. (1984). "Work incentives, hierarchy and internal labor markets," *Journal of Political Economy*, 92, 486–507

(1997). "Contracts, hold-ups and labor markets," *Journal of Economic Literature*, 1916–57

Malcomson, J. and McLeod, B. (1988). "Reputation and hierarchy in dynamic models of employment," *Journal of Political Economy*, 96, 832–54

Mankiw, G., Romer, D. and Weil, D. (1992). "A contribution to the empirics of economic growth," *Quarterly Journal of Economics*, 107

Marsden, D. (1990). "Institutions and labour mobility: occupational and internal labour markets in Britain, France, Italy and the UK," in C. Dell'Aringa and R. Brunetta (eds.), *Markets, Institutions and Cooperation: Labour Relations and Economic Performance*, London: Macmillan

Marshall, R. and Zarkin, G. (1987). "The effect of job tenure on wage offers," *Journal of Labor Economics*, 5, 301–24

Matsushige, T. (1995a). "Kako Kumitate gata Sangyo ni okeru Bunkei Daisotsu howaito cara no Ido to Shoshin," *JIL*, 68, Nihon Rodo Kenkyu Kiko

(1995b). "Denki B-sha no Daisotsu Danshi Jyugyo-in no Kinzoku 10-nen made no Idou to Sonogono Shoushin," in T. Tachibanaki (ed.), *Shoushin no Keizaigaku*, Tokyo: Toyo Keizai

McCue K. (1996). "Promotions and wage growth," *Journal of Labor Economics*, 2, 175–209

McLaughlin, J. (1988). "A survey on tournaments," in R. Ehrenberg (ed.), *Research in Labor Economics*, Ithaca: Cornell University Press

McLeod, B. (1986). "Behaviour and organization of the firms," *Journal of Comparative Economics*, 14, 207–20

Meyer, M. (1991). "Learning from coarse information: biased contests and career profiles," *Review of Economic Studies*, 58, 15–41

Mincer, J. (1989). "Human capital responses to technical change in the labor market," *NBER Working Paper*, 3207

Mincer, J. and Higuchi, Y. (1988). "Wage structures and labor turnover in the US and in Japan," *Journal of the Japanese and the International Economies*, 2, 97–133

Mincer, J. and Jovanovic, B. (1981). "Turnover and wage dynamics," in S. Rosen (ed.), *Studies in the Labor Market*, Chicago: University of Chicago Press

Moulton, B. (1990). "An illustration of a pitfall in estimating the effects of aggregate variables on micro units," *Review of Economics and Statistics*, 334–8

Nakatani, I. (1996). *Nihon Keizai no Rekishitekina Tenkan*, Tokyo: Toyo Keizai Shinposha

Nickell, S. (1998). "Product markets and labour markets," Oxford University, mimeo

Nishimura, K.G., Ohkusa, Y. and Ariga, K. (1999). "Estimating markups over marginal costs and returns to scale at firm level: a new approach applied to a panel of Japanese firms," *International Journal of Industrial Organization*, 17, 1077–1111

Odagiri, H. and Yamashita, T. (1987). "Price mark-ups, market structure and business fluctuations in Japanese manufacturing industries," *Journal of Industrial Economics*, 35, 317–31

Odaka, K. (1993). *Kigyounai Kyouiku no Jidai* (The Era of Enterprise Training), Tokyo: Iwanami

Oguchi, N., Kimura, Y. and Hatta, T. (1994). "Nihon no Koteki Nenkin no Saibunpai Koka," in T. Ishikawa (ed.), *Nihon no Shotoku to Tomi no Bunpai*, Tokyo: Tokyo University Press, 321–53

Ohashi, I. and Matsushige, Y. (1994). "The growth of the firm and promotions in the Japanese seniority system," in T. Tachibanaki, *Labour Market and Economic Performance*, London: Macmillan, 13–154

Ohkusa, Y. (1995). "An empirical test of incentives in the Japanese wage structure," Osaka City University, mimeo

Ohkusa, Y. and Ohta, S. (1994). "An empirical study of the wage–tenure profile in Japanese manufacturing," *Journal of the Japanese and the International Economies*, 8, 173–203

Ohkusa, Y. and Ohtake, F. (1996). "The relationship between supervisor and workers – the case of professional baseball in Japan," *Japan and the World Economies*, 8, 475–88

Ohkusa, Y., Brunello, G. and Ariga, K. (1997). "Occupational and internal labor markets in Japan," *Industrial Relations*, 36, 446–73

Ohtake, F. (1994), "Shoukaku no Kettei Youin-Satei to Kinzoku Nensu," Osaka University, mimeo

(1995). "The determinants of promotion: the effects of length of tenure and performance evaluation," *Keyzai Kenkyu*, 46, 241–8

Organization for Economic Cooperation and Development (OECD) (1991). *Employment Outlook*, Paris: OECD

Osawa, M. (1993). *Keizai Henka to Joshi Rodo*, Tokyo: Nihon Keizai Hyoronsha

Osterman, P. (1982). "Employment structures within firms," *British Journal of Industrial Relations*, 30, 349–61

(1987). "Choice of employment systems in internal labour markets," *Industrial Relations*, 26, 46–67

(1994). "Internal labor markets: theory and change," in C. Kerr and P. Staudothar, *Labor Economics and Industrial Relations*, Cambridge, MA: Harvard University Press

Pissarides, C. (1990). *Equilibrium Unemployment*, Oxford: Blackwell

278   Internal Labor Markets in Japan

Prais, S. J. (1990). "Productivity, education and training: Britain and other countries compared," London: National Institute of Economic and Social Research

Prendergast, C. (1990). "The economics of star treatment," Oxford University, mimeo

(1992). "Career development and specific human capital collection," *Journal of the Japanese and the International Economies*, 6, 207–27

(1998). "What happens within firms? A survey of empirical evidence on compensation policies," in D. Haltiwanger *et al.* (eds.), *Labor Statistics and Measurement Issues*, University of Chicago Press, 82–104

Rebick, M. (1993). "The Japanese approach to finding jobs for older workers," in O. Mitchell, *As the Workforce Ages*, Ithaca: ILR Press, 113–35

Rodosho (1997), *Rodo Hakusho*, Tokyo

Romu Kasei Kenkyujo (1997). *Jinji Romu Kanri sha Seido Jisshi Jokyo Chosa*, Tokyo

Rosen, S. (1982). "Authority, control and the distribution of earnings," *Bell Journal of Economics*, 13, 311–23

Rosenbaum, J. (1984). *Career Mobility in a Vertical Hierarchy*, New York: Academic Press

Saint Paul, G. (1997). *Dual Labor Markets*, Cambridge, MA: MIT Press

Sargan, D. (1984). "Wages and prices in the United Kingdom: a study in econometric methodology," in D. Hendry and K. Wallis (eds.), *Econometrics and Quantitative Economics*, Oxford: Blackwell (original version, 1964)

Sato, H. (1997). "Human resource management systems in large firms: the case of white-collar graduate employees," in M. Sako and H. Sato, *Japanese Labour and Management in Transition*, London: Routledge, 104–30

Seike, A. (1997). "Ageing workers," in M. Sako and H. Sato, *Japanese Labour and Management in Transition*, London: Routledge, 131–48

Sibert, W. S. and Addison, J. (1991). "Internal labour markets: causes and consequences," *Oxford Review of Economic Policy*, 7, 76–92

Stern, S. (1987). "Promotion and optimal retirement," *Journal of Labor Economics*, 6, 330–61

Shapiro, C. and Stiglitz, J. (1984). "Involuntary unemployment as a worker disciplinary device," *American Economic Review*, 74, 434–44

Sloane, P. and Theodossiou, I. (1993). "Gender and job tenure effects on earnings," *Oxford Bulletin of Economics and Statistics*, 55, 421–37

Spilerman, S. and Ishida, H. (1994). "Stratification and attainment in large Japanese firms," Columbia University, mimeo

Tachibanaki, T. (ed.) (1992). *Satei, Shoushin, Chingin Kettei*, Tokyo: Yuhikaku

(ed.) (1995). *Shoushin no Keizaigaku*, Tokyo: Toyo Keizai Shinposha

(1996). *Wage Determination and Distribution in Japan*, New York: Oxford University Press

Tachibanaki, T. and Ohta, S. (1996). "Wage differentials by industry and the size of firm, and labor market in Japan," in T. Tachibanaki (ed.), *Labor Market* and *Economic Performance: Europe, Japan and the USA*, New York: St. Martin's Press

Takeuchi, Y. (1995). *Nihon no Meritocracy*, Tokyo: Tokyo Daigaku Shuppankai

Taubman, P. and Watcher, M. (1986). "Segmented labour markets," in O. Ashenfelter and R. Layard, *Handbook of Labor Economics*, Amsterdam: North-Holland

Tomita, Y. (1992). "Shousin no Shikami: Satei to Kinzoku nensuu no Eikyou," in T. Tachibanaki (ed.), *Satei, Shousin, Chingin Kettei*, Tokyo: Yuhikaku

Topel, R. (1991). "Specific capital, mobility and wages: wages rise with job seniority, *Journal of Political Economy*, 99, 145–76

Wadhwani, S. and Wall, M. (1991). "A direct test of the efficiency wage model using UK micro-data," *Oxford Economic Papers*, 43, 529–48

Waldman, M. (1984). "Worker allocation, hierarchies and the wage distribution," *Review of Economic Studies*, 51, 95–109

Williamson, O. (1985). *The Economic Institutions of Capitalism: Firms, Markets and Relational Contracts*, New York: Macmillan

Womack, J., Jones, D. and Roos, D. (1991). *The Machine that Changes the World*, New York: Rawson Associates

Yashiro, A. (1995). *Dai Kigyo Howaito Cara no Kiaria*, Tokyo: Nihon Rodo Kenkyu Kiko

Yoshikawa, H. (1995). *Macroeconomics and the Japanese Economy*, Oxford: Oxford University Press

Yoshino, M. Y. (1968). *Japan's Managerial System: Tradition and Innovation*, Cambridge, MA: MIT Press

Author Index

Subject Index

ability
  innate 40–3, 47–9, 52–9, 66–7,
    102, 103, 106, 124, 126,
    150–2, 158, 160, 255
  distribution 56, 66
ABO (acronym for a sample firm)
    122, 127, 128, 149, 158, 163–8
adverse selection 99, 243
age group 79, 100, 104, 111, 191,
    197, 207, 21824, 238, 251, 260,
    262
ageing, Japanese labor force xi, 1,
    2, 8, 9, 189, 190, 196, 202, 203,
    226, 227, 237–41, 242
agency explanation 98
agency relationship 243
agency theory xi
Anglo-Saxon (system, economies)
    9, 15, 202, 270
appreciation of Yen 193–4, 209
asset value of (un)employment 19,
    23, 24, 26, 221, 222
  of vacancy 19, 27
assignment to positions, 98
attrition rate 147
  see also survival rate

bang-bang solution 45
bargaining power 182

Basic Survey on the Wage
    Structure 207, 224, 227
benchmarking (in promotion
    policy) 140, 157, 165
BGH (acronym for a sample firm)
    163–7,
blue collar (jobs, workers) 71, 87,
    91, 120, 128, 206
bounded rationality 13
British Household Panel Survey
    (BHPS) 97,112
bubble economy in late 1980s,
    Japan, xi, 104, 190, 194, 195,
    210
bucho (department head or
    director), 96, 104, 105, 114,
    128, 191, 194, 196, 208, 218,
    230
burst of the bubble economy in
    early 1990s, Japan 1, 30, 120,
    181, 207, 209, 219, 259
business cycle fluctuation 8, 213,
    242, 256–9, 263

career 3, 36, 39, 47, 60, 70, 124,
    144, 166, 206, 250
  development 5, 168, 199, 269
  differentiation 124
  dynamics 38
  history 122, 159

net experience 229–36
New Earnings Survey (NES) 111
new school graduate 128, 131, 165,
    166, 167, 189, 190, 197, 203,
    204, 209, 269
Nihon Keizai Shinbun, 171

occupation-specific tenure 4, 70–5,
    79, 82, 92
occupational labor market 4, 8, 15,
    19, 35–7, 38, 68–71, 71, 82, 92,
    96, 241
    see also ILM type of firm, OLM
    type of firm
oil shock xi, 1, 104
older worker 7, 191, 227
OLM type of firm, 15, 17, 20–3, 28,
    29, 34, 37, 38, 41, 47, 48, 50,
    52–9, 67–9, 71, 72, 74–6, 79,
    82, 86, 90, 98, 99,162
    see also ILM type of firm,
    occupational labor market
ordinary least squares (OLS) 107,
    229
orthogonal 73, 239
over-identifying restriction (test)
    103, 107, 232, 233

panel regression 156
partial equilibrium model 38, 40
paternalism
    corporate 69
    in employment system 268
Penrose effect, 184
perfect substitute 43, 47, 64
personnel
    data (file) xi, 5, 121, 124, 128,
        146, 159, 162, 165, 168
    department (division) 128, 149,
        165, 166, 191
    evaluation 165, 166, 192, 193,
        196, 198, 199

management 35, 128
    record 150
Peter Principle, 35
port(s) of entry (jobs) 1, 4, 5, 8, 82,
    13, 37, 60, 68, 121, 133, 165–8,
    164, 257
pre-job experience 100, 108, 109
previous labor market experience
    7, 131, 158, 160, 197, 203, 218,
    240
primary sector, 9, 208
probit 108, 109, 149, 162, 163
    ordered probit 108, 109, 110,
        111
product market competition 169,
    170, 176, 177
productivity growth 2, 3, 13–15,
    21, 22, 29, 30, 32, 97, 227
profit 33, 52, 170, 246, 267
    profit center 127
promotion, 1–7, 13, 18, 21, 25, 27,
    28, 32, 35–8, 46–50, 52, 55–60,
    66, 68, 70, 86, 96, 105, 111,
    119, 120, 121–30, 134–68, 143,
    145, 162, 163, 181, 182, 190,
    194–200, 218–225, 219, 227,
    241, 242–50, 252, 254, 257,
    260, 265, 269
    candidate 58
    history 128, 149, 159
    ladder 3, 13, 36, 38–40, 60, 119
    policy 3, 60, 123, 126, 134, 142,
        144, 157–9 165, 167, 195–9
    probability 58, 59, 149–52, 156,
        196, 224, 225, 227, 242,
        246–52, 254, 266
    race 138, 144
    rate 7, 8, 195, 201, 216, 218–24,
        242, 251, 252–4
    timing 3, 36, 60
    tournament 125, 126, 142, 149,
        157, 227, 243, 245

wage–tenure profile, 6, 170, 172, 177, 179, 181, 196, 226, 227, 237, 242
see also earnings profile
Weibull distribution 101, 160–162

white collar (worker) 6, 73, 120, 128, 131, 167, 169, 191, 201, 206

X-inefficiency, 181